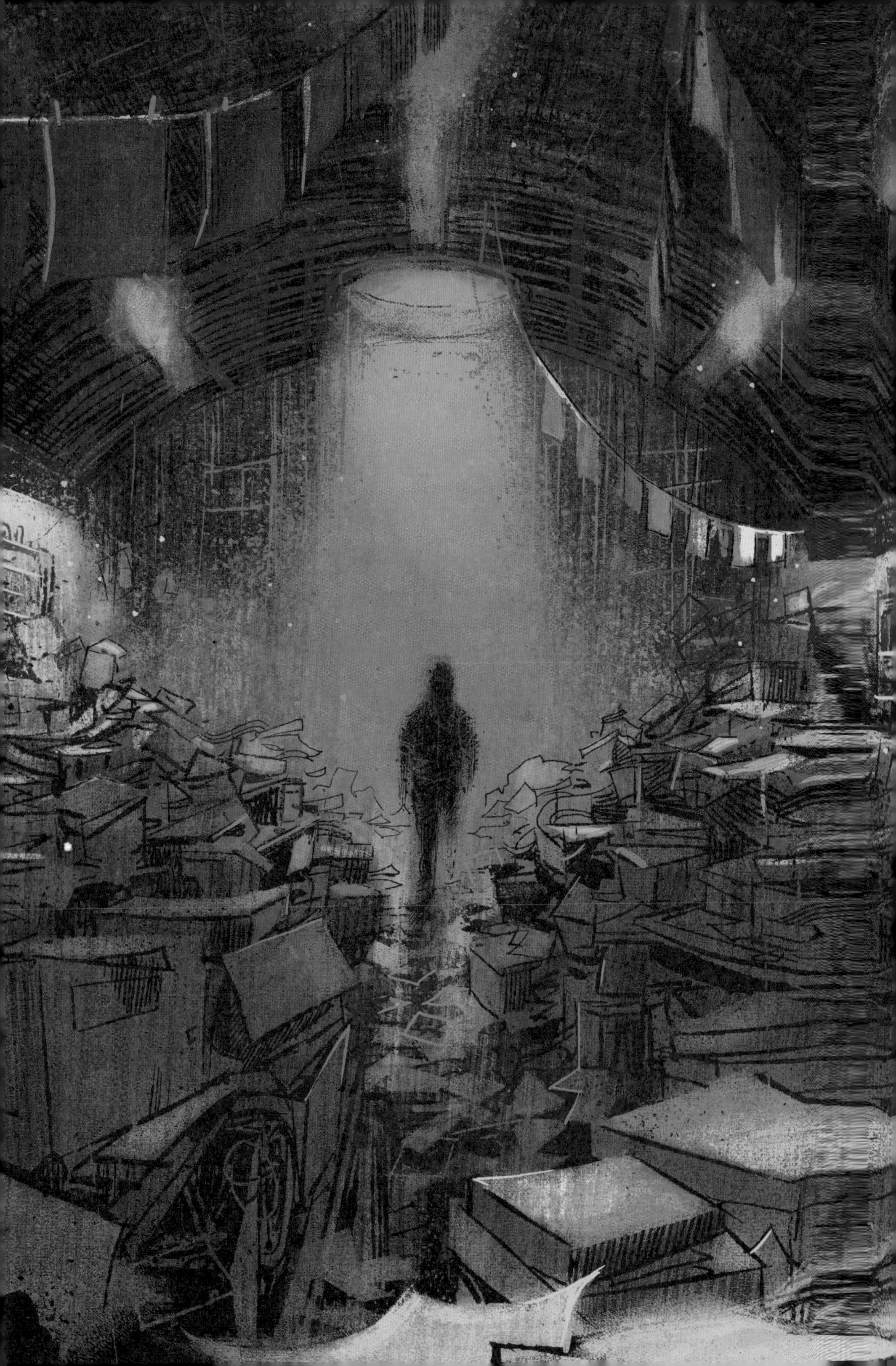

# THE BUNKER

VOLUME 1

Written by
**Joshua Hale Fialkov**

Illustrated, Colored, and Lettered by
**Joe Infurnari**

Edited by
**James Lucas Jones and Robin Herrera**

Designed by
**Jason Storey**

# PUBLISHED BY ONI PRESS, INC.

Publisher, Joe Nozemack
Editor In Chief, James Lucas Jones
Director of Sales, Cheyenne Allott
Director of Publicity, John Schork
Editor, Charlie Chu
Associate Editor, Robin Herrera
Production Manager, Troy Look
Senior Graphic Designer, Jason Storey
Administrative Assistant, Ari Yarwood
Inventory Coordinator, Brad Rooks
Office Assistant, Jung Lee
Production Assistant, Jared Jones

VOLUME 1

This volume collects issues 1-4 of the
Oni Press series *The Bunker*

ONIPRESS.COM
FACEBOOK.COM/ONIPRESS • TWITTER.COM/ONIPRESS • ONIPRESS.TUMBLR.COM
THEFIALKOV.COM / @JOSHFIALKOV • JOEINFURNARI.COM / @INFURNARI

FIRST EDITION:            LIBRARY OF CONGRESS CONTROL NUMBER:            ISBN 978-1-62010-164-3
JULY 2014                          2014932053                           eISBN 978-1-62010-165-0

10 8 6 4 2 1 3 5 7 9

PRINTED IN CHINA

For the future and whatever
she may bring.

—JHF

For my father, Nicoló Infurnari.
I'll see you tomorrow, Dad.

—JI

# CHAPTER

01

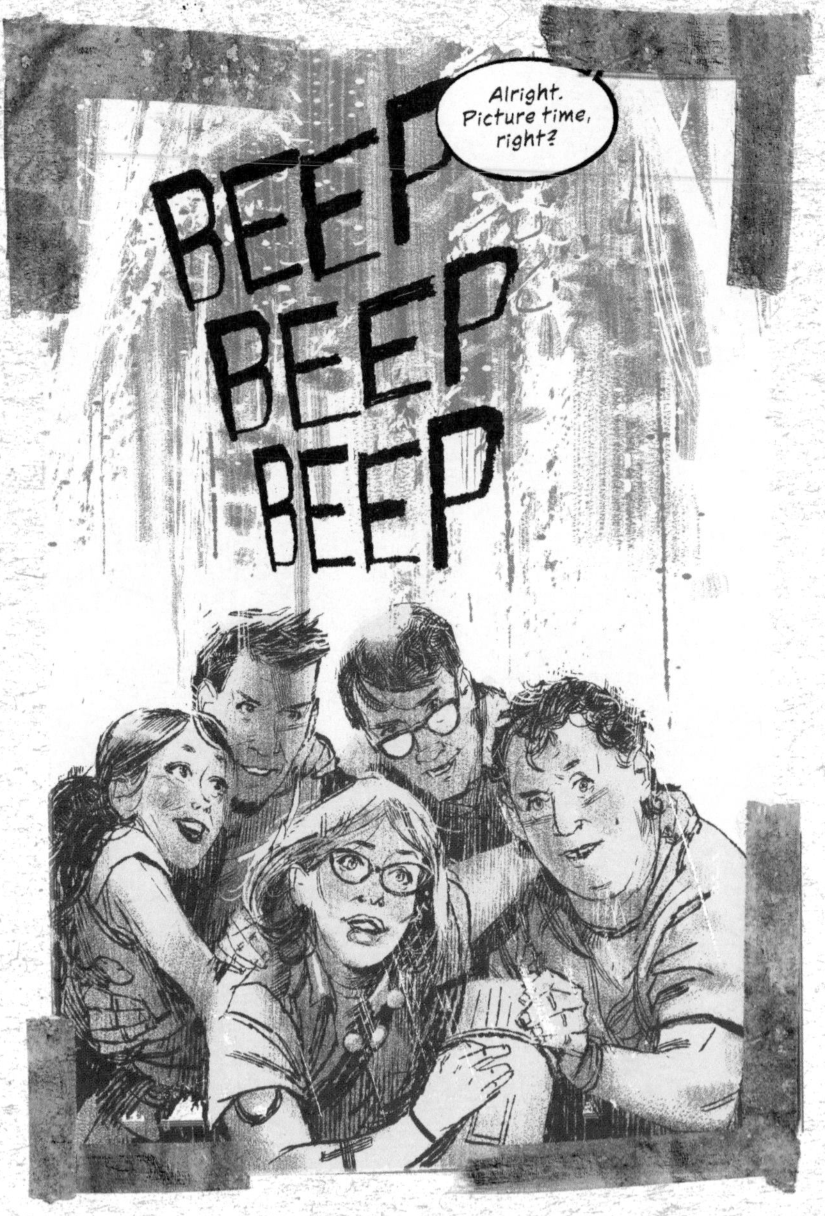
Alright. Picture time, right?
BEEP BEEP BEEP

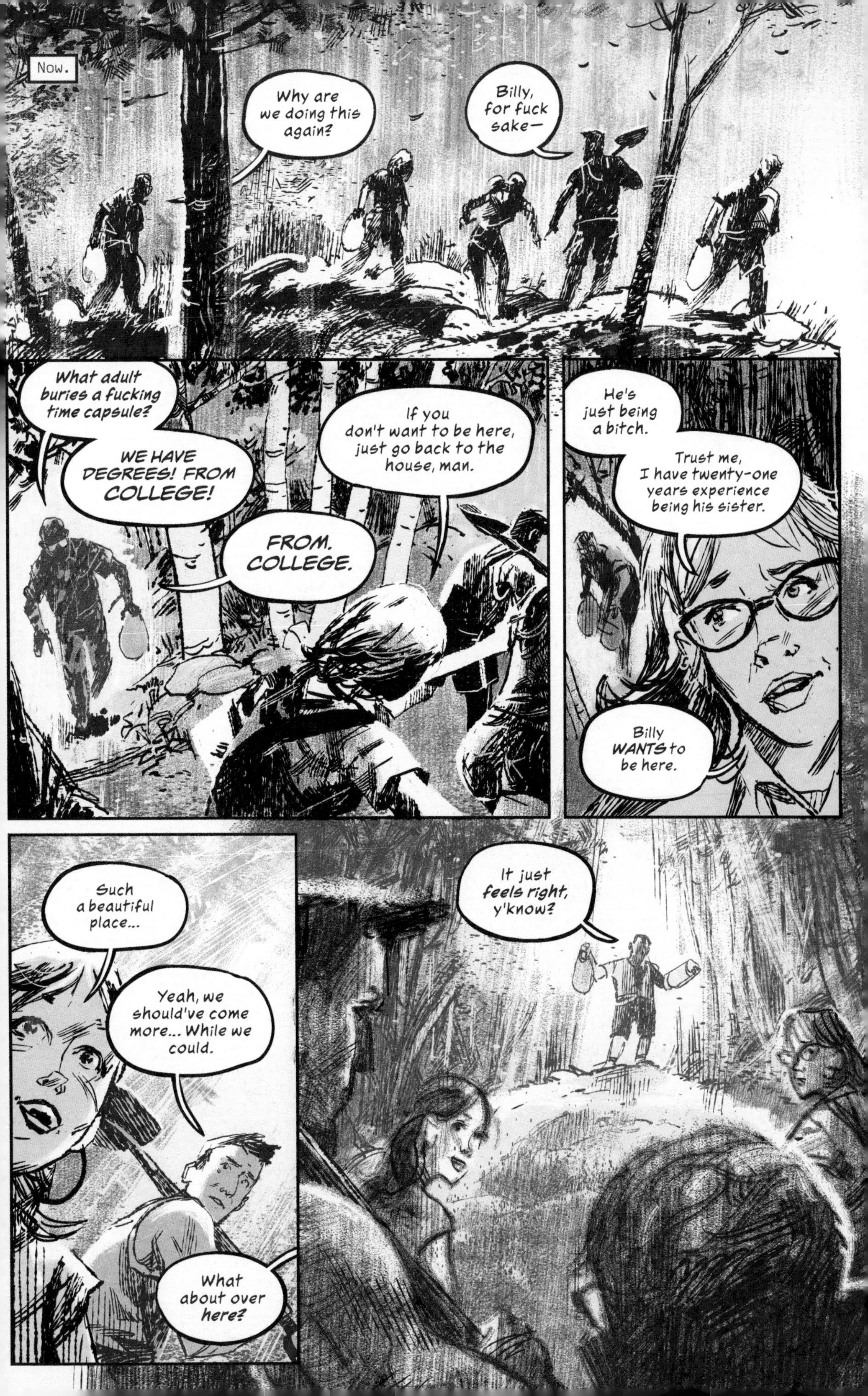
Now.
Why are we doing this again?
Billy, for fuck sake—
What adult buries a fucking time capsule?
WE HAVE DEGREES! FROM COLLEGE!
FROM. COLLEGE.
If you don't want to be here, just go back to the house, man.
He's just being a bitch.
Trust me, I have twenty-one years experience being his sister.
Billy WANTS to be here.
Such a beautiful place...
Yeah, we should've come more... While we could.
What about over here?
It just feels right, y'know?

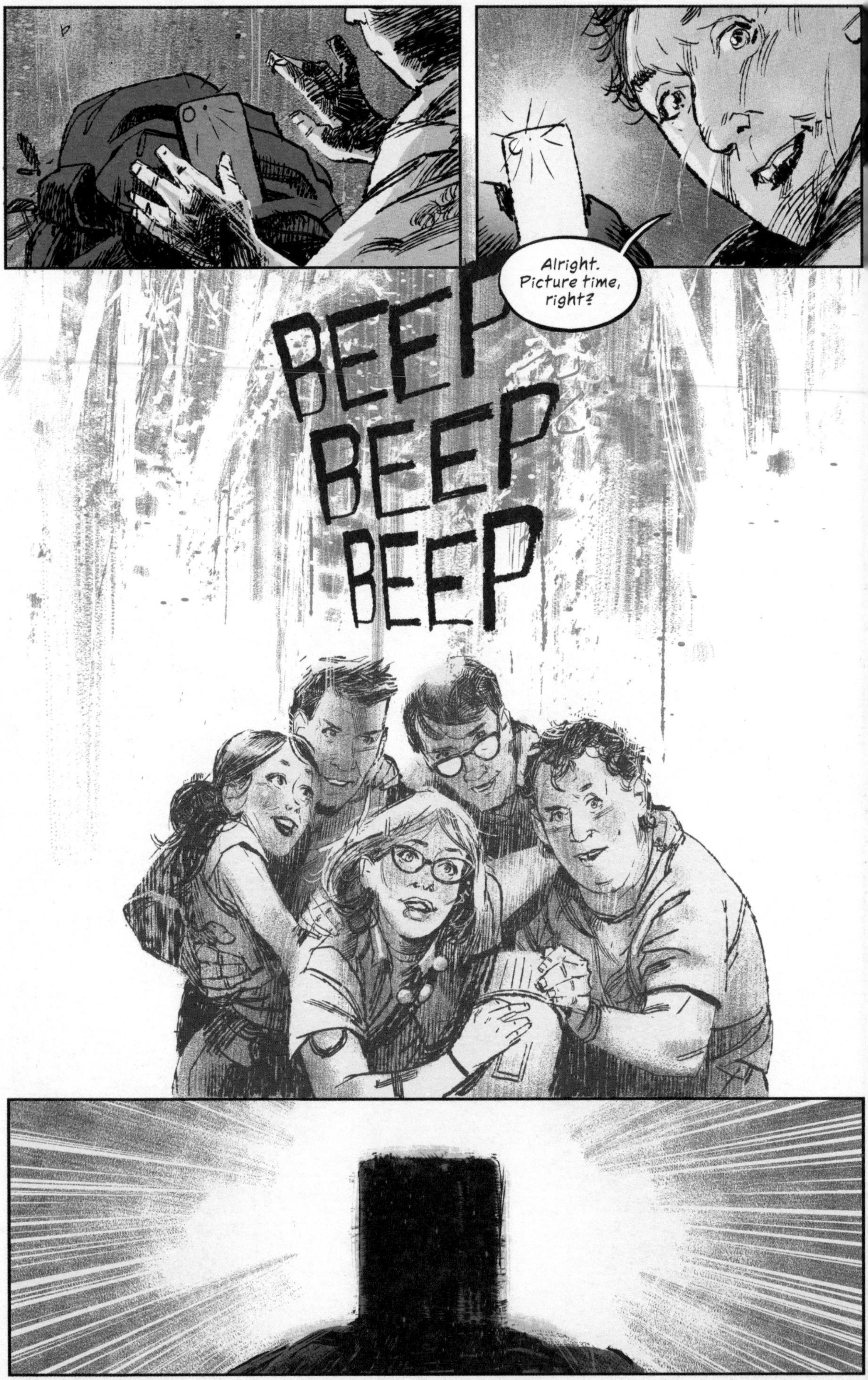
Alright. Picture time, right?
BEEP
BEEP
BEEP

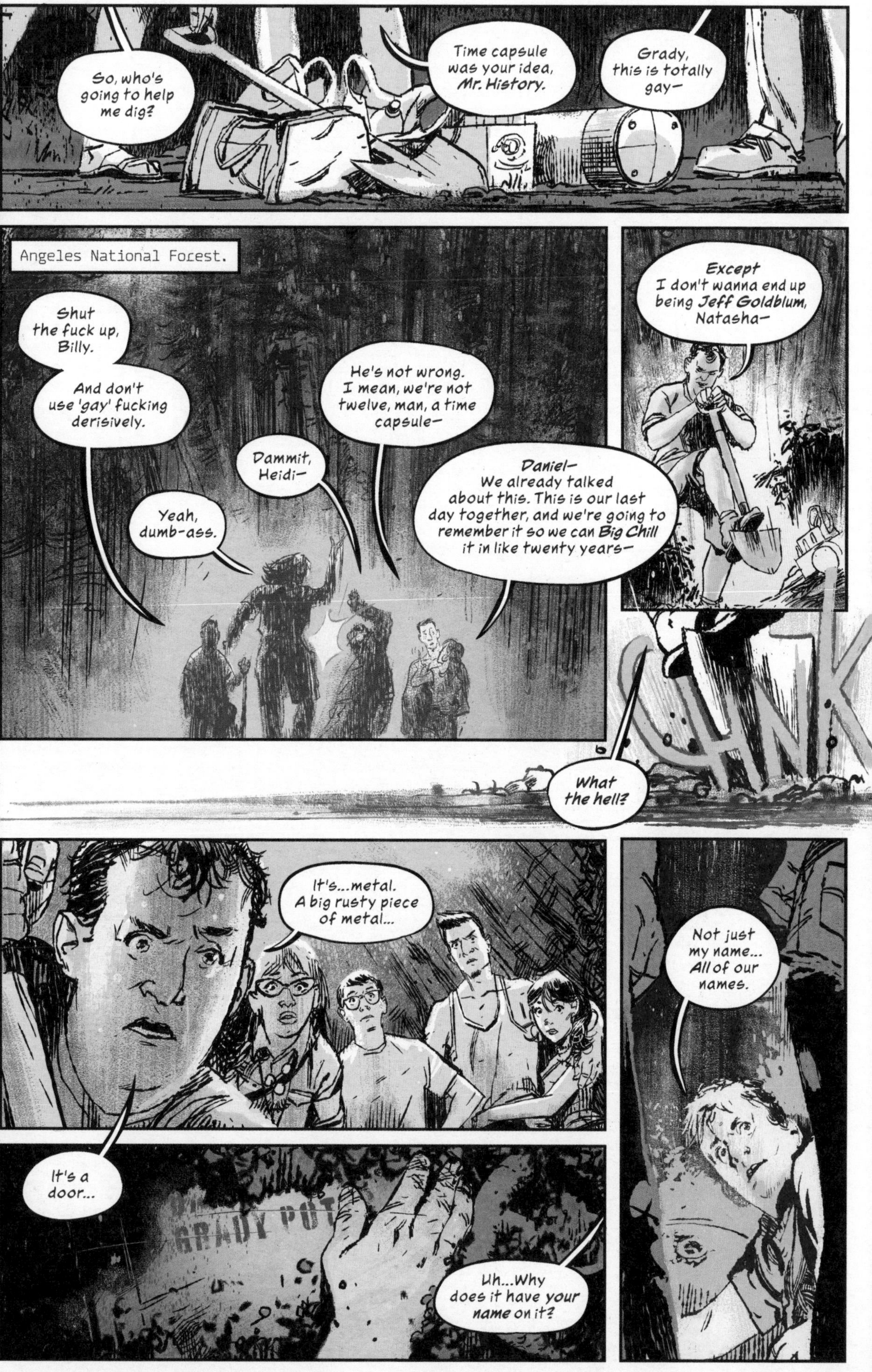
So, who's going to help me dig?
Time capsule was your idea, Mr. History.
Grady, this is totally gay—
Angeles National Forest.
Shut the fuck up, Billy.
And don't use 'gay' fucking derisively.
He's not wrong. I mean, we're not twelve, man, a time capsule—
Dammit, Heidi—
Yeah, dumb-ass.
Daniel— We already talked about this. This is our last day together, and we're going to remember it so we can Big Chill it in like twenty years—
Except I don't wanna end up being Jeff Goldblum, Natasha—
CHNK
What the hell?
It's...metal. A big rusty piece of metal...
Not just my name... All of our names.
It's a door...
GRADY POT
Uh...Why does it have your name on it?

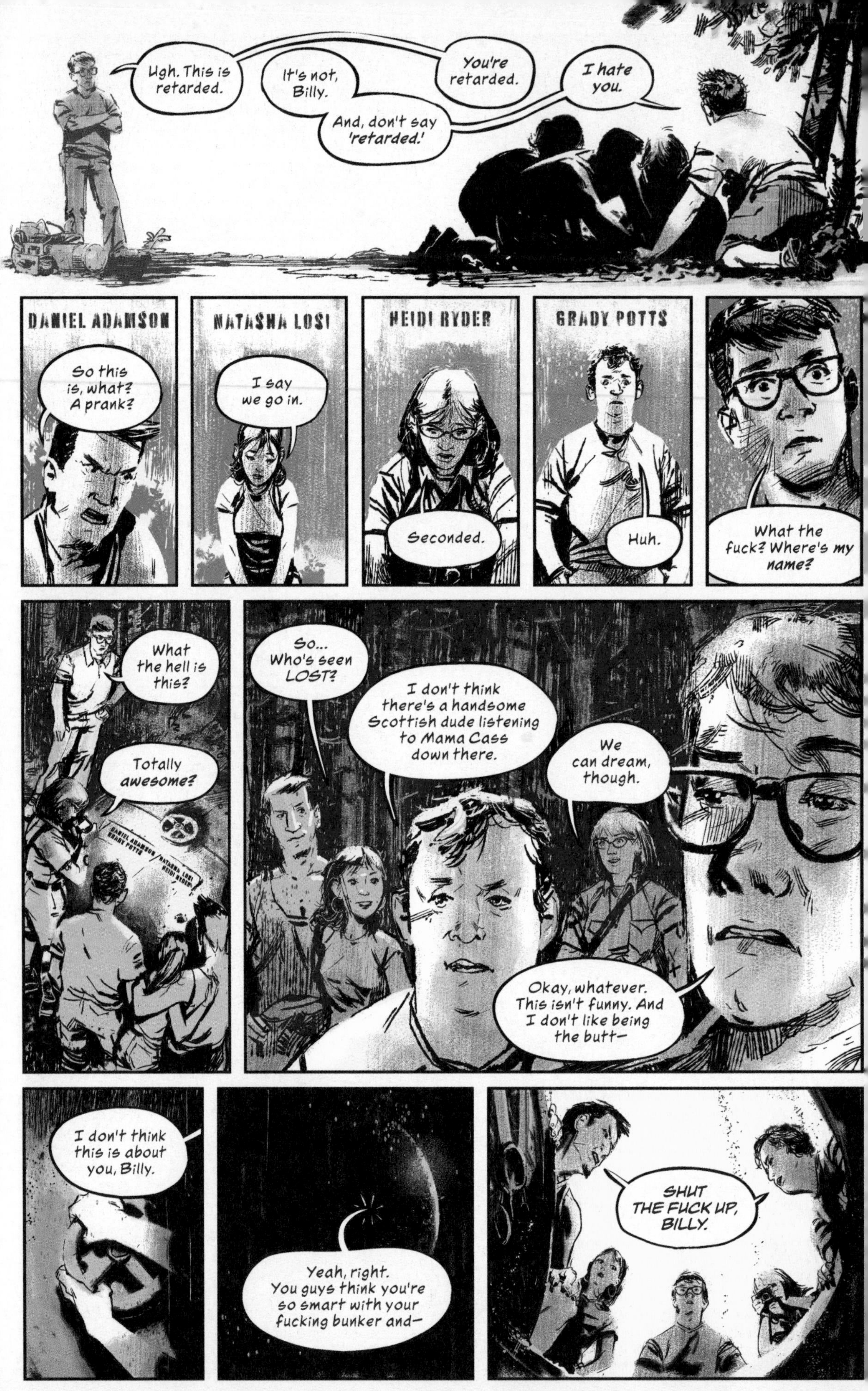
Ugh. This is retarded.
It's not, Billy.
And, don't say 'retarded.'
You're retarded.
I hate you.
DANIEL ADAMSON
So this is, what? A prank?
NATASHA LOSI
I say we go in.
HEIDI RYDER
Seconded.
GRADY POTTS
Huh.
What the fuck? Where's my name?
What the hell is this?
Totally awesome?
DANIEL ADAMSON / NATASHA LOSI
GRADY POTTS / HEIDI RYDER
So... Who's seen LOST?
I don't think there's a handsome Scottish dude listening to Mama Cass down there.
We can dream, though.
Okay, whatever. This isn't funny. And I don't like being the butt—
I don't think this is about you, Billy.
Yeah, right. You guys think you're so smart with your fucking bunker and—
SHUT THE FUCK UP, BILLY.

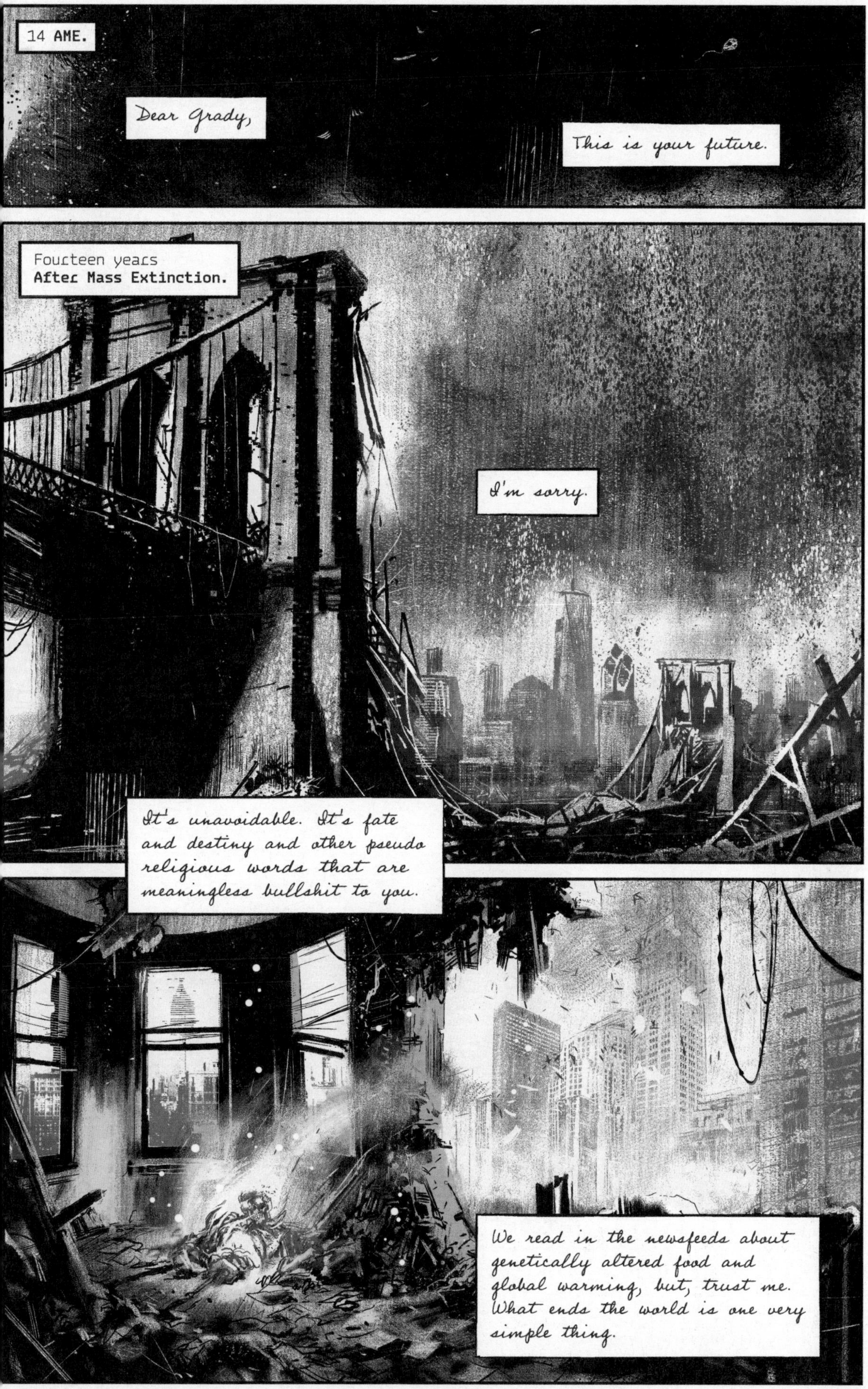
14 AME.
Dear Grady,
This is your future.
Fourteen years After Mass Extinction.
I'm sorry.
It's unavoidable. It's fate and destiny and other pseudo religious words that are meaningless bullshit to you.
We read in the newsfeeds about genetically altered food and global warming, but, trust me. What ends the world is one very simple thing.

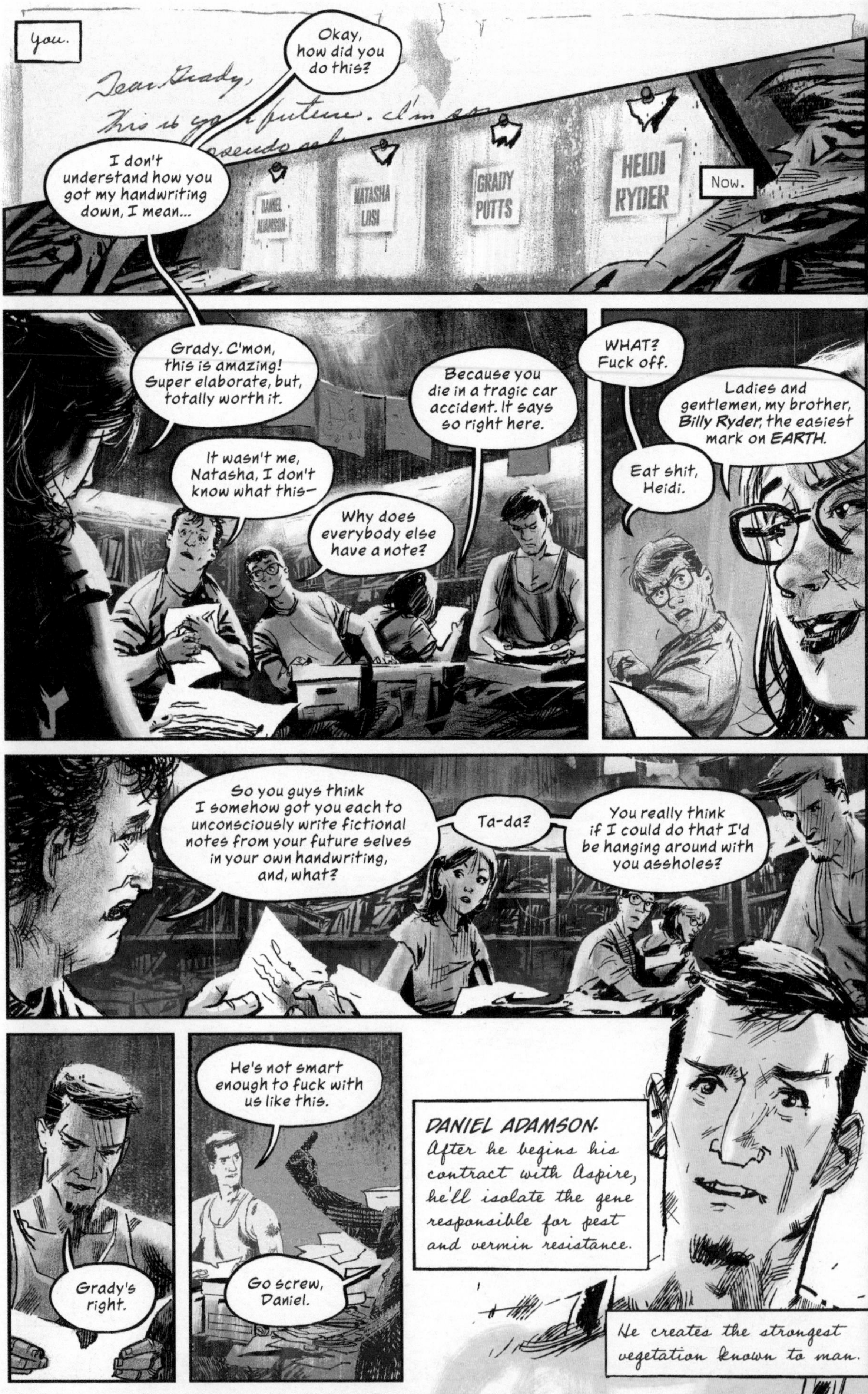

You.
Okay, how did you do this?
DANIEL ADAMSON
NATASHA LOSI
GRADY PUTTS
HEIDI RYDER
I don't understand how you got my handwriting down, I mean...
Now.
Grady. C'mon, this is amazing! Super elaborate, but, totally worth it.
It wasn't me, Natasha, I don't know what this–
Why does everybody else have a note?
Because you die in a tragic car accident. It says so right here.
WHAT? Fuck off.
Ladies and gentlemen, my brother, *Billy Ryder*, the easiest mark on *EARTH*.
Eat shit, Heidi.
So you guys think I somehow got you each to unconsciously write fictional notes from your future selves in your own handwriting, and, what?
Ta-da?
You really think if I could do that I'd be hanging around with you assholes?
Grady's right.
He's not smart enough to fuck with us like this.
Go screw, Daniel.
DANIEL ADAMSON. After he begins his contract with Aspire, he'll isolate the gene responsible for pest and vermin resistance.
He creates the strongest vegetation known to man.

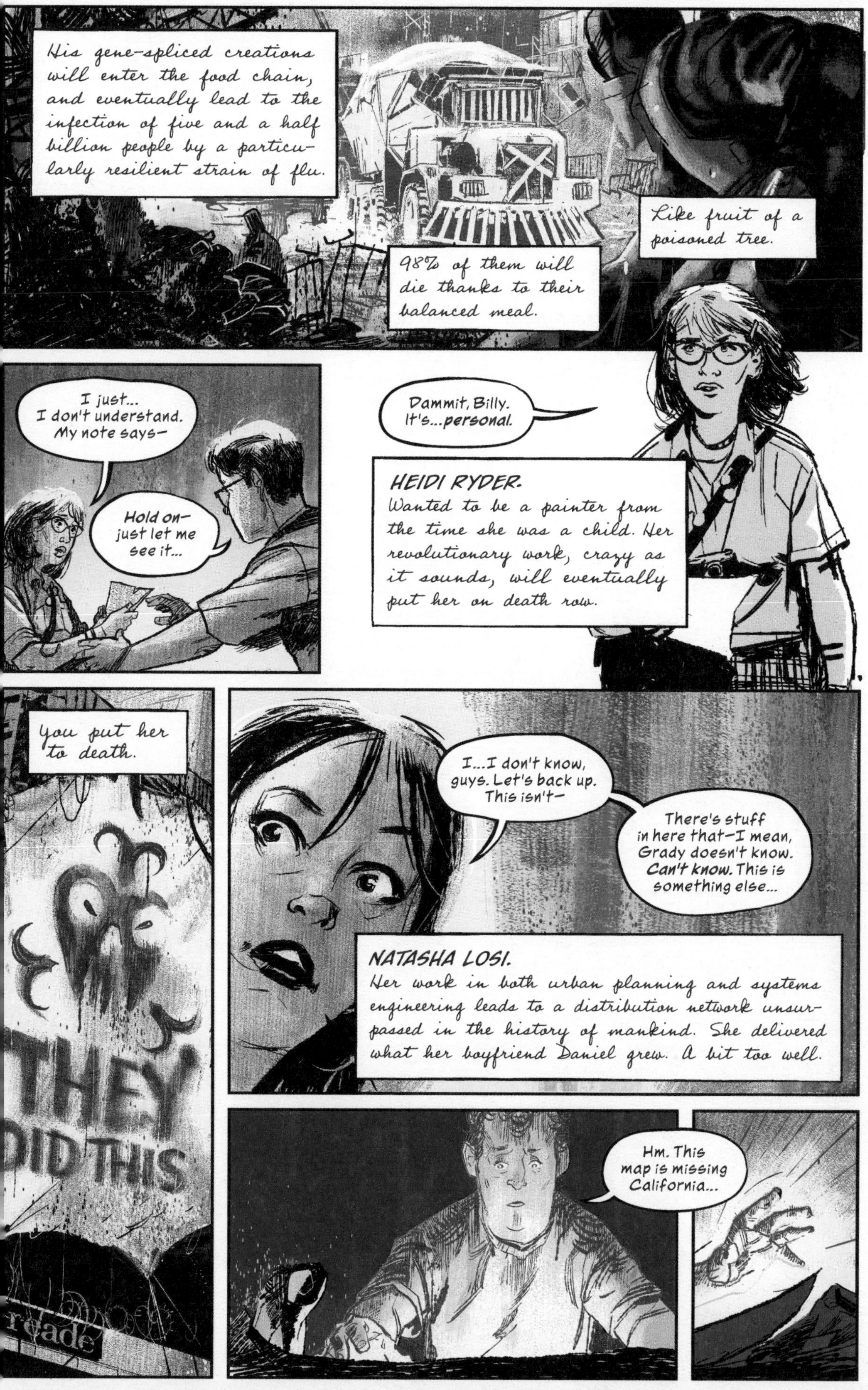

His gene-spliced creations will enter the food chain, and eventually lead to the infection of five and a half billion people by a particularly resilient strain of flu.
98% of them will die thanks to their balanced meal.
Like fruit of a poisoned tree.
I just... I don't understand. My note says—
Hold on— just let me see it...
Dammit, Billy. It's...personal.
HEIDI RYDER.
Wanted to be a painter from the time she was a child. Her revolutionary work, crazy as it sounds, will eventually put her on death row.
You put her to death.
THEY DID THIS
I...I don't know, guys. Let's back up. This isn't—
There's stuff in here that—I mean, Grady doesn't know. Can't know. This is something else...
NATASHA LOSI.
Her work in both urban planning and systems engineering leads to a distribution network unsurpassed in the history of mankind. She delivered what her boyfriend Daniel grew. A bit too well.
Hm. This map is missing California...

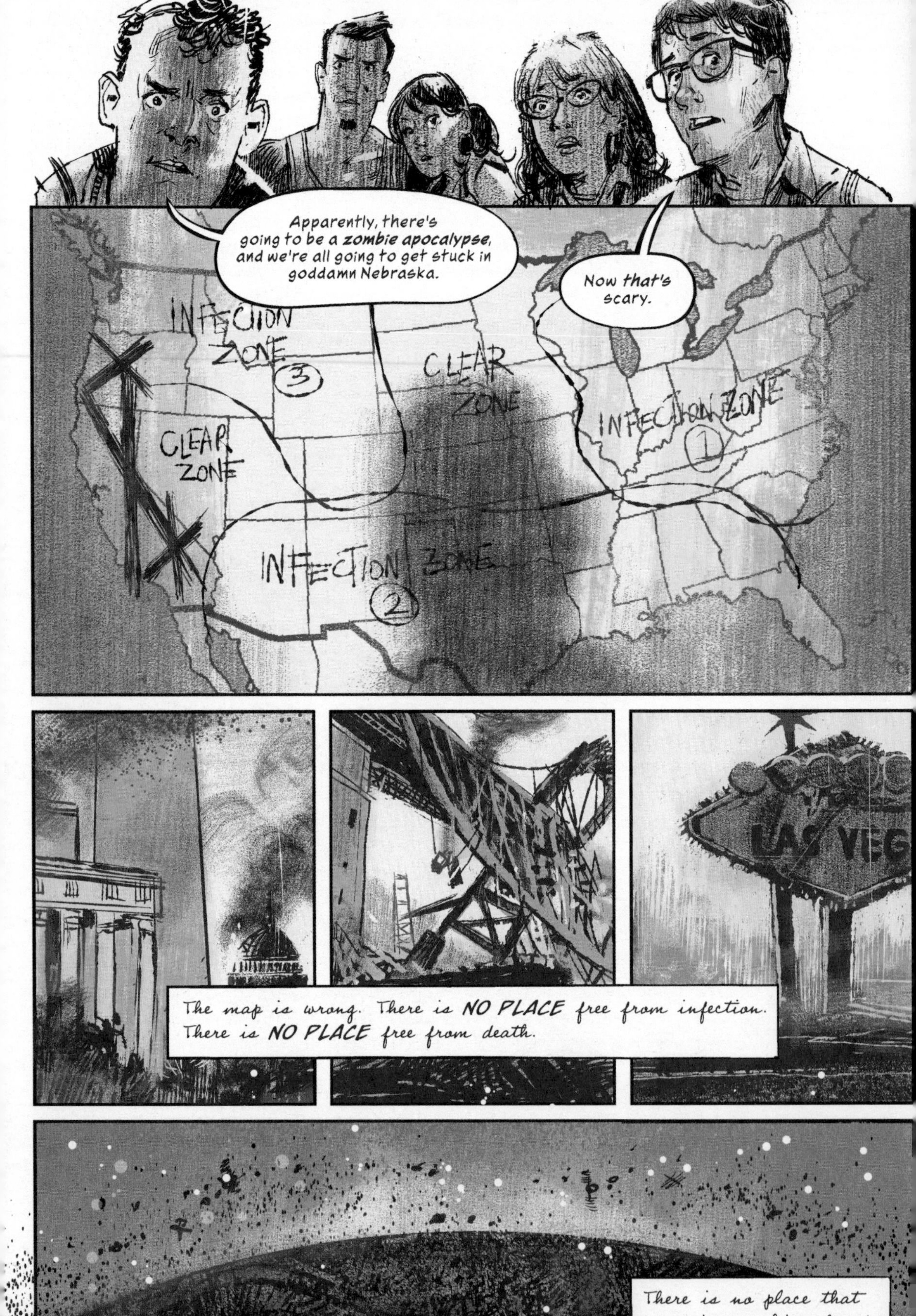
Apparently, there's going to be a zombie apocalypse, and we're all going to get stuck in goddamn Nebraska.
Now that's scary.
INFECTION ZONE 3
CLEAR ZONE
CLEAR ZONE
INFECTION ZONE 1
INFECTION ZONE 2
LAS VEG
The map is wrong. There is NO PLACE free from infection. There is NO PLACE free from death.
There is no place that your icy fucking hand hasn't turned to SHIT.

We wrote these letters to tell you that it's not too late.

To inspire a future we hope can be made.

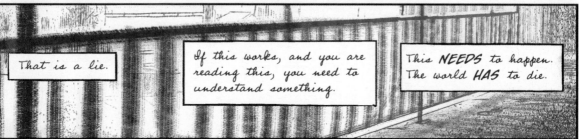

That is a lie.

If this works, and you are reading this, you need to understand something.

This **NEEDS** to happen. The world **HAS** to die.

If these billions don't die...

...then, we all do.

I've seen what happens. **WE'VE** seen what happens.

I have, you will.

You have no choice but to destroy the people you love, let everyone you cared for rot away, otherwise, there will be nothing left.

Mr. President, do we need to move?

Yes. They'll be here soon.

They *who*, sir?

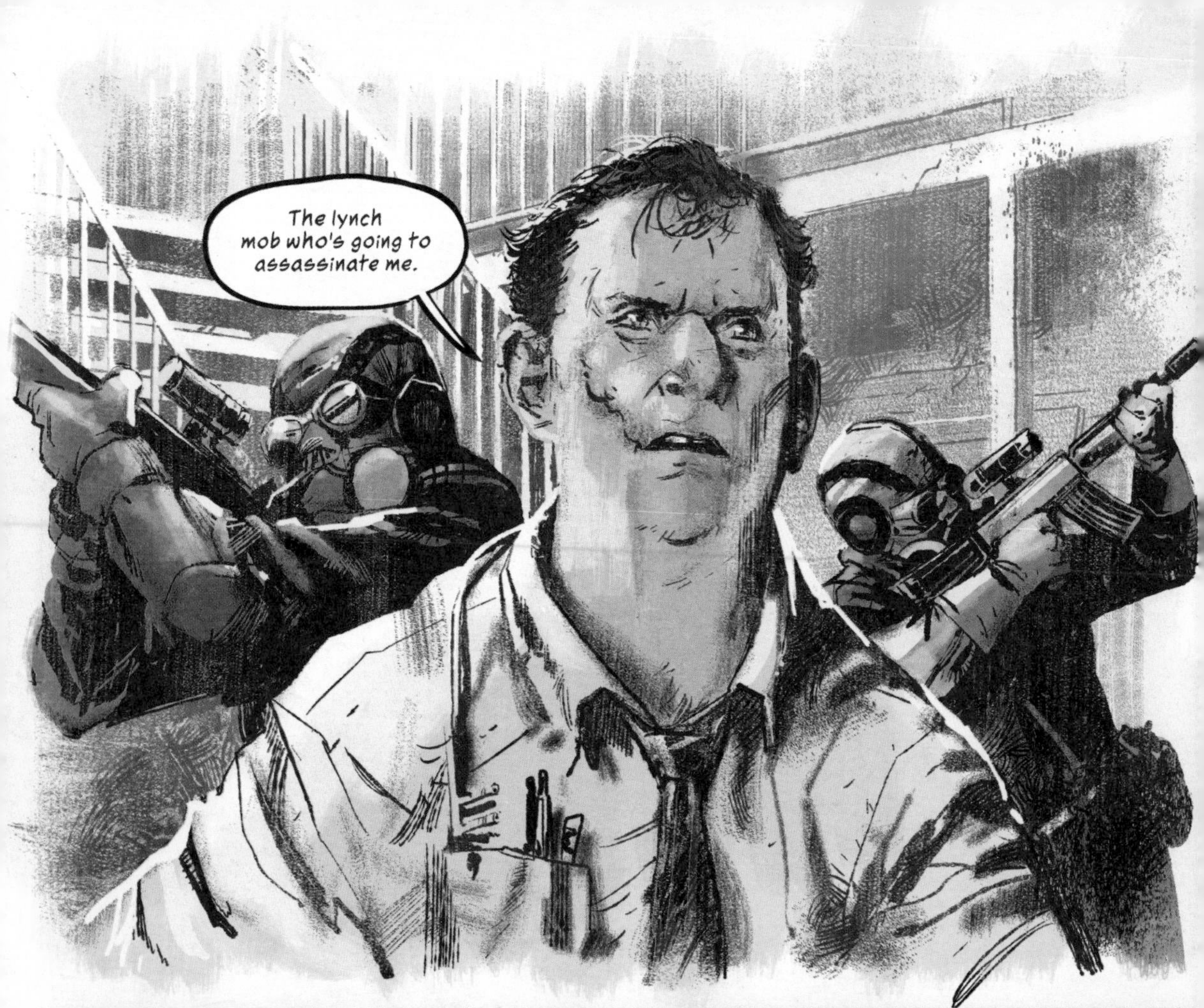
The lynch mob who's going to assassinate me.

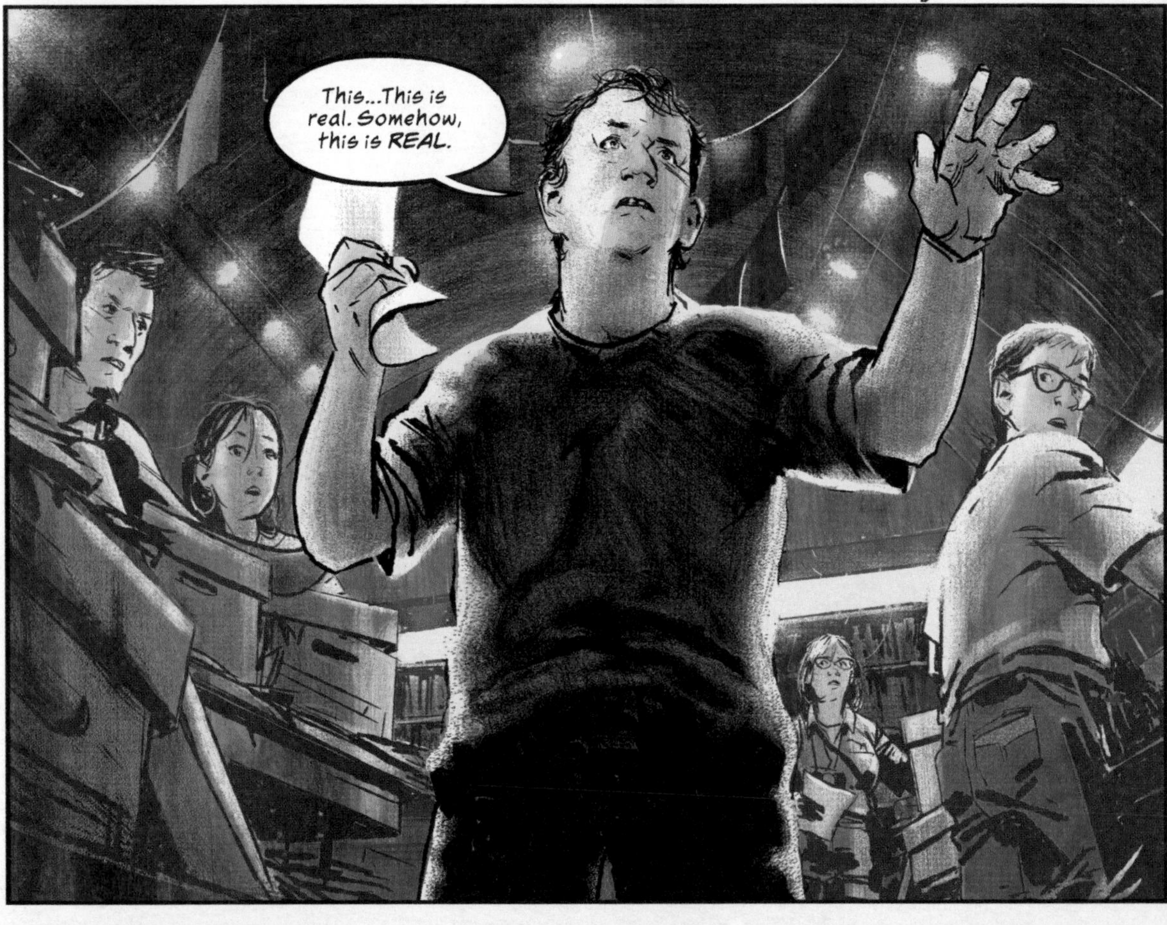
This...This is real. Somehow, this is REAL.

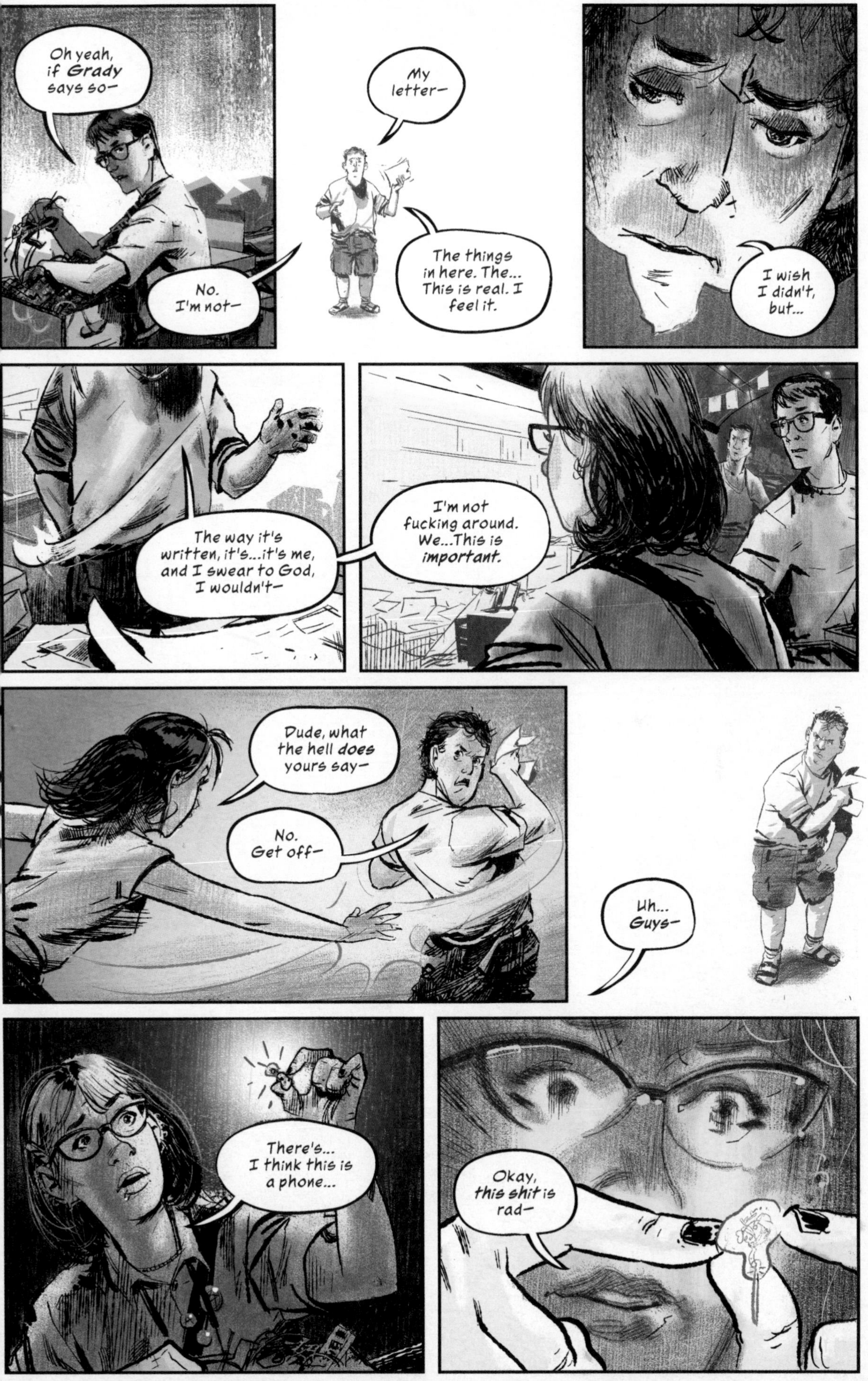
Oh yeah, if Grady says so–
My letter–
No. I'm not–
The things in here. The... This is real. I feel it.
I wish I didn't, but...
The way it's written, it's...it's me, and I swear to God, I wouldn't–
I'm not fucking around. We...This is important.
Dude, what the hell does yours say–
No. Get off–
Uh... Guys–
There's... I think this is a phone...
Okay, this shit is rad–

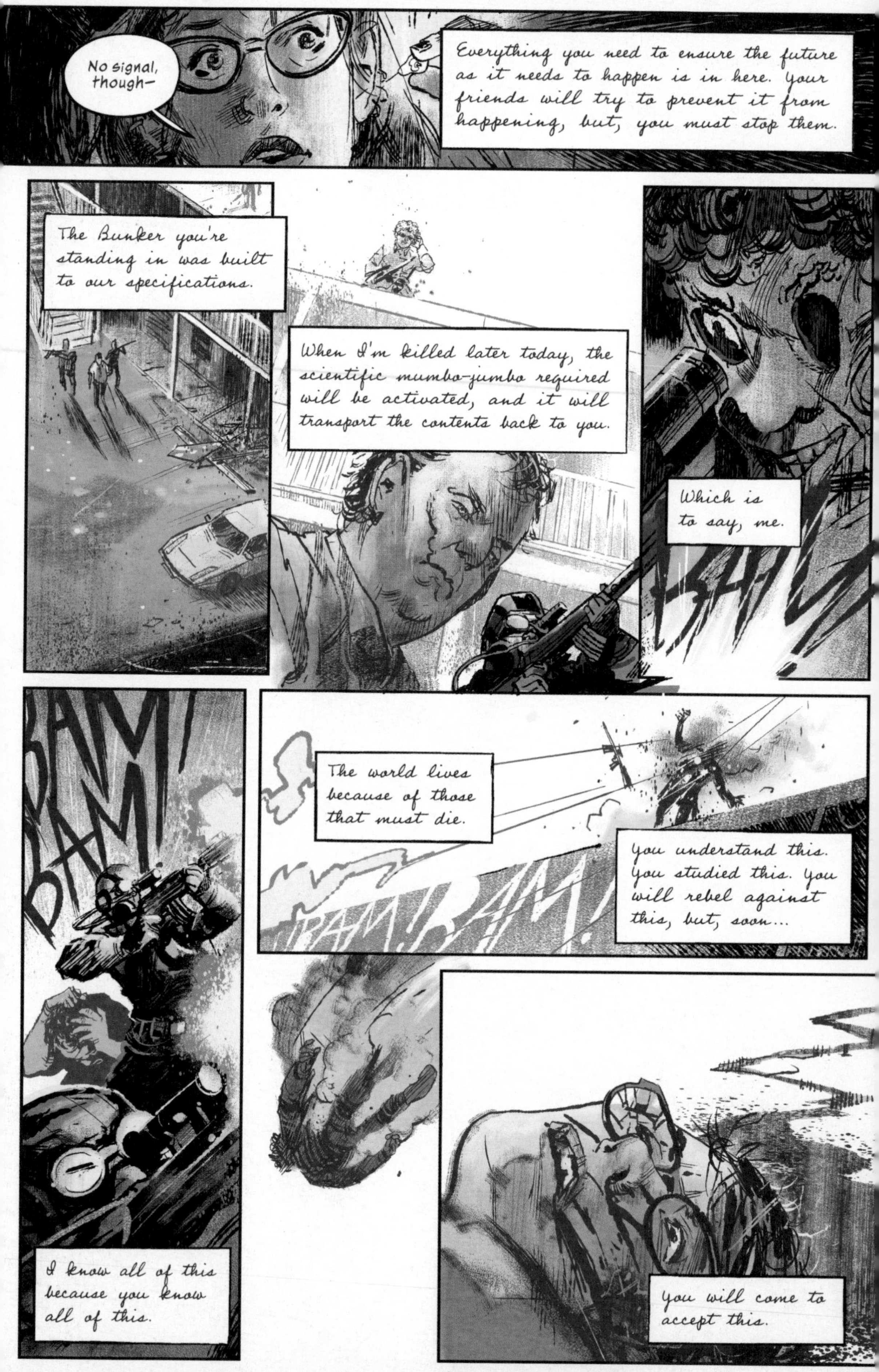
No signal, though—
Everything you need to ensure the future as it needs to happen is in here. Your friends will try to prevent it from happening, but, you must stop them.
The Bunker you're standing in was built to our specifications.
When I'm killed later today, the scientific mumbo-jumbo required will be activated, and it will transport the contents back to you.
Which is to say, me.
BAM!
BAM!
BAM!
BAM!
The world lives because of those that must die.
BAM! BAM!
You understand this. You studied this. You will rebel against this, but, soon...
I know all of this because you know all of this.
You will come to accept this.

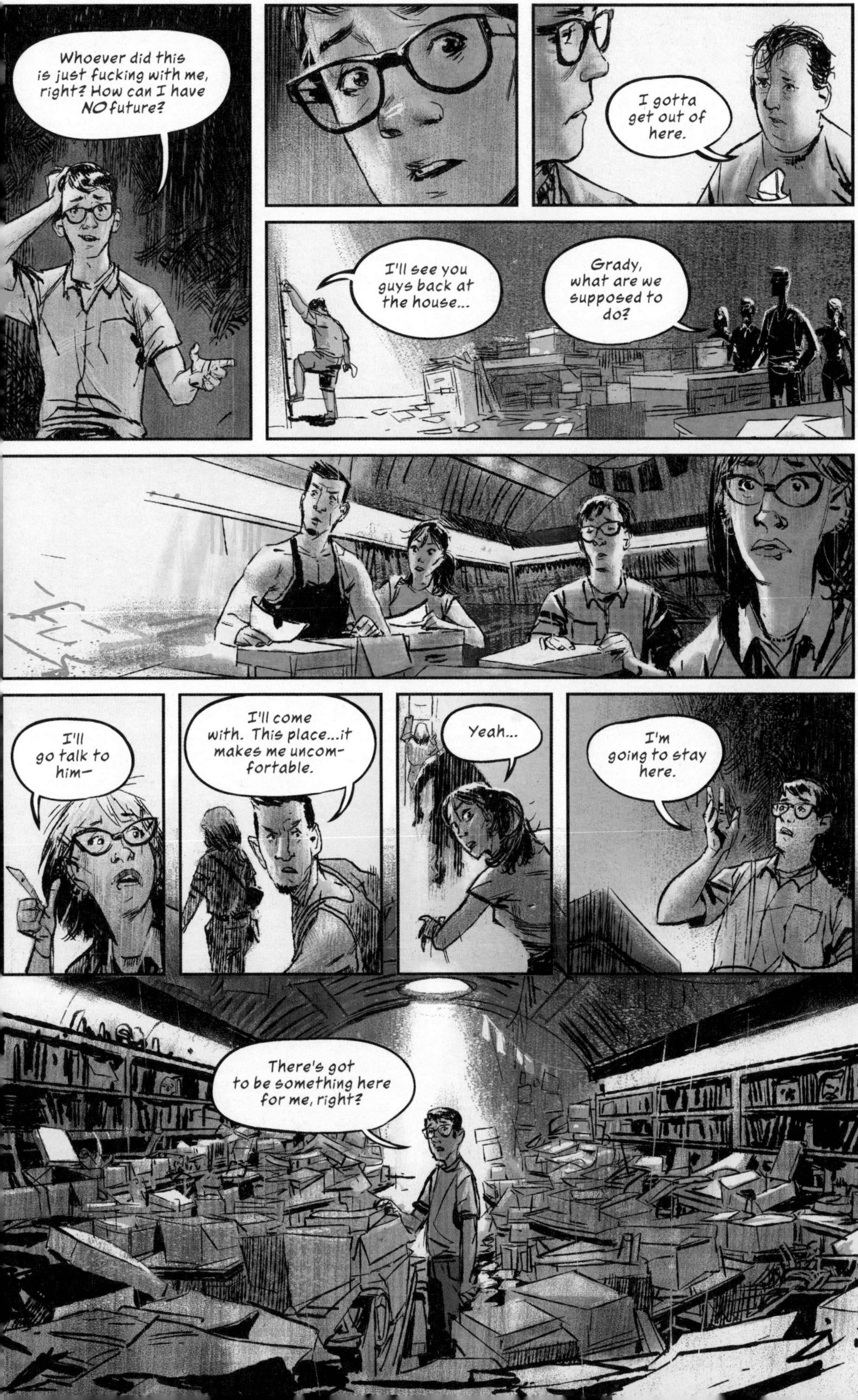
Whoever did this is just fucking with me, right? How can I have NO future?
I gotta get out of here.
I'll see you guys back at the house...
Grady, what are we supposed to do?
I'll go talk to him—
I'll come with. This place...it makes me uncom-fortable.
Yeah...
I'm going to stay here.
There's got to be something here for me, right?

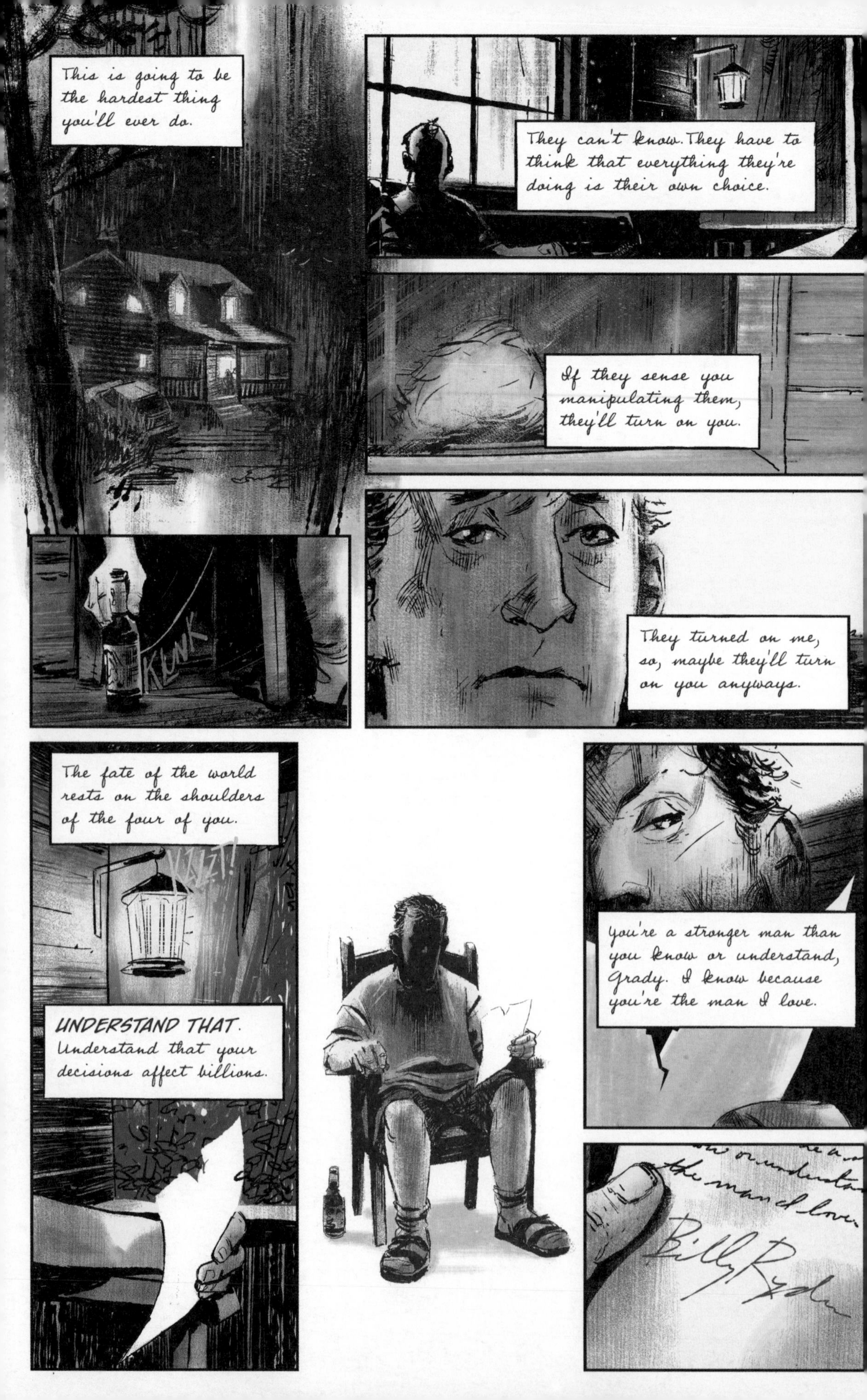
This is going to be the hardest thing you'll ever do.
They can't know. They have to think that everything they're doing is their own choice.
If they sense you manipulating them, they'll turn on you.
KLUNK
They turned on me, so, maybe they'll turn on you anyways.
The fate of the world rests on the shoulders of the four of you.
VZZZT!
UNDERSTAND THAT. Understand that your decisions affect billions.
You're a stronger man than you know or understand, Grady. I know because you're the man I love.
Billy Ryder

Dear Heidi,

I know you won't believe this is real, because, hell, I barely believe it's real. So, I know proving it is the key. You need to believe, and...

...I'm sorry.

This is getting to you before you've come to terms with what he did to you, and I'm sorry to make you leap over all of the years of therapy.

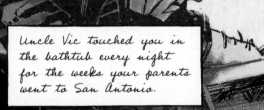

Uncle Vic touched you in the bathtub every night for the weeks your parents went to San Antonio.

You feel like somehow this is your fault, and it isn't. You'll spend thousands on therapy to get there, but, well, nobody knows but you.

And I'm YOU.

Now.

This is fucking weird.

Heidi? You okay?

Huh? Yeah. I just—

Never mind.

I'm freaked out, too. I mean, my letter says I cause a plague... Which y'know, not great, right.

No. It's not that stuff that bothers me.

Daniel... Something happened to me when I was a kid, and nobody knows except the... other person.

Oh.

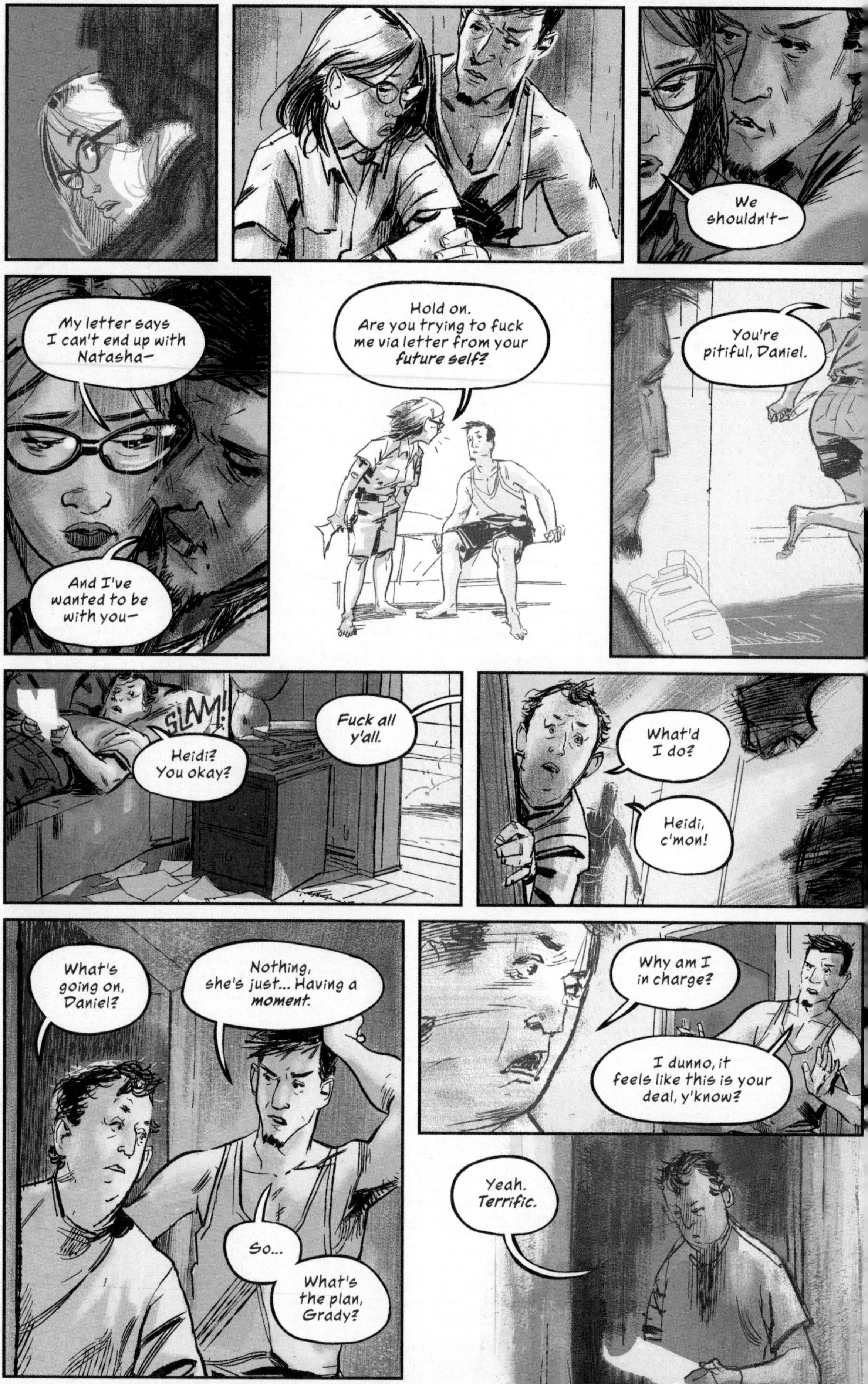
We shouldn't—
My letter says I can't end up with Natasha—
And I've wanted to be with you—
Hold on. Are you trying to fuck me via letter from your *future self?*
You're pitiful, Daniel.
SLAM!
Heidi? You okay?
Fuck all y'all.
What'd I do?
Heidi, c'mon!
What's going on, Daniel?
Nothing, she's just... Having a *moment.*
So...
What's the plan, Grady?
Why am I in charge?
I dunno, it feels like this is your deal, y'know?
Yeah. *Terrific.*

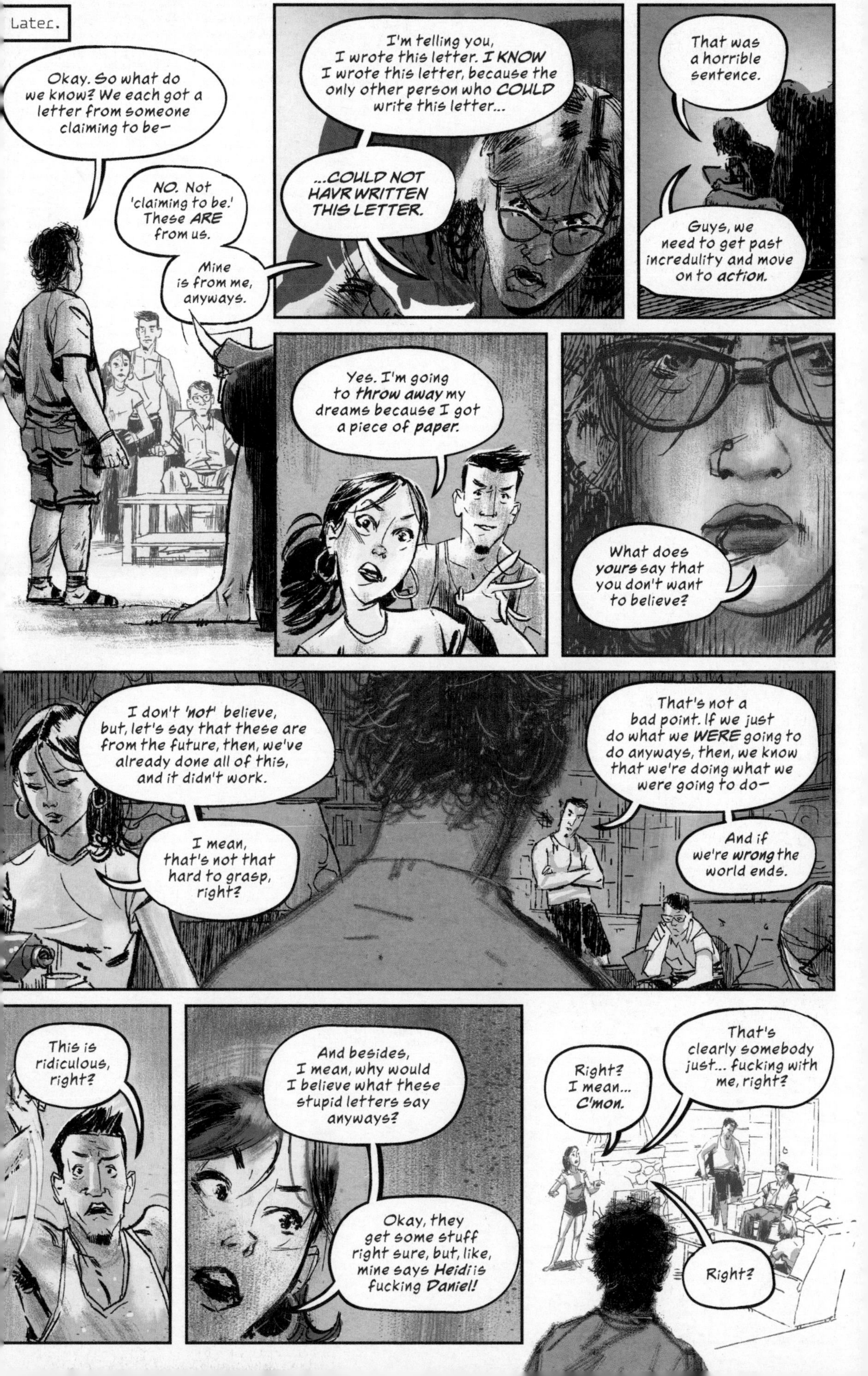

Later.
Okay. So what do we know? We each got a letter from someone claiming to be—
NO. Not 'claiming to be.' These ARE from us.
Mine is from me, anyways.
I'm telling you, I wrote this letter. I KNOW I wrote this letter, because the only other person who COULD write this letter...
...COULD NOT HAVR WRITTEN THIS LETTER.
That was a horrible sentence.
Guys, we need to get past incredulity and move on to action.
Yes. I'm going to throw away my dreams because I got a piece of paper.
What does yours say that you don't want to believe?
I don't 'not' believe, but, let's say that these are from the future, then, we've already done all of this, and it didn't work.
I mean, that's not that hard to grasp, right?
That's not a bad point. If we just do what we WERE going to do anyways, then, we know that we're doing what we were going to do—
And if we're wrong the world ends.
This is ridiculous, right?
And besides, I mean, why would I believe what these stupid letters say anyways?
Okay, they get some stuff right sure, but, like, mine says Heidi is fucking Daniel!
Right? I mean... C'mon.
That's clearly somebody just... fucking with me, right?
Right?

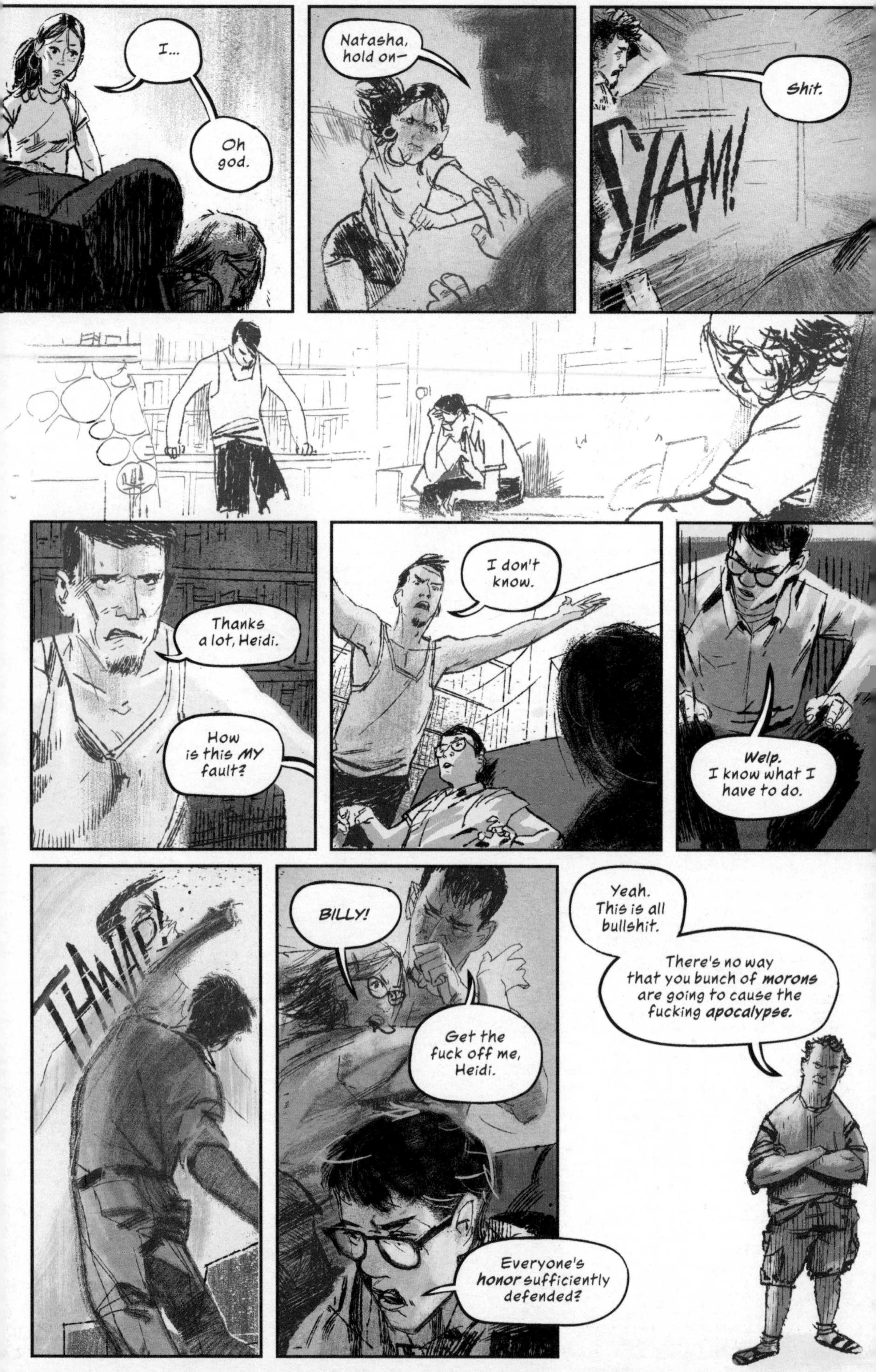

I...
Oh god.
Natasha, hold on–
Shit.
SLAM!
Thanks a lot, Heidi.
How is this MY fault?
I don't know.
Welp. I know what I have to do.
THWAP!
BILLY!
Get the fuck off me, Heidi.
Everyone's honor sufficiently defended?
Yeah. This is all bullshit.
There's no way that you bunch of morons are going to cause the fucking apocalypse.

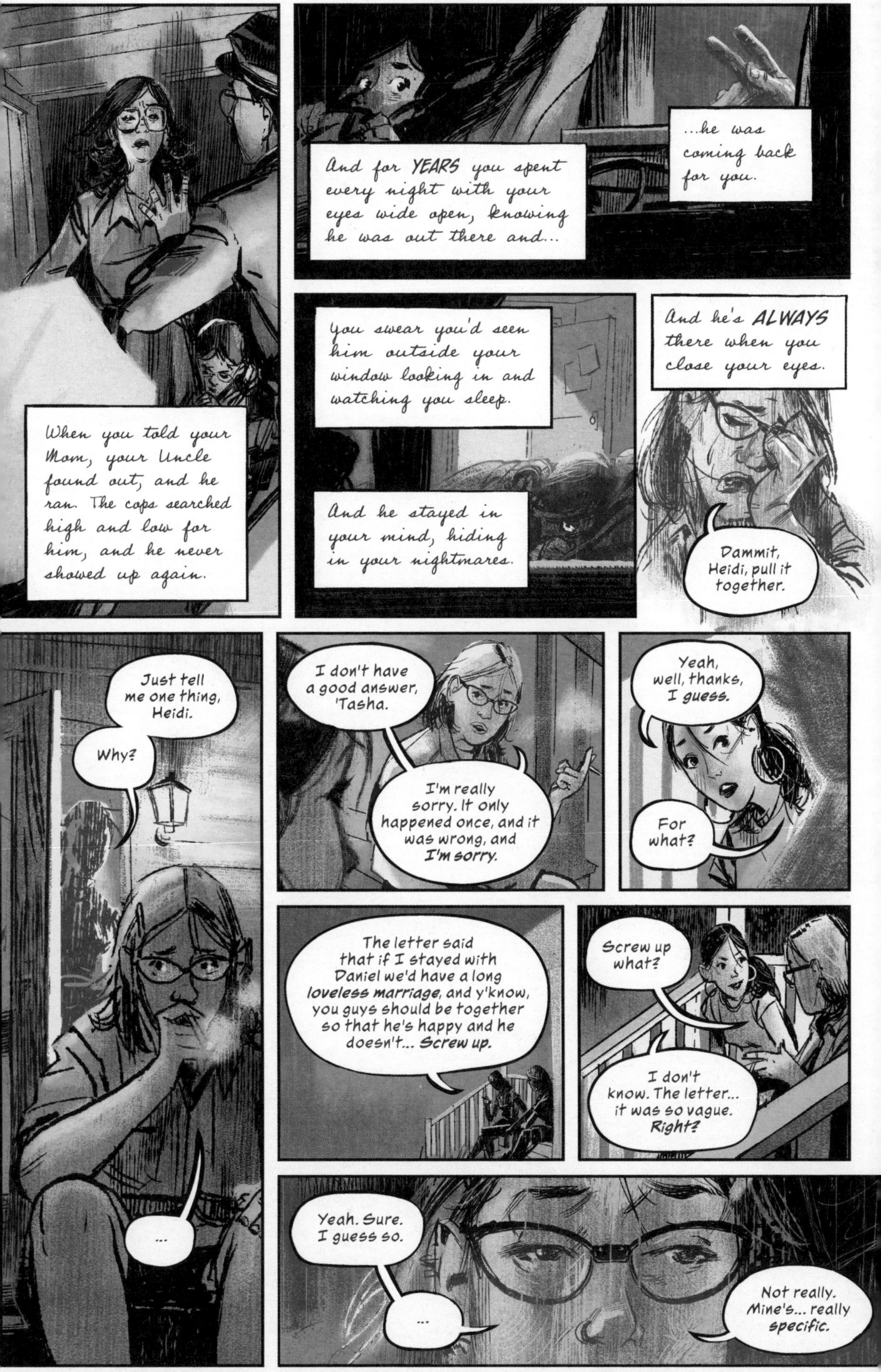
And for YEARS you spent every night with your eyes wide open, knowing he was out there and...
...he was coming back for you.
When you told your Mom, your Uncle found out, and he ran. The cops searched high and low for him, and he never showed up again.
You swear you'd seen him outside your window looking in and watching you sleep.
And he stayed in your mind, hiding in your nightmares.
And he's ALWAYS there when you close your eyes.
Dammit, Heidi, pull it together.
Just tell me one thing, Heidi.
Why?
...
I don't have a good answer, 'Tasha.
I'm really sorry. It only happened once, and it was wrong, and I'm sorry.
Yeah, well, thanks, I guess.
For what?
The letter said that if I stayed with Daniel we'd have a long loveless marriage, and y'know, you guys should be together so that he's happy and he doesn't... Screw up.
Screw up what?
I don't know. The letter... it was so vague. Right?
Yeah. Sure. I guess so.
...
Not really. Mine's... really specific.

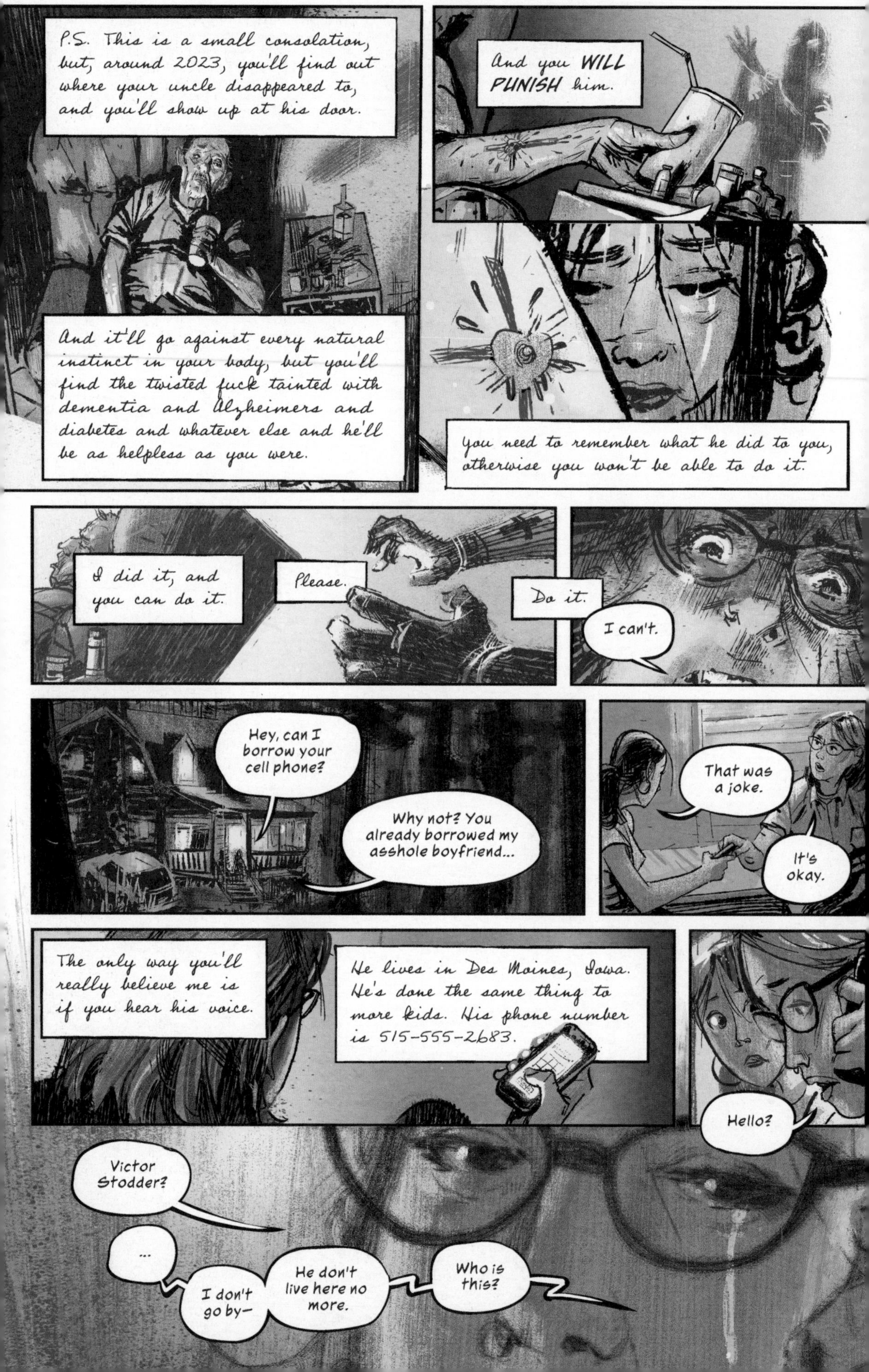
P.S. This is a small consolation, but, around 2023, you'll find out where your uncle disappeared to, and you'll show up at his door.
And it'll go against every natural instinct in your body, but you'll find the twisted fuck tainted with dementia and Alzheimers and diabetes and whatever else and he'll be as helpless as you were.
And you WILL PUNISH him.
You need to remember what he did to you, otherwise you won't be able to do it.
I did it, and you can do it.
Please.
Do it.
I can't.
Hey, can I borrow your cell phone?
Why not? You already borrowed my asshole boyfriend...
That was a joke.
It's okay.
The only way you'll really believe me is if you hear his voice.
He lives in Des Moines, Iowa. He's done the same thing to more kids. His phone number is 515-555-2683.
Hello?
Victor Stodder?
...
I don't go by—
He don't live here no more.
Who is this?

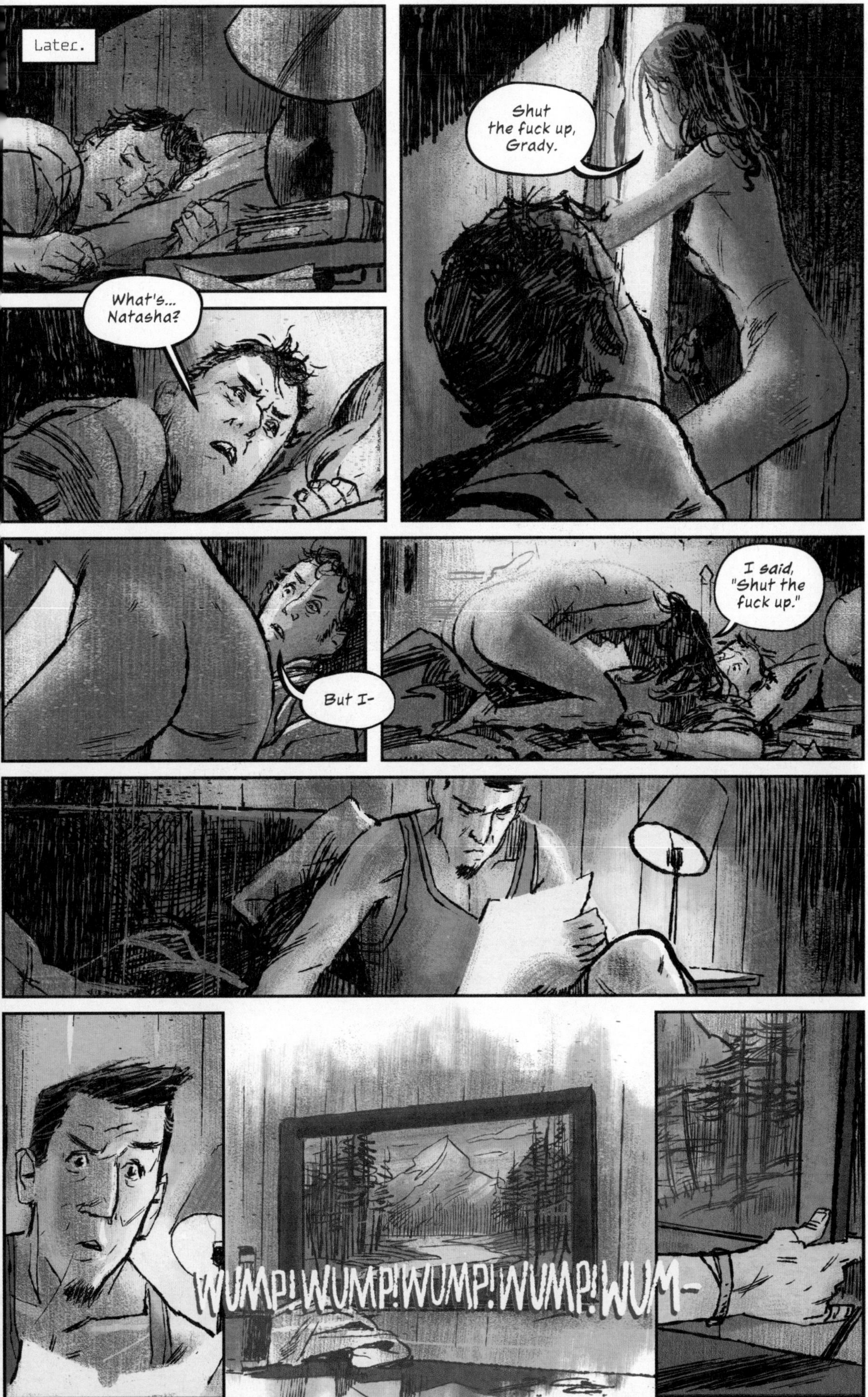

Later.
Shut the fuck up, Grady.
What's... Natasha?
But I-
I said, "Shut the fuck up."
WUMP! WUMP! WUMP! WUMP! WUM-

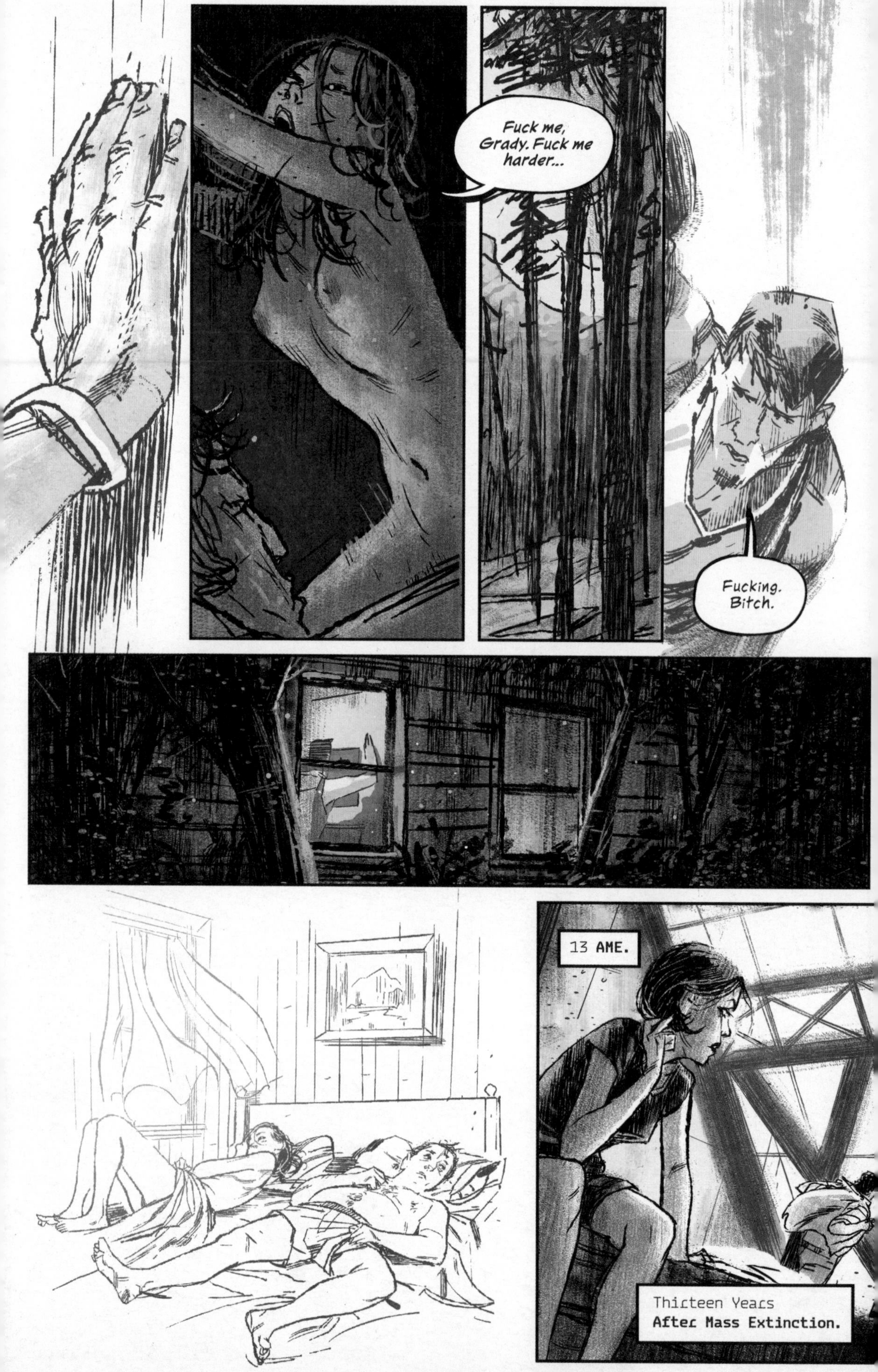
Fuck me, Grady. Fuck me harder...
Fucking. Bitch.
13 AME.
Thirteen Years
After Mass Extinction.

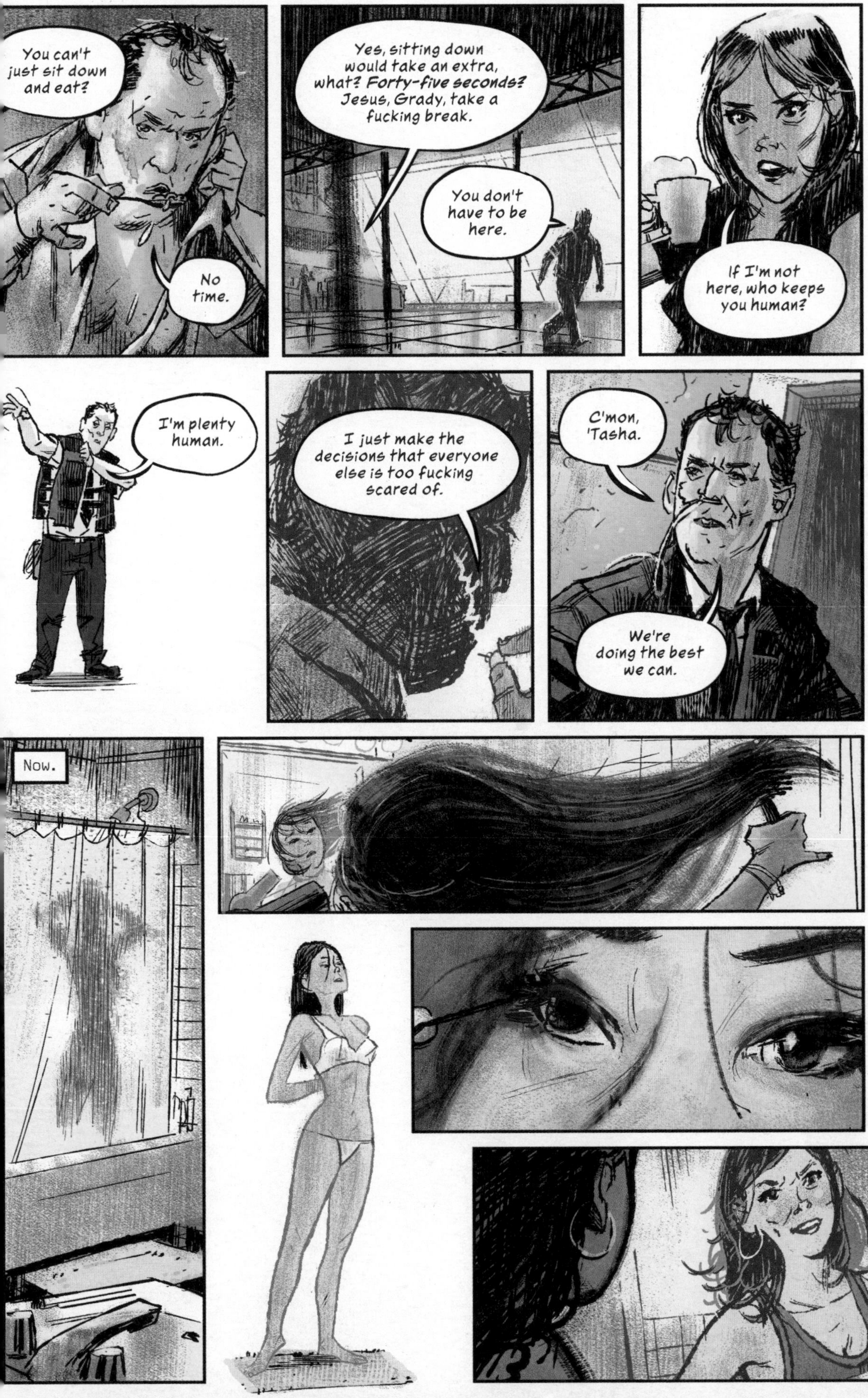
You can't just sit down and eat?
No time.
Yes, sitting down would take an extra, what? *Forty-five seconds?* Jesus, Grady, take a fucking break.
You don't have to be here.
If I'm not here, who keeps you human?
I'm plenty human.
I just make the decisions that everyone else is too fucking scared of.
C'mon, 'Tasha.
We're doing the best we can.
Now.

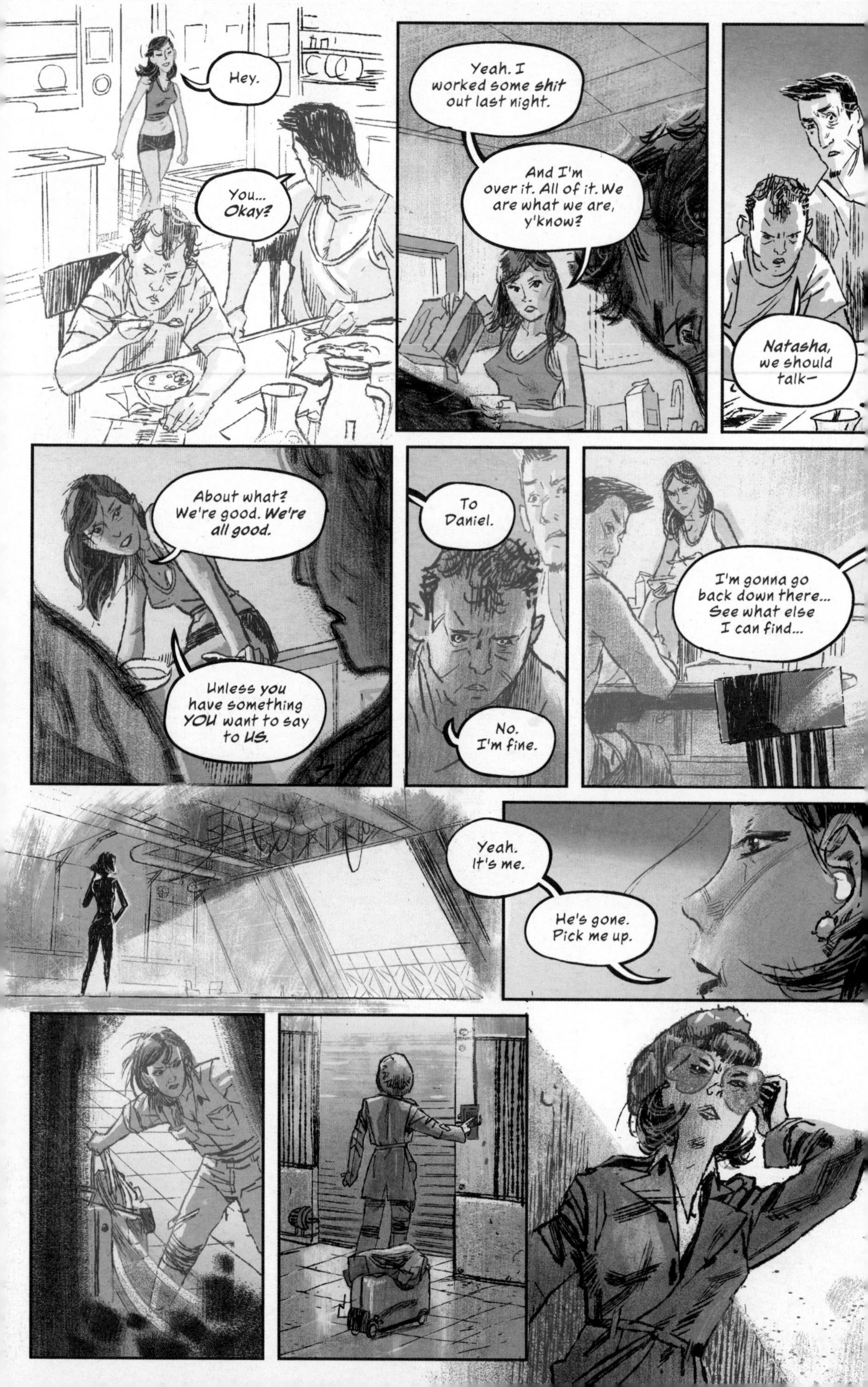
Hey.
You... Okay?
Yeah. I worked some shit out last night.
And I'm over it. All of it. We are what we are, y'know?
Natasha, we should talk—
About what? We're good. We're all good.
Unless you have something YOU want to say to US.
To Daniel.
No. I'm fine.
I'm gonna go back down there... See what else I can find...
Yeah. It's me.
He's gone. Pick me up.

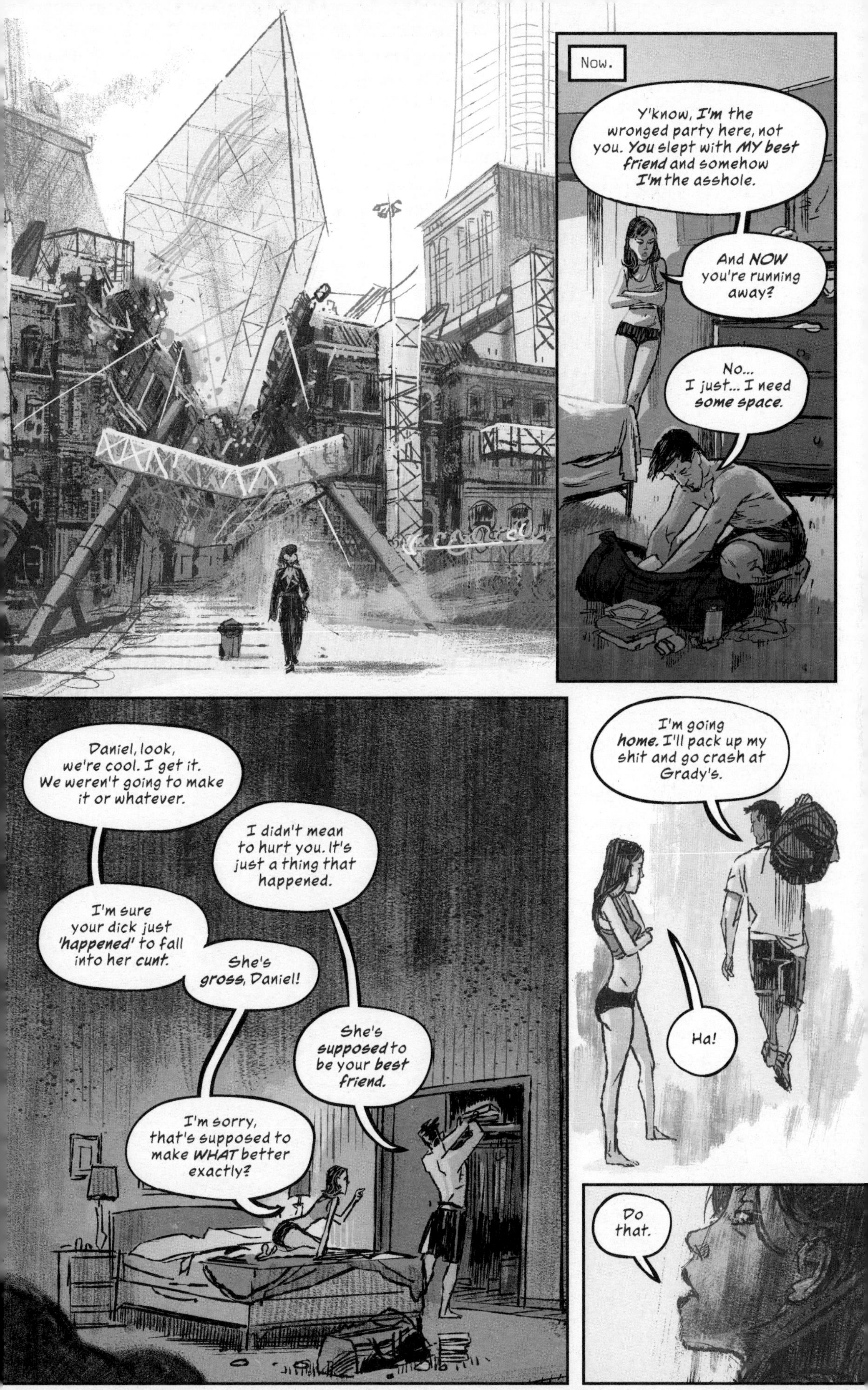
Now.
Y'know, I'm the wronged party here, not you. You slept with MY best friend and somehow I'm the asshole.
And NOW you're running away?
No... I just... I need some space.
Daniel, look, we're cool. I get it. We weren't going to make it or whatever.
I didn't mean to hurt you. It's just a thing that happened.
I'm sure your dick just 'happened' to fall into her cunt.
She's gross, Daniel!
She's supposed to be your best friend.
I'm sorry, that's supposed to make WHAT better exactly?
I'm going home. I'll pack up my shit and go crash at Grady's.
Ha!
Do that.

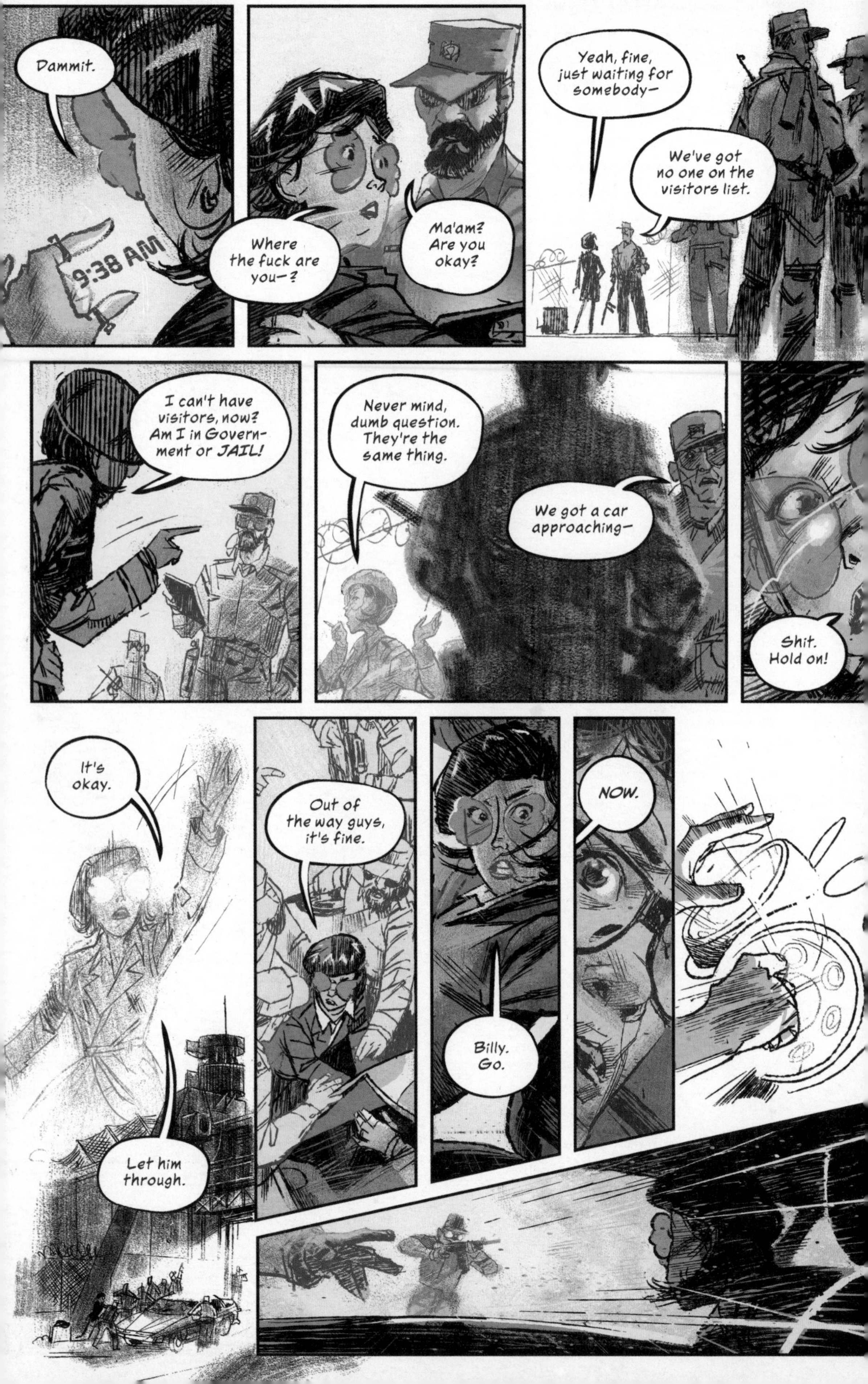
Dammit.
9:38 AM
Where the fuck are you—?
Ma'am? Are you okay?
Yeah, fine, just waiting for somebody—
We've got no one on the visitors list.
I can't have visitors, now? Am I in Govern-ment or JAIL!
Never mind, dumb question. They're the same thing.
We got a car approaching—
Shit. Hold on!
It's okay.
Let him through.
Out of the way guys, it's fine.
Billy. Go.
NOW.

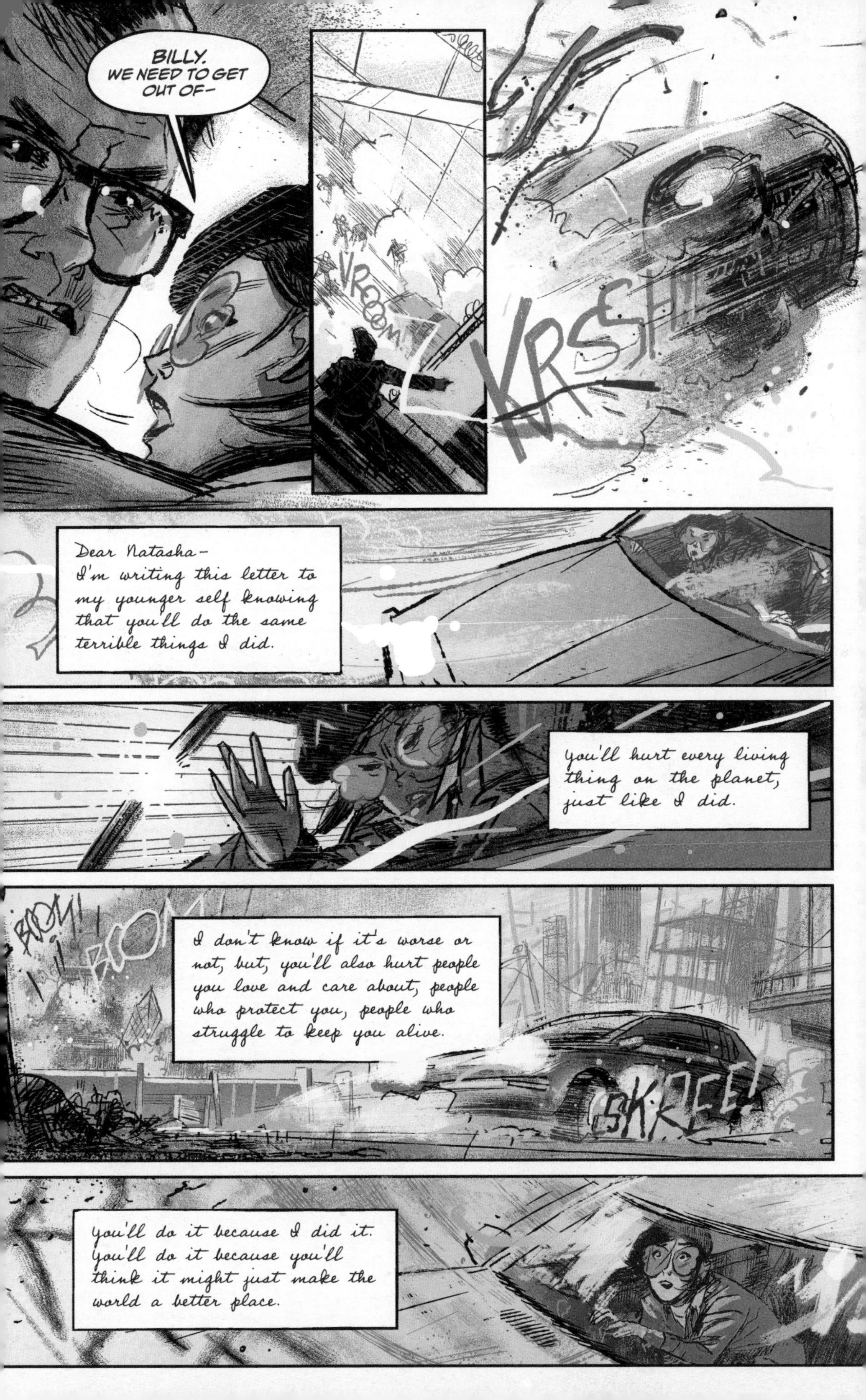
BILLY. WE NEED TO GET OUT OF–
VROOOM
KRSSH
Dear Natasha–
I'm writing this letter to my younger self knowing that you'll do the same terrible things I did.
You'll hurt every living thing on the planet, just like I did.
BOOM!
BOOM!
I don't know if it's worse or not, but, you'll also hurt people you love and care about, people who protect you, people who struggle to keep you alive.
SKREE!
You'll do it because I did it. You'll do it because you'll think it might just make the world a better place.

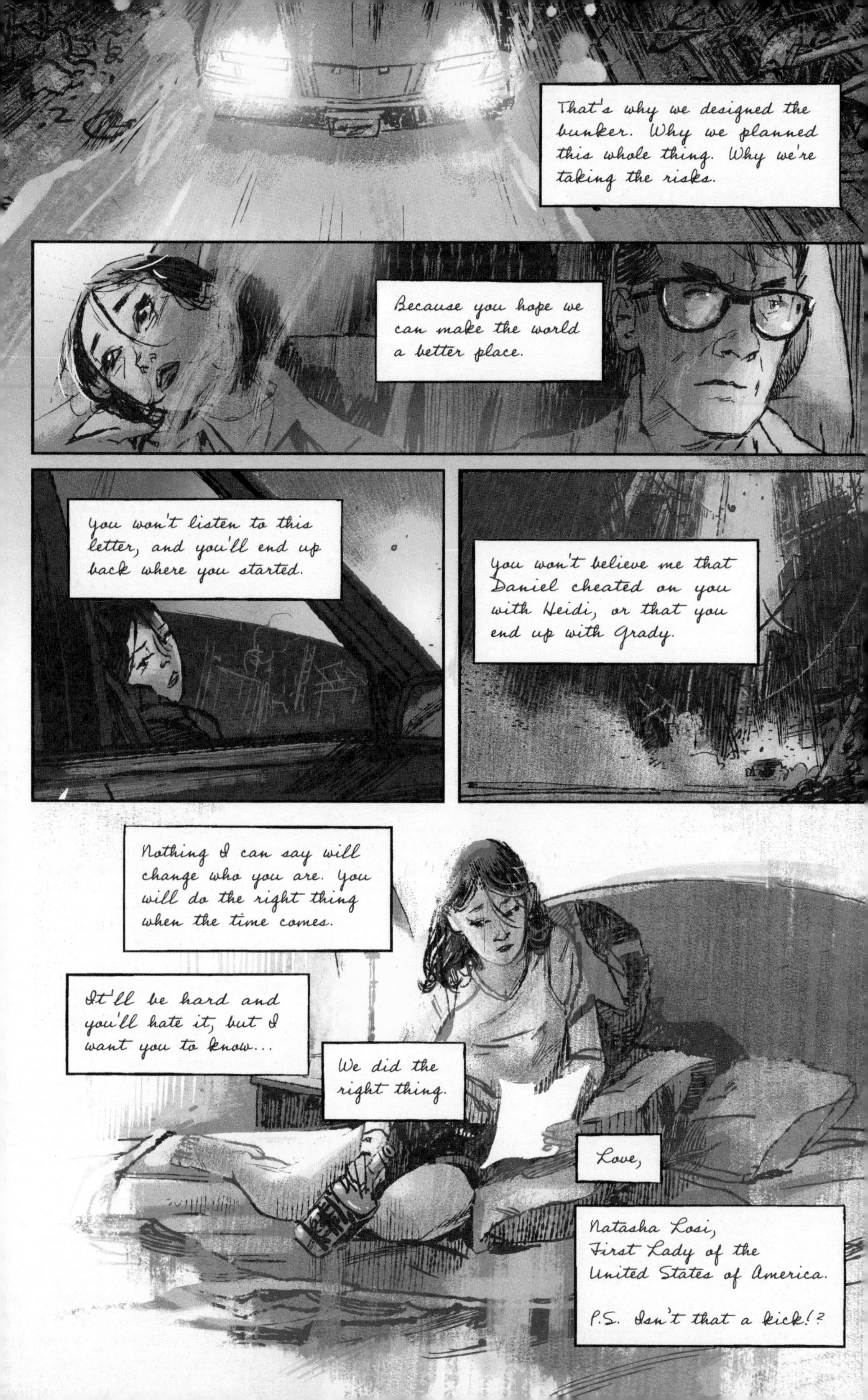
That's why we designed the bunker. Why we planned this whole thing. Why we're taking the risks.
Because you hope we can make the world a better place.
You won't listen to this letter, and you'll end up back where you started.
You won't believe me that Daniel cheated on you with Heidi, or that you end up with Grady.
Nothing I can say will change who you are. You will do the right thing when the time comes.
It'll be hard and you'll hate it, but I want you to know...
We did the right thing.
Love,
Natasha Losi, First Lady of the United States of America.
P.S. Isn't that a kick!?

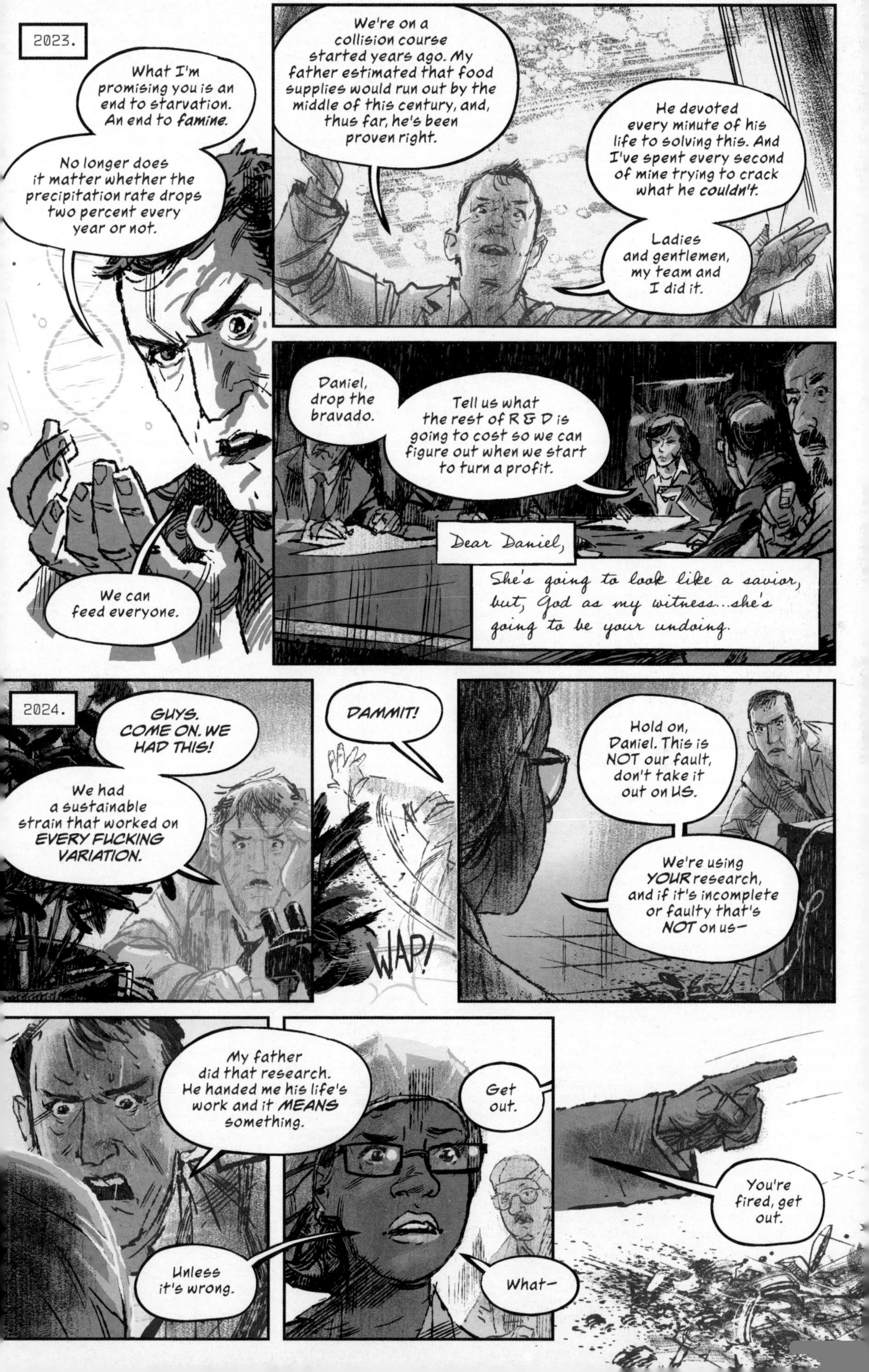
2023.
What I'm promising you is an end to starvation. An end to famine.
No longer does it matter whether the precipitation rate drops two percent every year or not.
We can feed everyone.
We're on a collision course started years ago. My father estimated that food supplies would run out by the middle of this century, and, thus far, he's been proven right.
He devoted every minute of his life to solving this. And I've spent every second of mine trying to crack what he couldn't.
Ladies and gentlemen, my team and I did it.
Daniel, drop the bravado.
Tell us what the rest of R & D is going to cost so we can figure out when we start to turn a profit.
Dear Daniel,
She's going to look like a savior, but, God as my witness...she's going to be your undoing.
2024.
GUYS. COME ON. WE HAD THIS!
We had a sustainable strain that worked on EVERY FUCKING VARIATION.
DAMMIT!
WAP!
Hold on, Daniel. This is NOT our fault, don't take it out on US.
We're using YOUR research, and if it's incomplete or faulty that's NOT on us—
My father did that research. He handed me his life's work and it MEANS something.
Unless it's wrong.
Get out.
What—
You're fired, get out.

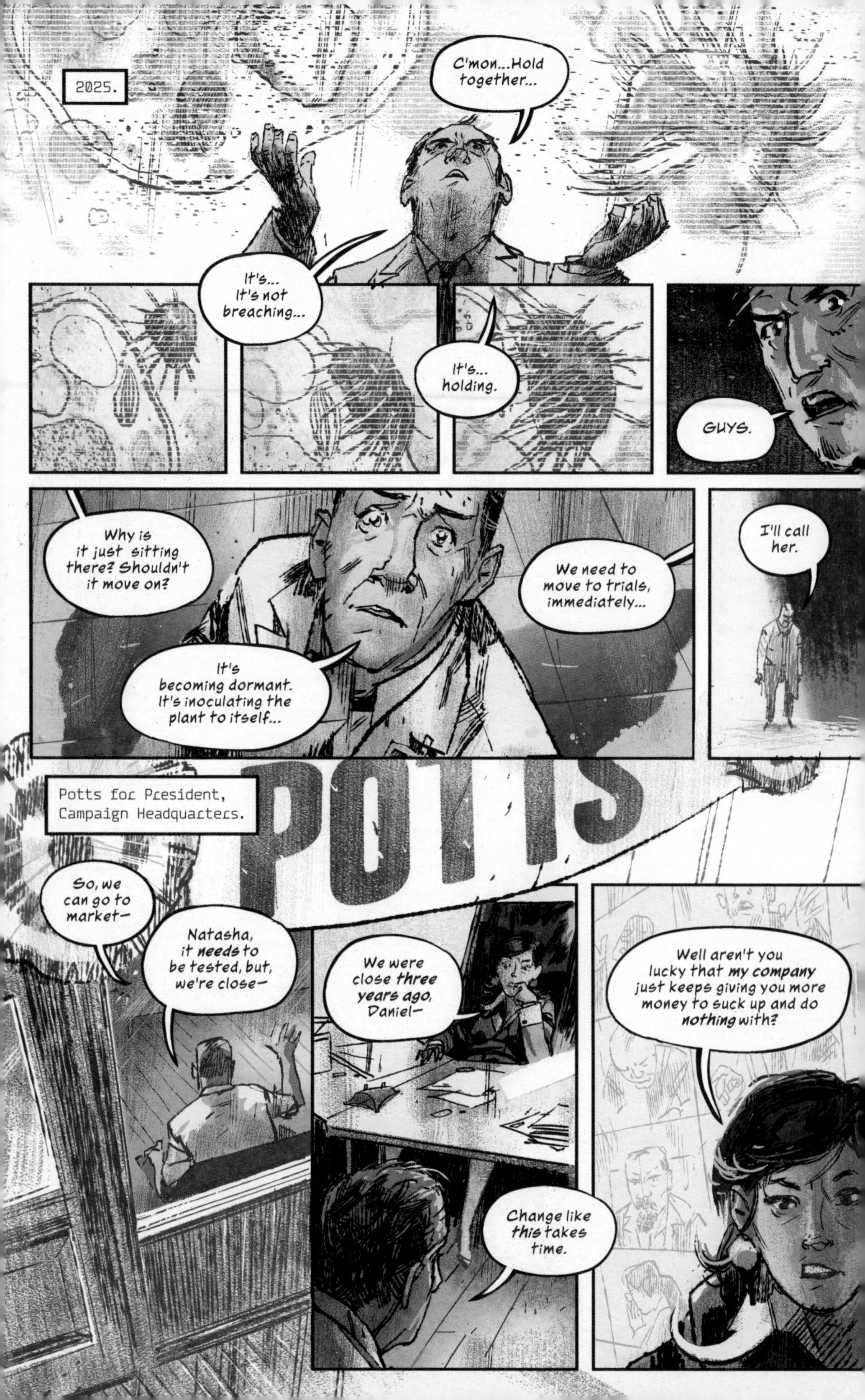
2025.
C'mon...Hold together...
It's... It's not breaching...
It's... holding.
GUYS.
Why is it just sitting there? Shouldn't it move on?
It's becoming dormant. It's inoculating the plant to itself...
We need to move to trials, immediately...
I'll call her.
Potts for President, Campaign Headquarters.
POTTS
So, we can go to market—
Natasha, it **needs** to be tested, but, we're close—
We were close **three years ago**, Daniel—
Change like **this** takes time.
Well aren't you lucky that **my company** just keeps giving you more money to suck up and do **nothing** with?

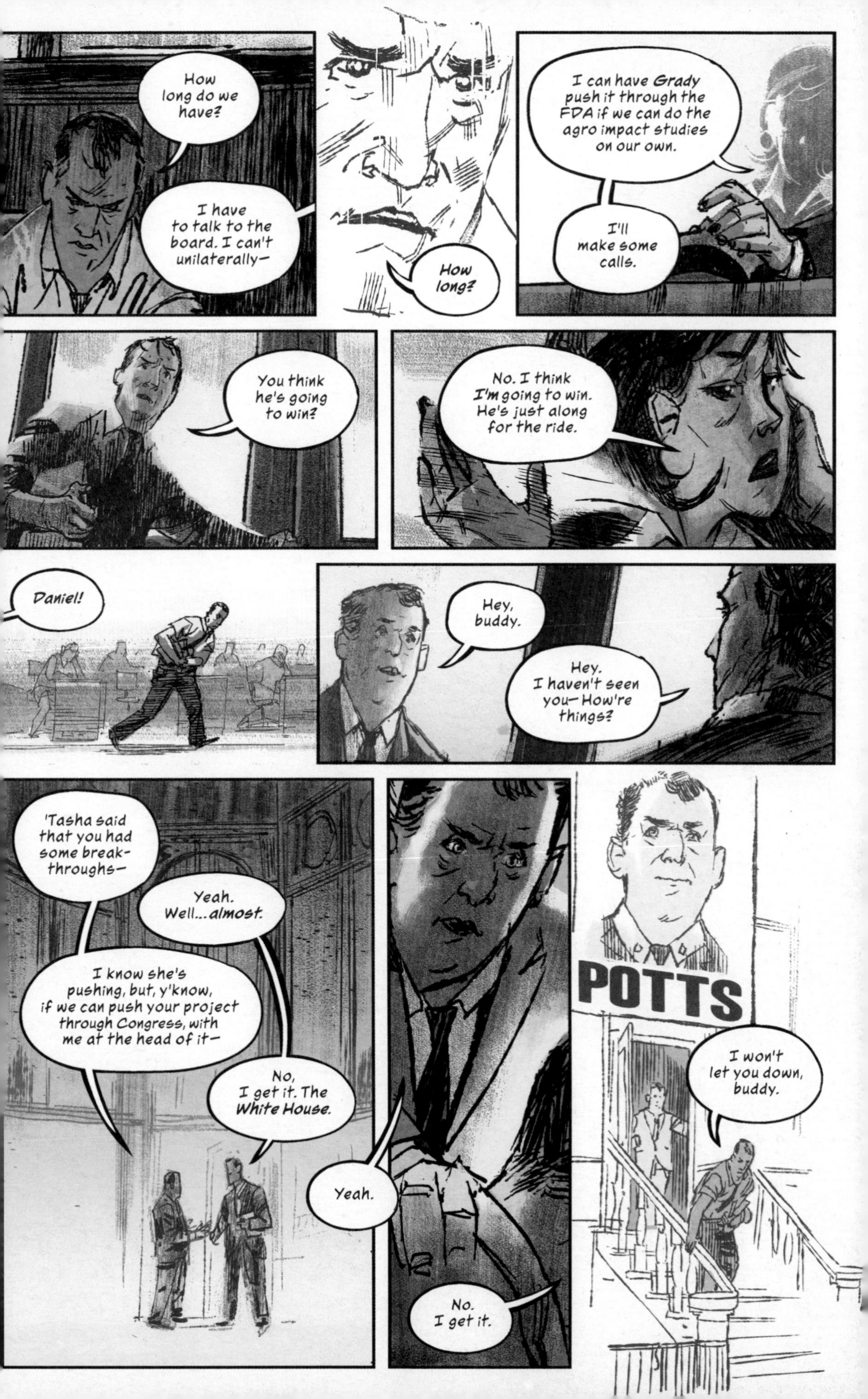
How long do we have?
I have to talk to the board. I can't unilaterally—
How long?
I can have Grady push it through the FDA if we can do the agro impact studies on our own.
I'll make some calls.
You think he's going to win?
No. I think I'm going to win. He's just along for the ride.
Daniel!
Hey, buddy.
Hey. I haven't seen you— How're things?
'Tasha said that you had some break-throughs—
Yeah. Well... almost.
I know she's pushing, but, y'know, if we can push your project through Congress, with me at the head of it—
No, I get it. The White House.
Yeah.
No. I get it.
POTTS
I won't let you down, buddy.

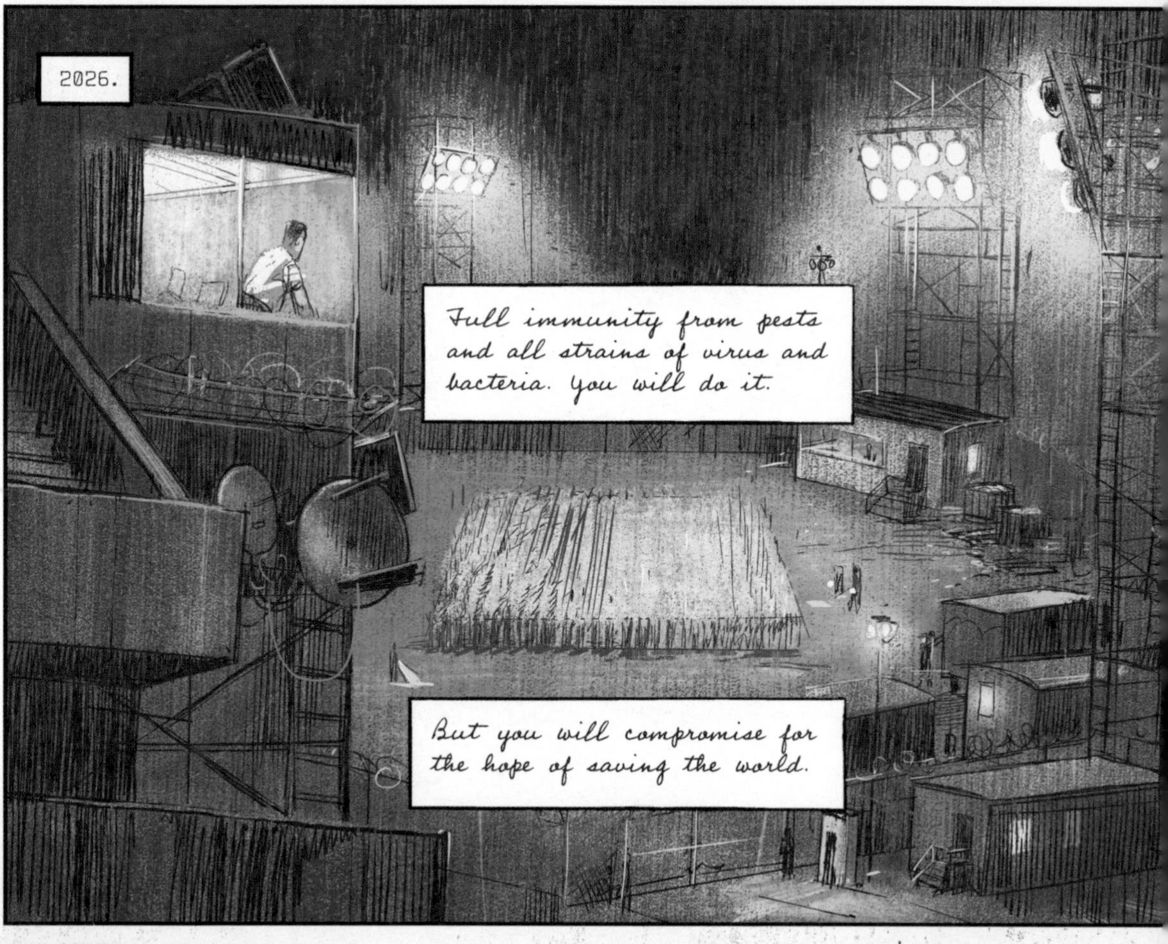
2026.
Full immunity from pests and all strains of virus and bacteria. You will do it.
But you will compromise for the hope of saving the world.

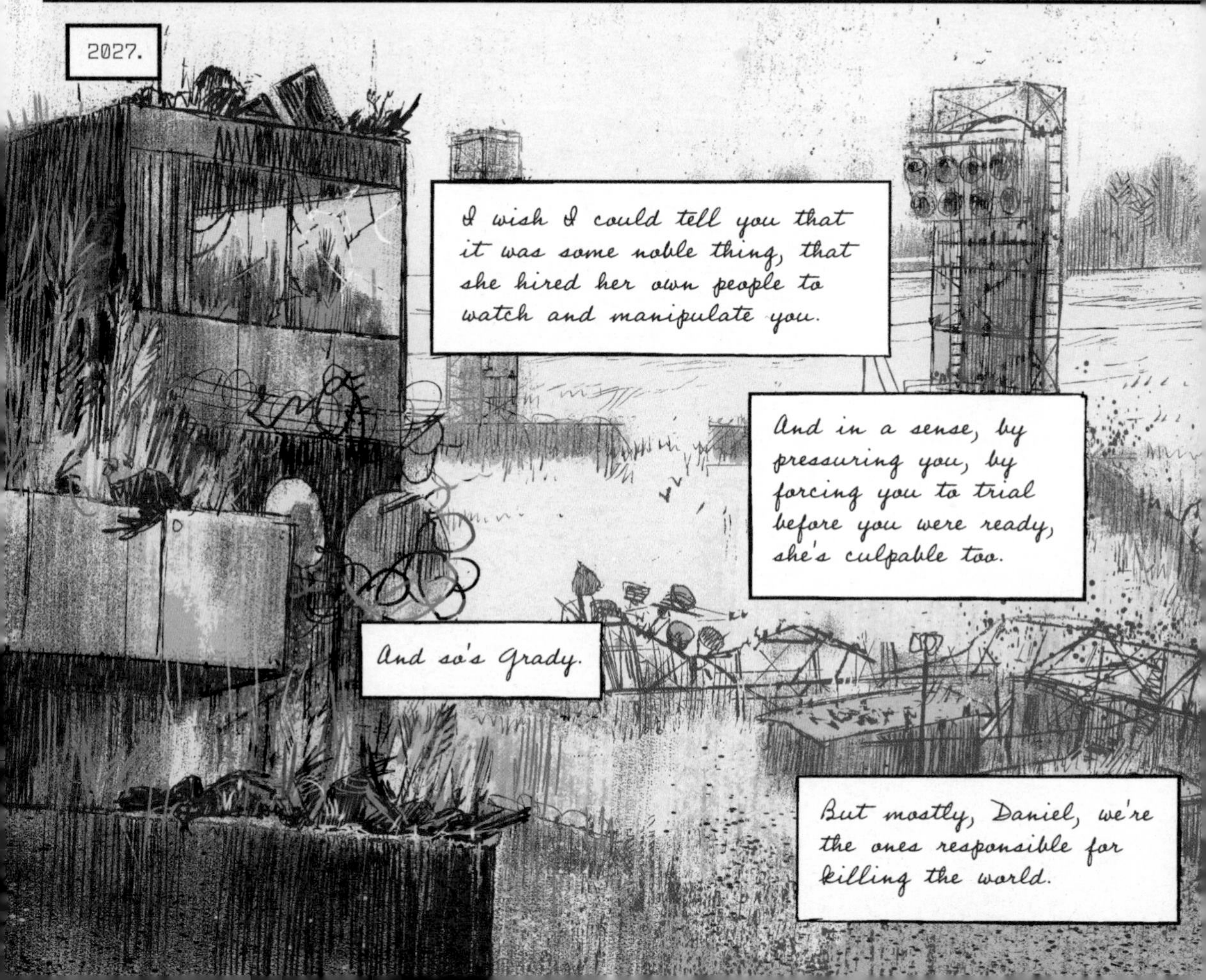
2027.
I wish I could tell you that it was some noble thing, that she hired her own people to watch and manipulate you.
And in a sense, by pressuring you, by forcing you to trial before you were ready, she's culpable too.
And so's Grady.
But mostly, Daniel, we're the ones responsible for killing the world.

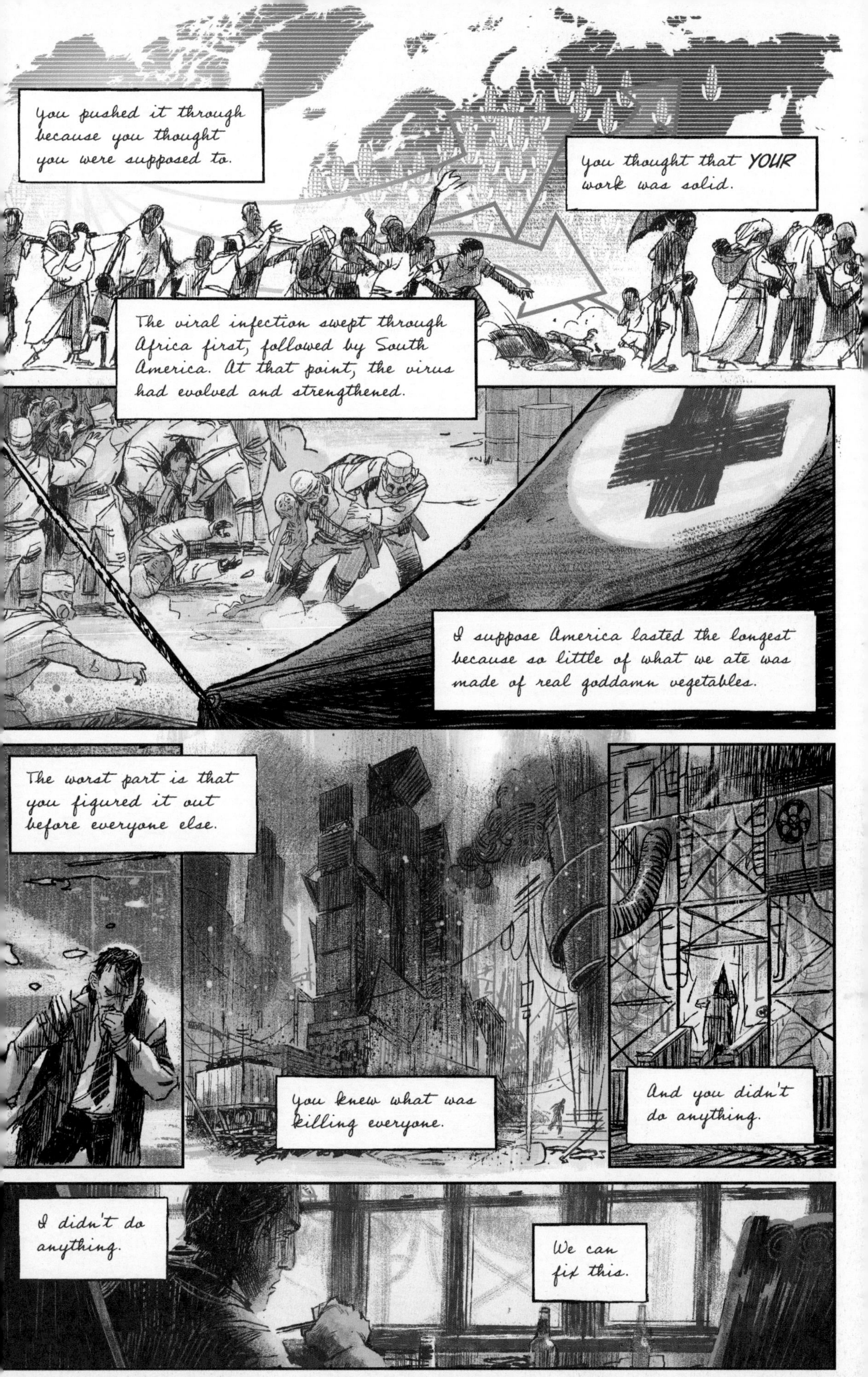
You pushed it through because you thought you were supposed to.
You thought that YOUR work was solid.
The viral infection swept through Africa first, followed by South America. At that point, the virus had evolved and strengthened.
I suppose America lasted the longest because so little of what we ate was made of real goddamn vegetables.
The worst part is that you figured it out before everyone else.
You knew what was killing everyone.
And you didn't do anything.
I didn't do anything.
We can fix this.

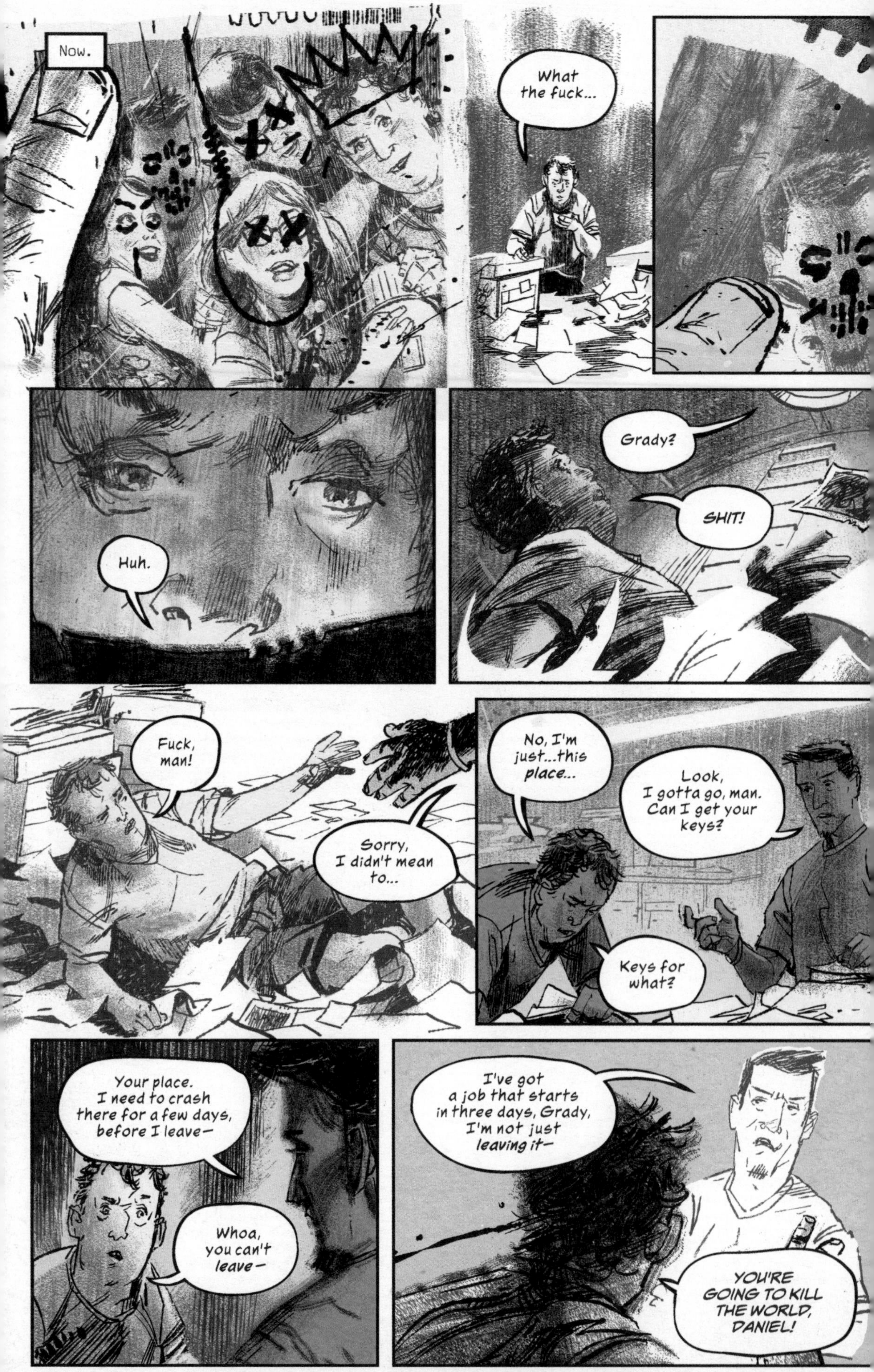
Now.
What the fuck...
Huh.
Grady?
SHIT!
Fuck, man!
Sorry, I didn't mean to...
No, I'm just...this place...
Look, I gotta go, man. Can I get your keys?
Keys for what?
Your place. I need to crash there for a few days, before I leave—
Whoa, you can't leave—
I've got a job that starts in three days, Grady, I'm not just leaving it—
YOU'RE GOING TO KILL THE WORLD, DANIEL!

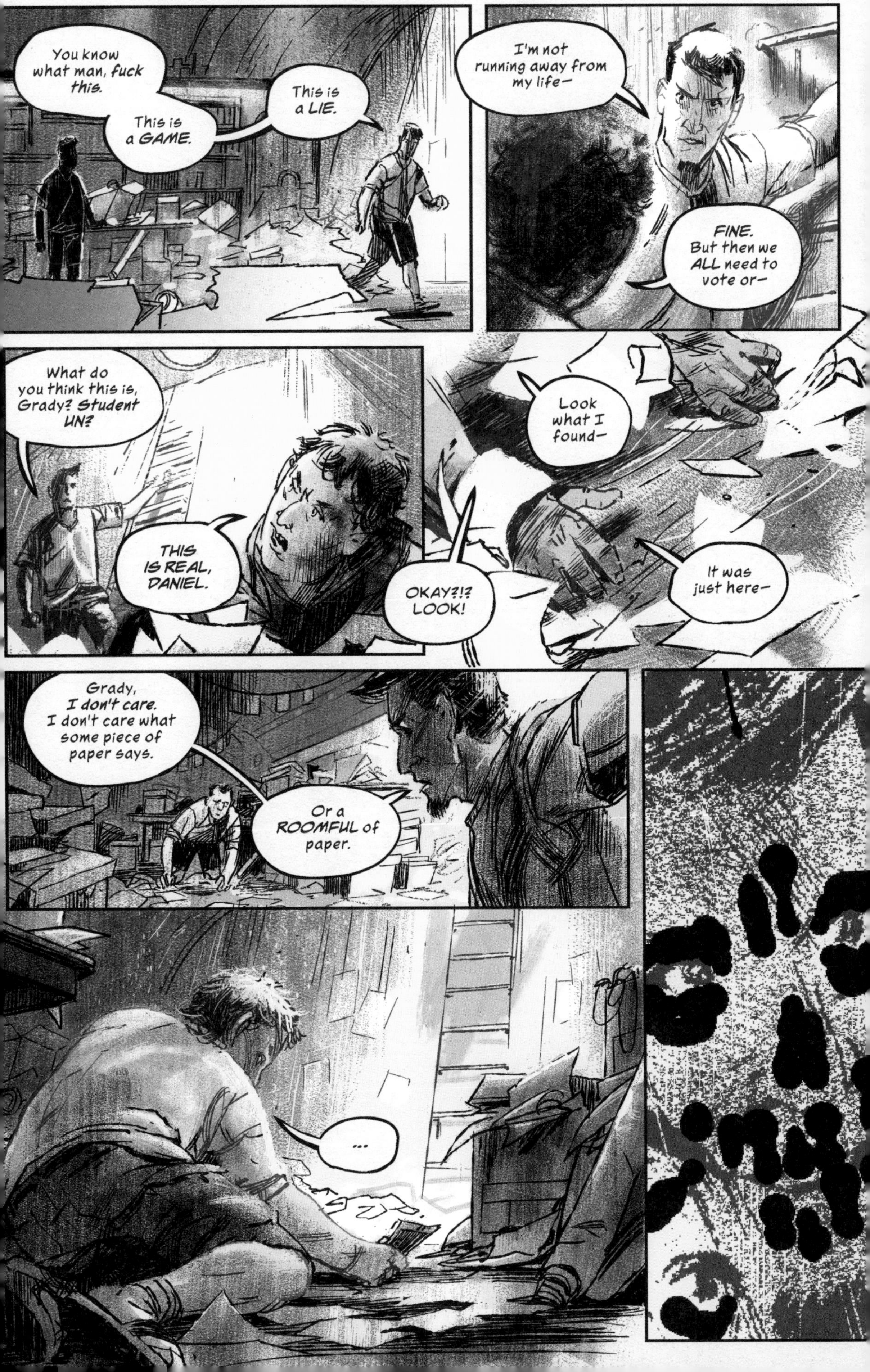
You know what man, fuck this.
This is a GAME.
This is a LIE.
I'm not running away from my life—
FINE. But then we ALL need to vote or—
What do you think this is, Grady? Student UN?
THIS IS REAL, DANIEL.
OKAY?!? LOOK!
Look what I found—
It was just here—
Grady, I don't care. I don't care what some piece of paper says.
Or a ROOMFUL of paper.
...

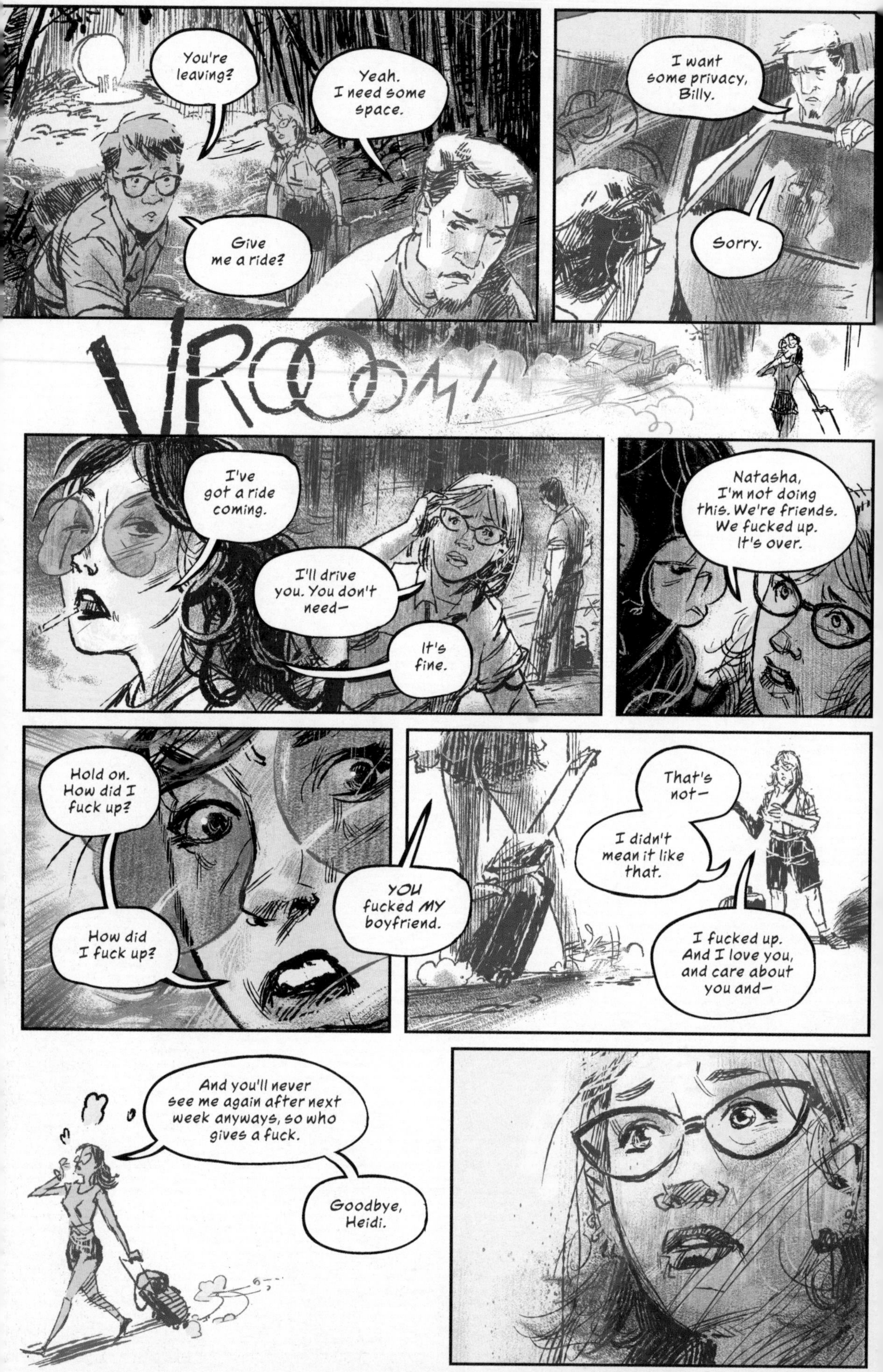
You're leaving?
Yeah. I need some space.
Give me a ride?
I want some privacy, Billy.
Sorry.
VROOOOM!
I've got a ride coming.
I'll drive you. You don't need—
It's fine.
Natasha, I'm not doing this. We're friends. We fucked up. It's over.
Hold on. How did I fuck up?
How did I fuck up?
YOU fucked MY boyfriend.
That's not—
I didn't mean it like that.
I fucked up. And I love you, and care about you and—
And you'll never see me again after next week anyways, so who gives a fuck.
Goodbye, Heidi.

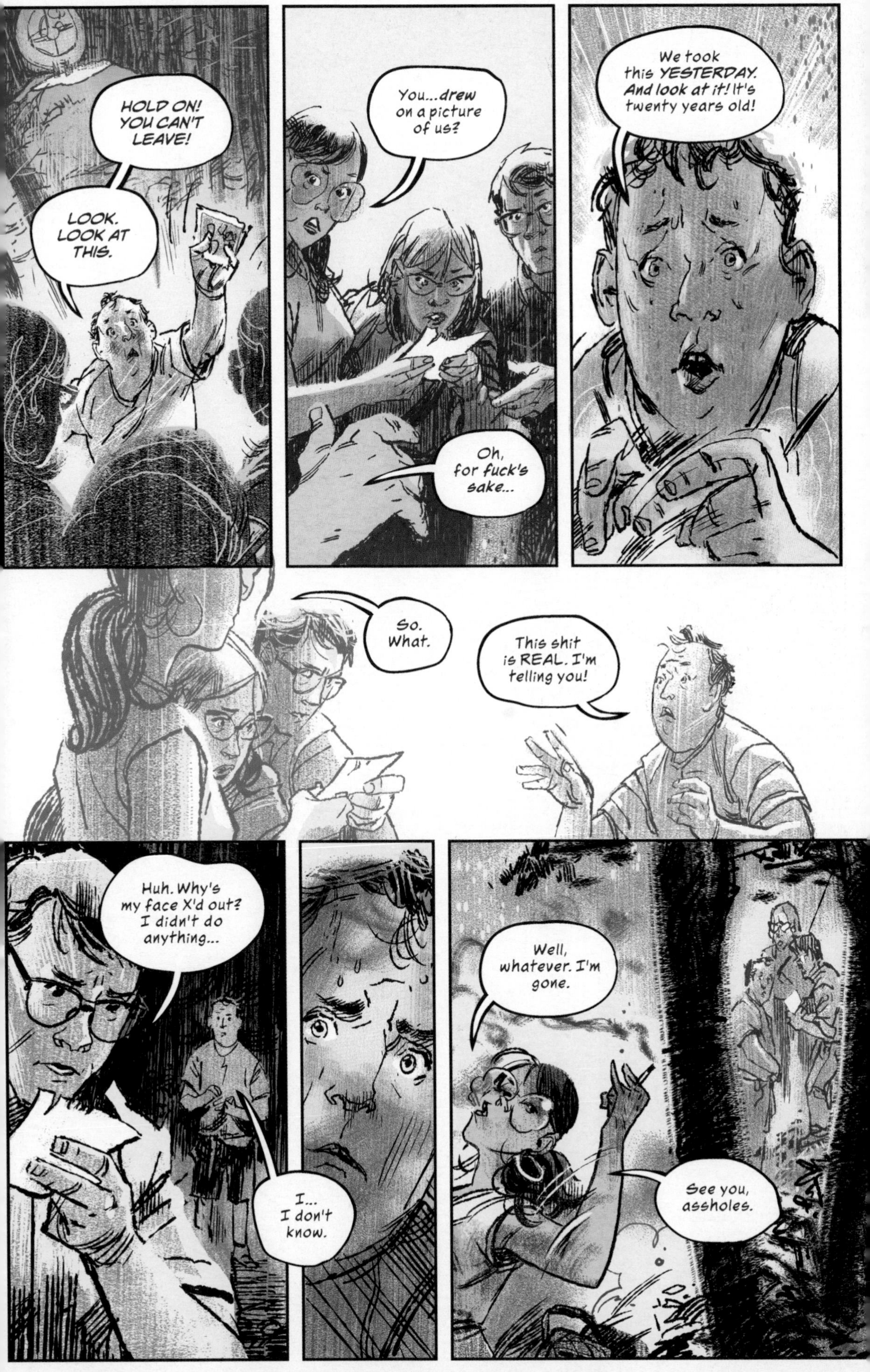
HOLD ON! YOU CAN'T LEAVE!
LOOK. LOOK AT THIS.
You...drew on a picture of us?
Oh, for fuck's sake...
We took this YESTERDAY. And look at it! It's twenty years old!
So. What.
This shit is REAL. I'm telling you!
Huh. Why's my face X'd out? I didn't do anything...
I... I don't know.
Well, whatever. I'm gone.
See you, assholes.

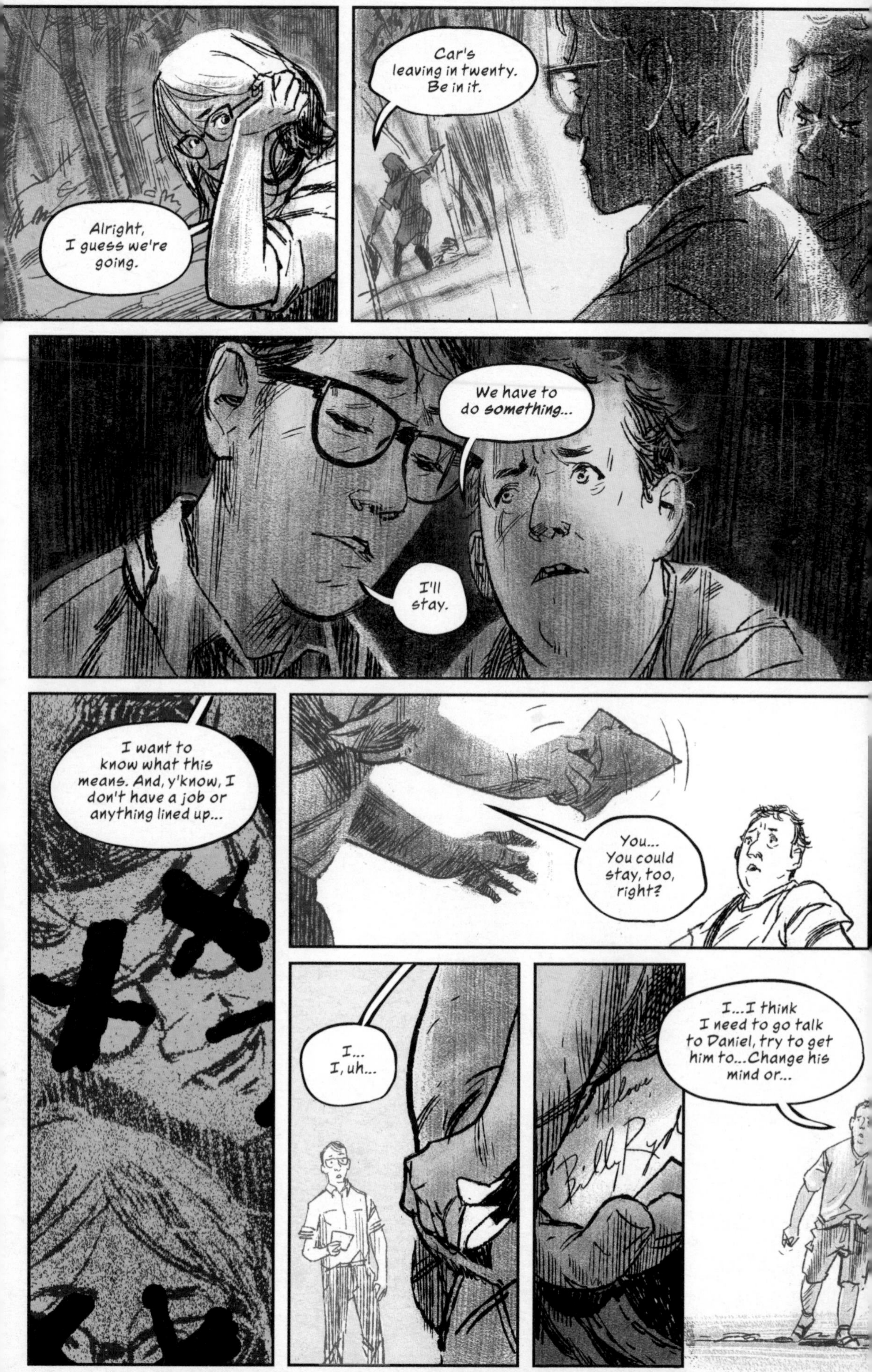
Alright, I guess we're going.
Car's leaving in twenty. Be in it.
We have to do *something*...
I'll stay.
I want to know what this means. And, y'know, I don't have a job or anything lined up...
You... You could stay, too, right?
I... I, uh...
I...I think I need to go talk to Daniel, try to get him to...Change his mind or...

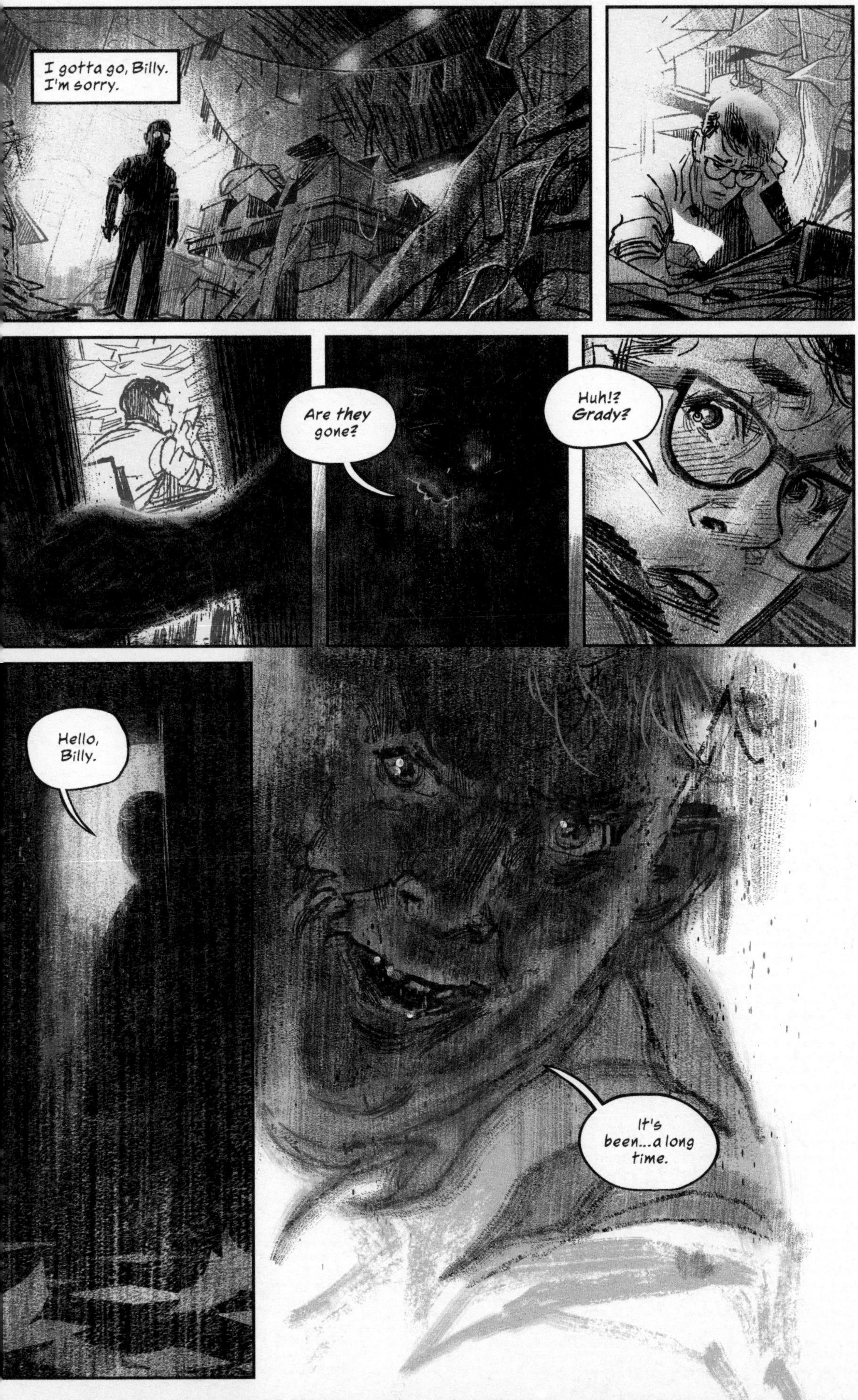
I gotta go, Billy. I'm sorry.
Are they gone?
Huh!? Grady?
Hello, Billy.
It's been...a long time.

# CHAPTER
## 02

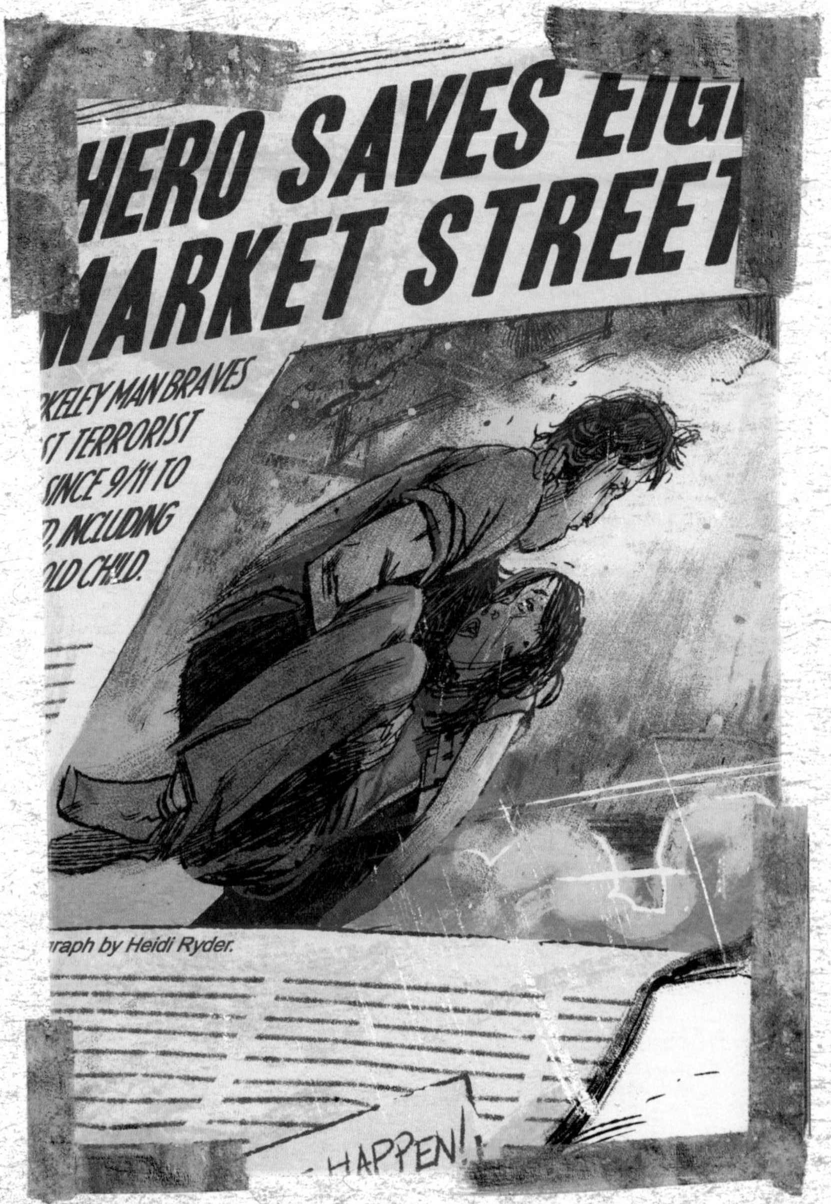

HERO SAVES EIG
ARKET STREET
RKELEY MAN BRAVES
ST TERRORIST
SINCE 9/11 TO
D, INCLUDING
OLD CHILD.
raph by Heidi Ryder.
HAPPEN!

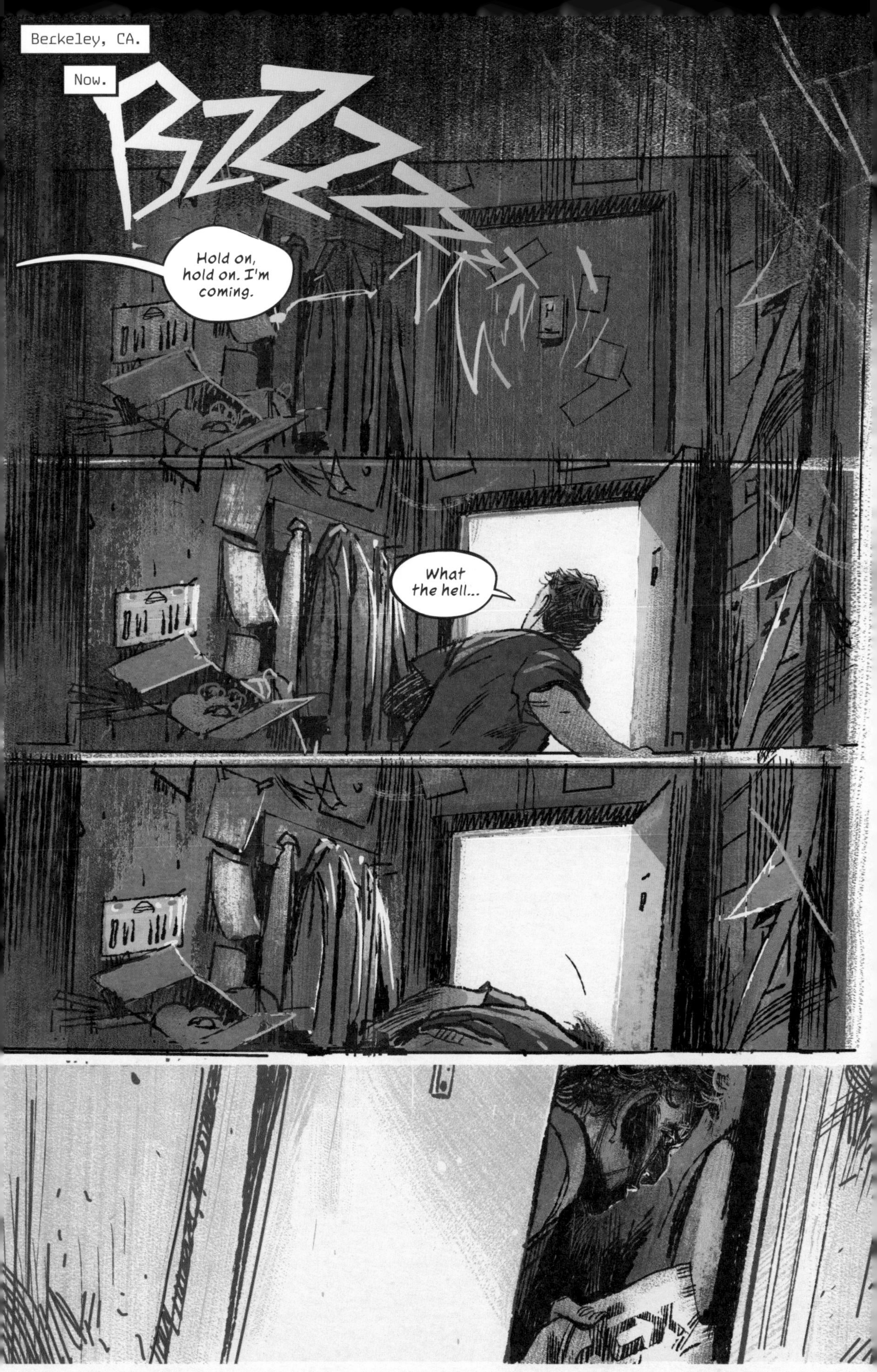
Berkeley, CA.
Now.
BZZZZ
Hold on, hold on. I'm coming.
What the hell...

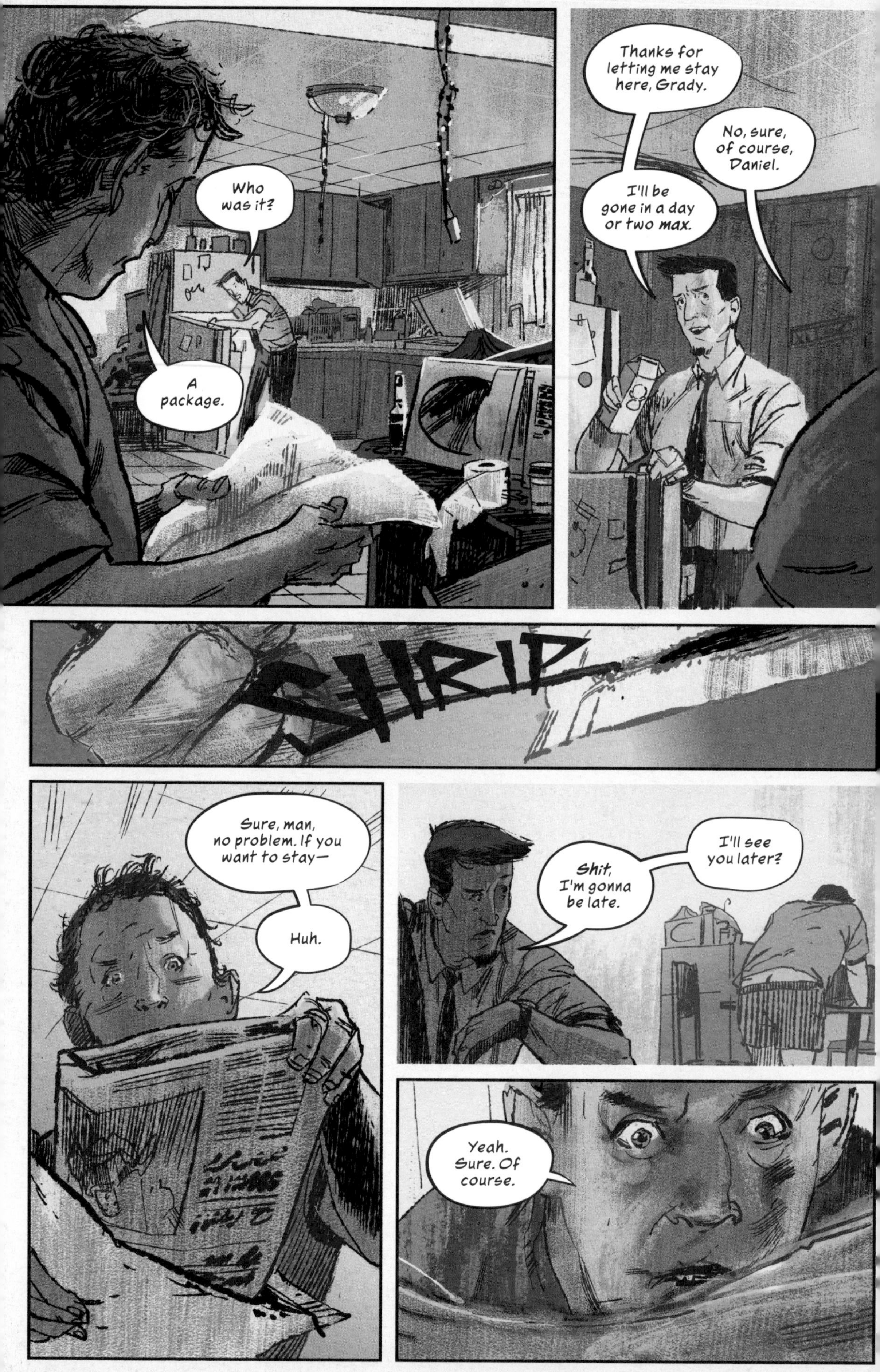
Who was it?
A package.
Thanks for letting me stay here, Grady.
I'll be gone in a day or two *max*.
No, sure, of course, Daniel.
SHRIP
Sure, man, no problem. If you want to stay—
Huh.
*Shit*, I'm gonna be late.
I'll see you later?
Yeah. Sure. Of course.

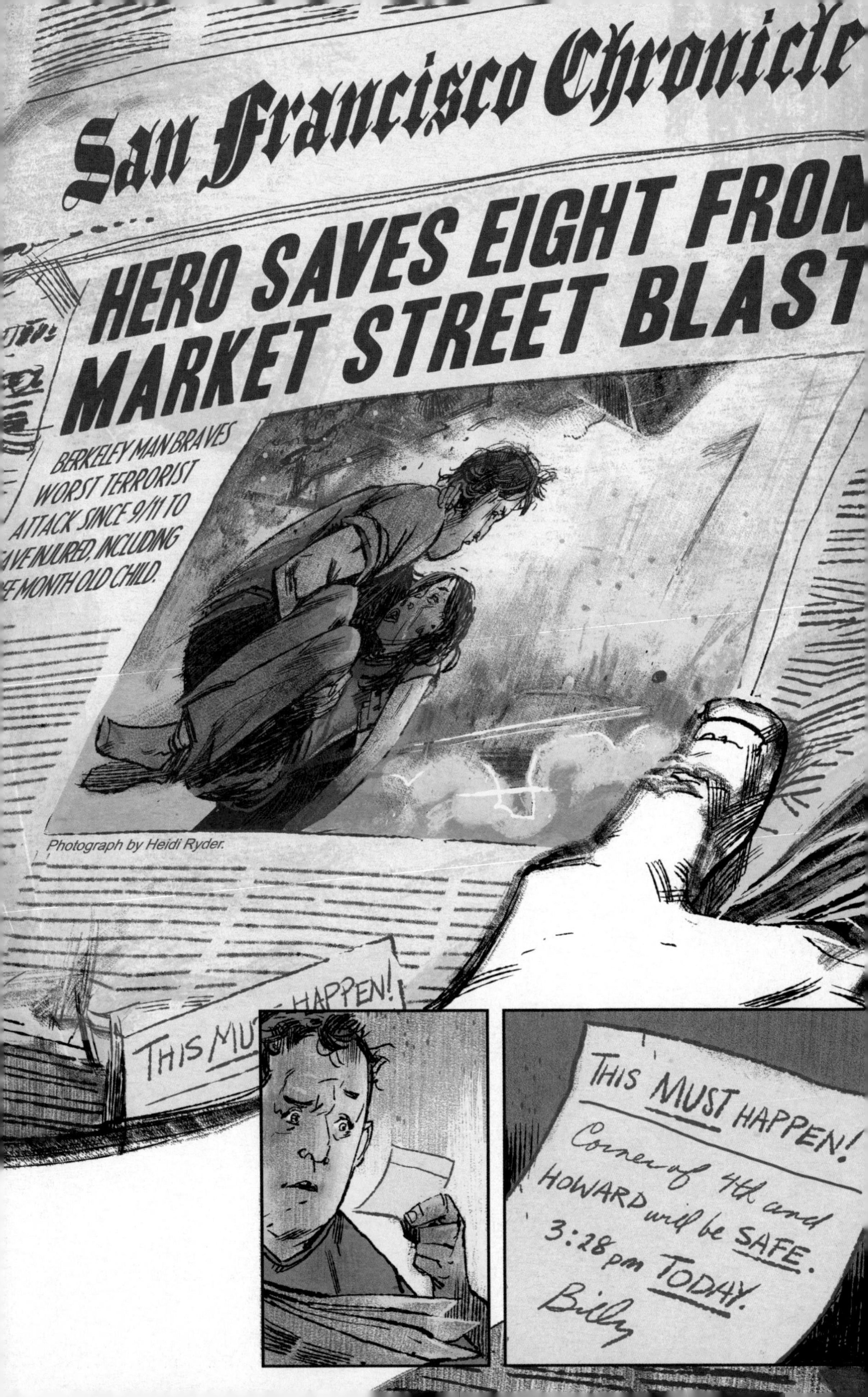
San Francisco Chronicle
HERO SAVES EIGHT FROM MARKET STREET BLAST
BERKELEY MAN BRAVES WORST TERRORIST ATTACK SINCE 9/11 TO SAVE INJURED, INCLUDING MONTH OLD CHILD.
Photograph by Heidi Ryder.
THIS MUST HAPPEN!
THIS MUST HAPPEN! Corner of 4th and HOWARD will be SAFE. 3:28 pm TODAY. Billy

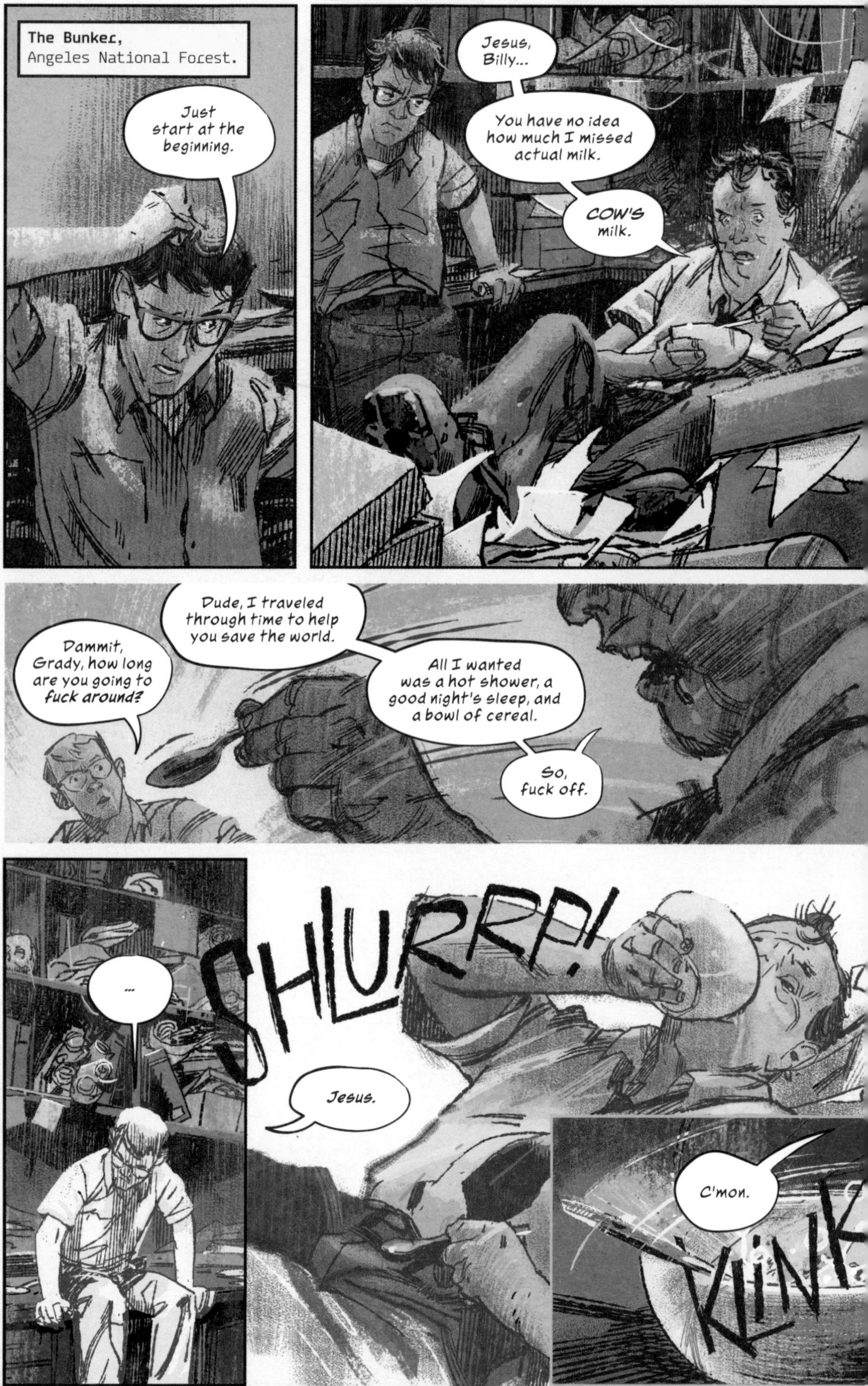
The Bunker,
Angeles National Forest.
Just start at the beginning.
Jesus, Billy...
You have no idea how much I missed actual milk.
COW'S milk.
Dude, I traveled through time to help you save the world.
Dammit, Grady, how long are you going to fuck around?
All I wanted was a hot shower, a good night's sleep, and a bowl of cereal.
So, fuck off.
...
SHLURRP!
Jesus.
C'mon.
KLINK

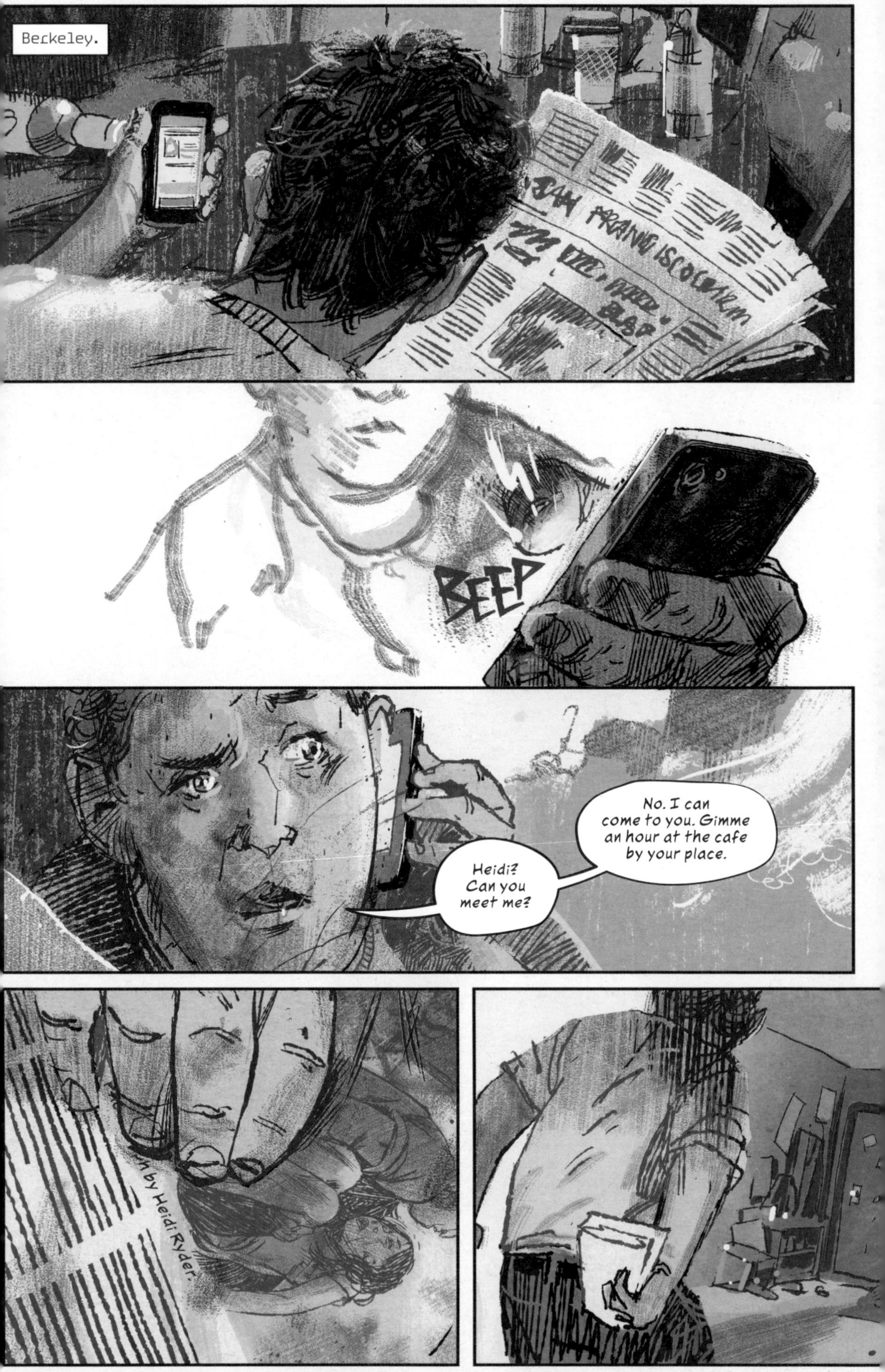
Berkeley.
BEEP
Heidi? Can you meet me?
No. I can come to you. Gimme an hour at the cafe by your place.
by Heidi Ryder.

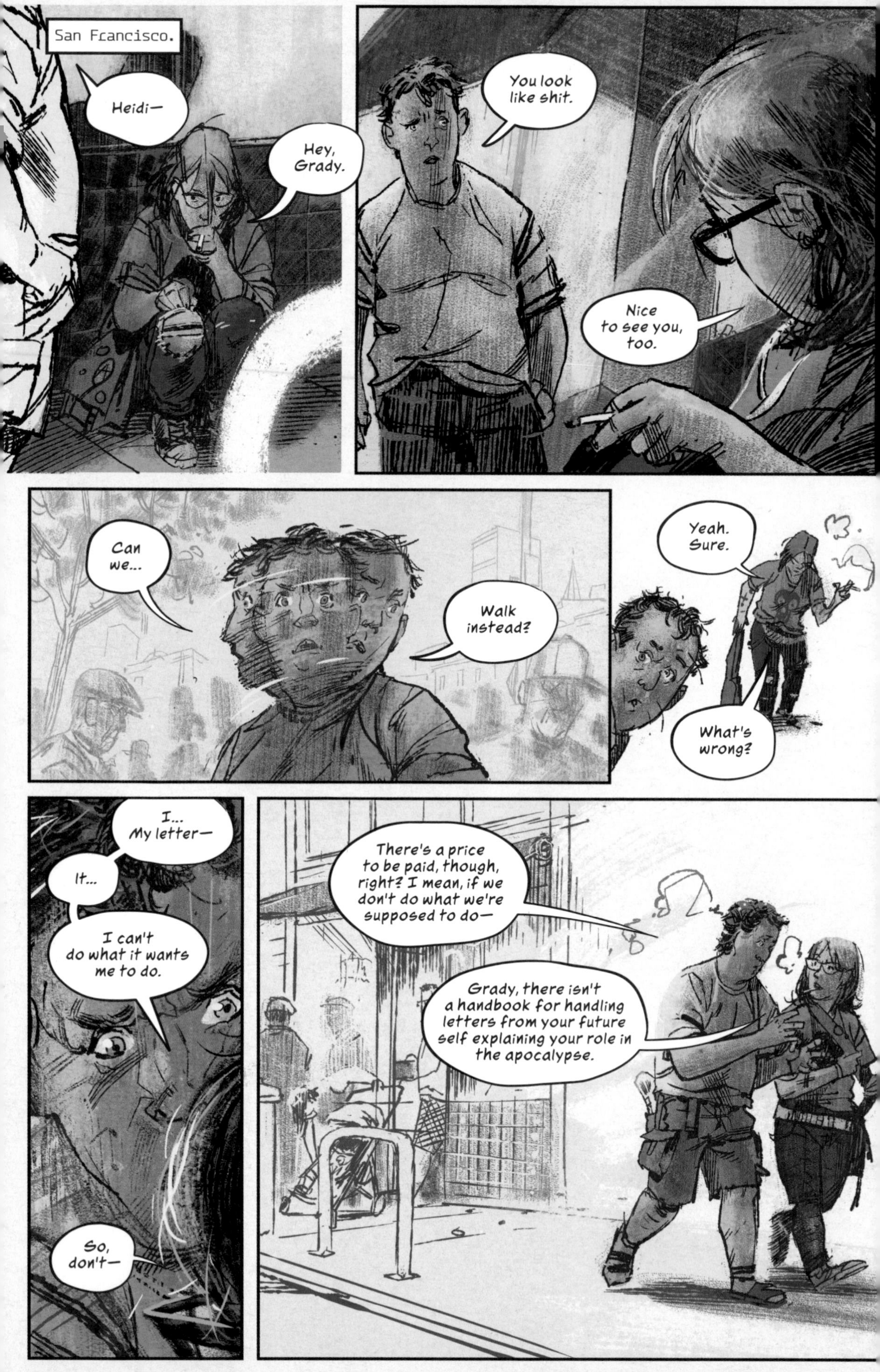
San Francisco.
Heidi—
Hey, Grady.
You look like shit.
Nice to see you, too.
Can we...
Walk instead?
Yeah. Sure.
What's wrong?
I... My letter—
It...
I can't do what it wants me to do.
So, don't—
There's a price to be paid, though, right? I mean, if we don't do what we're supposed to do—
Grady, there isn't a handbook for handling letters from your future self explaining your role in the apocalypse.

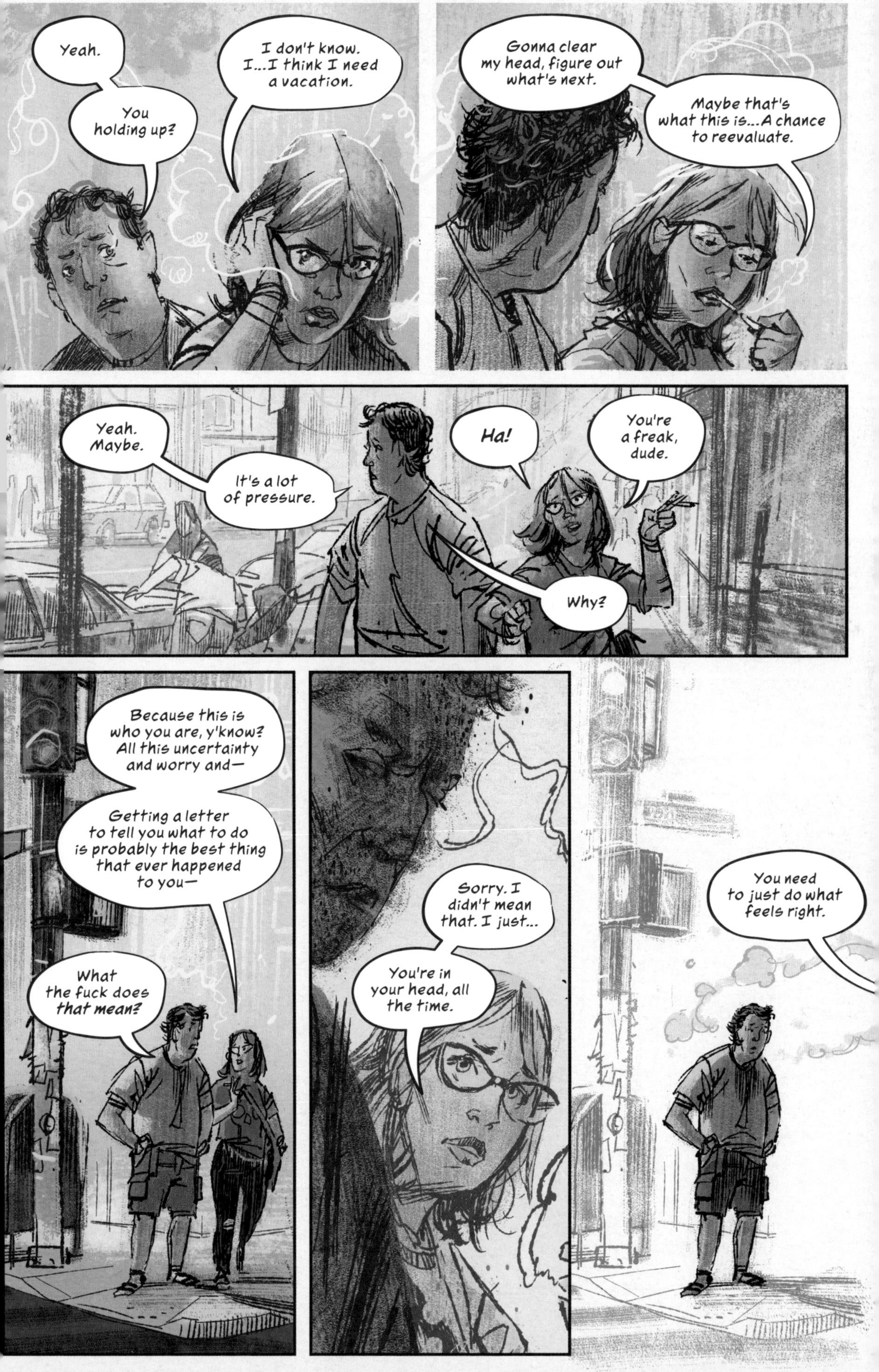
Yeah.
You holding up?
I don't know. I...I think I need a vacation.
Gonna clear my head, figure out what's next.
Maybe that's what this is...A chance to reevaluate.
Yeah. Maybe.
It's a lot of pressure.
Ha!
You're a freak, dude.
Why?
Because this is who you are, y'know? All this uncertainty and worry and—
Getting a letter to tell you what to do is probably the best thing that ever happened to you—
What the fuck does that mean?
Sorry. I didn't mean that. I just...
You're in your head, all the time.
You need to just do what feels right.

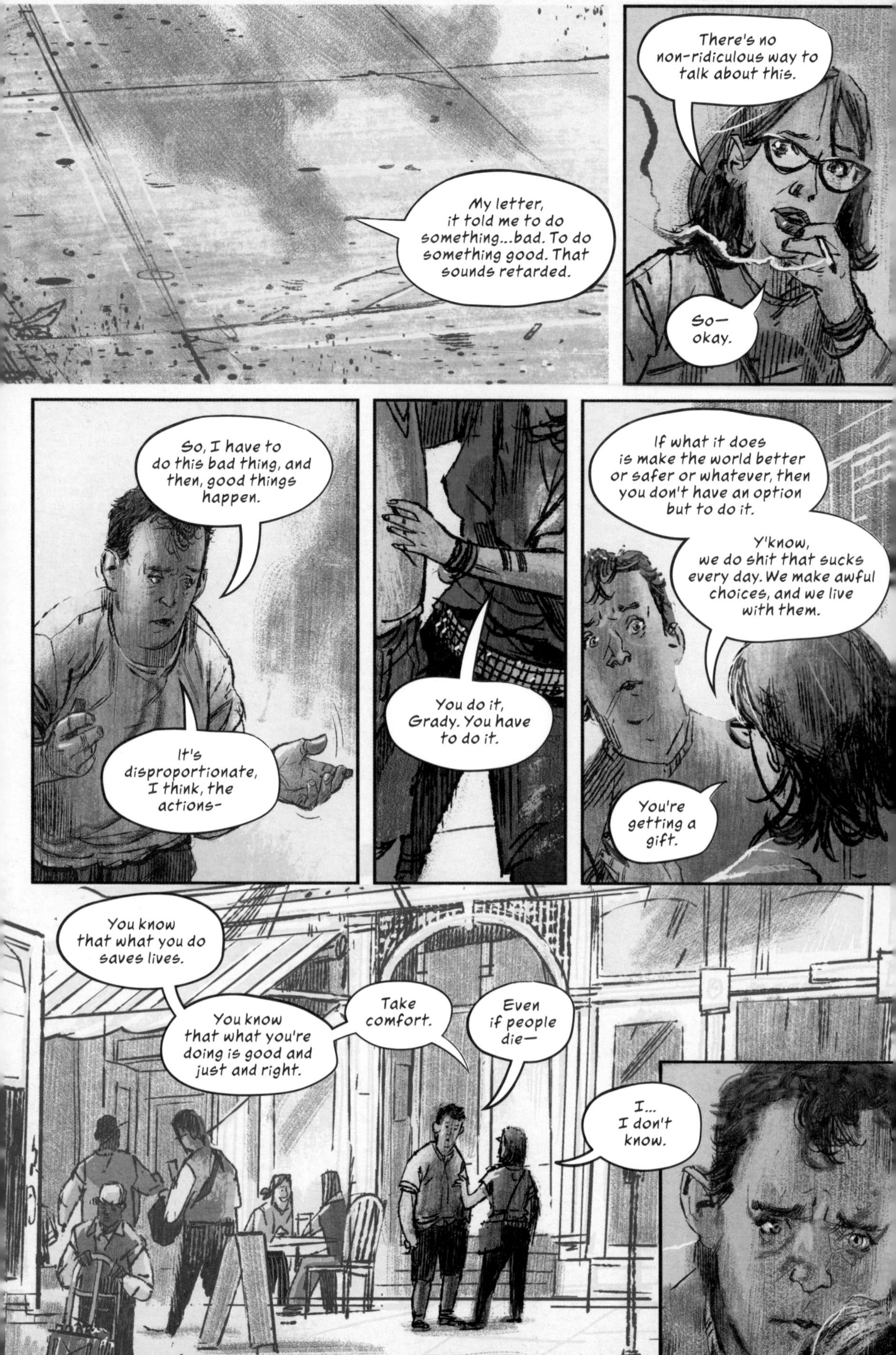
My letter, it told me to do something...bad. To do something good. That sounds retarded.
There's no non-ridiculous way to talk about this.
So— okay.
So, I have to do this bad thing, and then, good things happen.
It's disproportionate, I think, the actions-
You do it, Grady. You have to do it.
If what it does is make the world better or safer or whatever, then you don't have an option but to do it.
Y'know, we do shit that sucks every day. We make awful choices, and we live with them.
You're getting a gift.
You know that what you do saves lives.
You know that what you're doing is good and just and right.
Take comfort.
Even if people die—
I... I don't know.

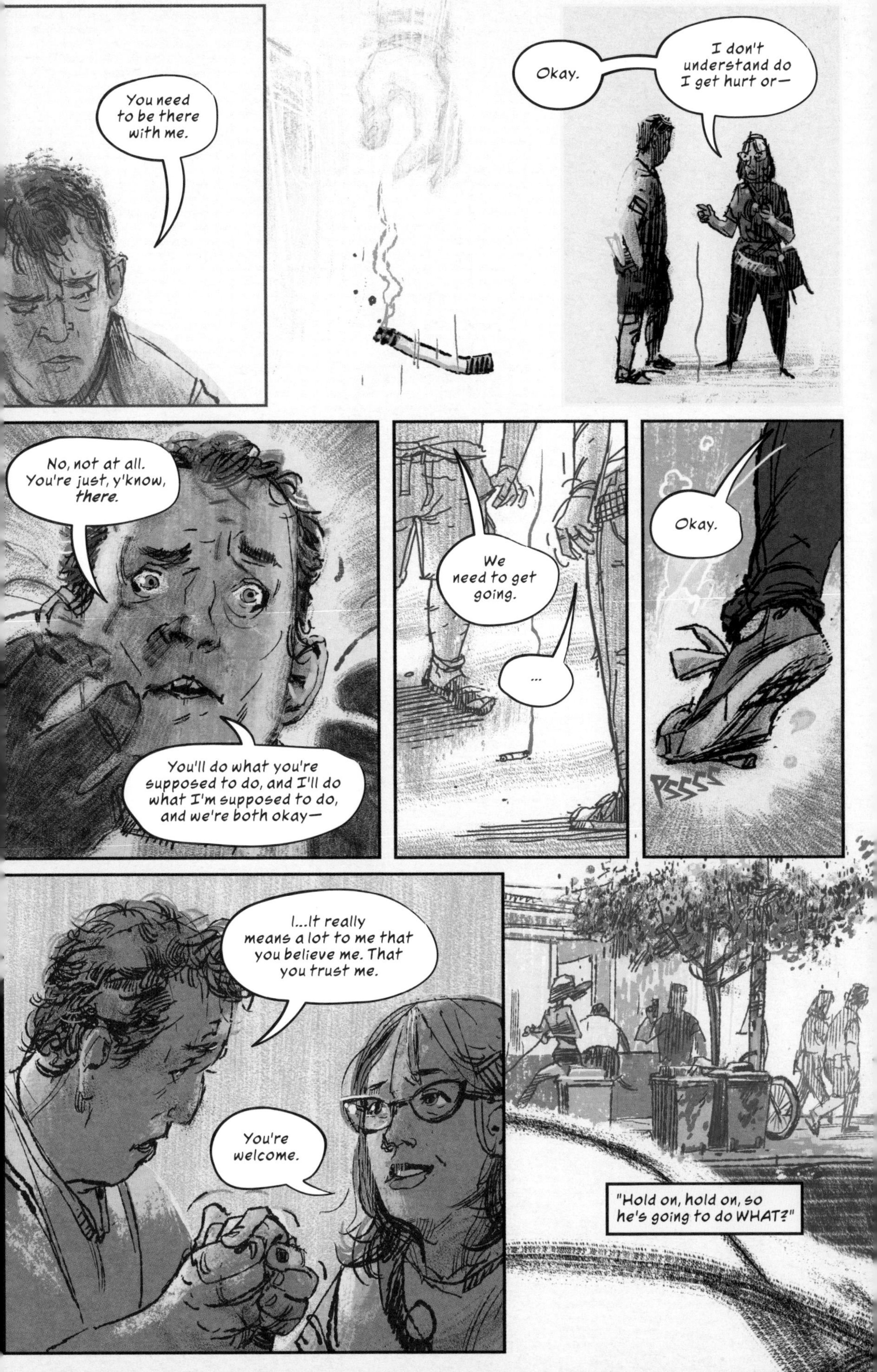
You need to be there with me.
Okay.
I don't understand do I get hurt or—
No, not at all. You're just, y'know, there.
You'll do what you're supposed to do, and I'll do what I'm supposed to do, and we're both okay—
We need to get going.
...
Okay.
PSSSS
I...It really means a lot to me that you believe me. That you trust me.
You're welcome.
"Hold on, hold on, so he's going to do WHAT?"

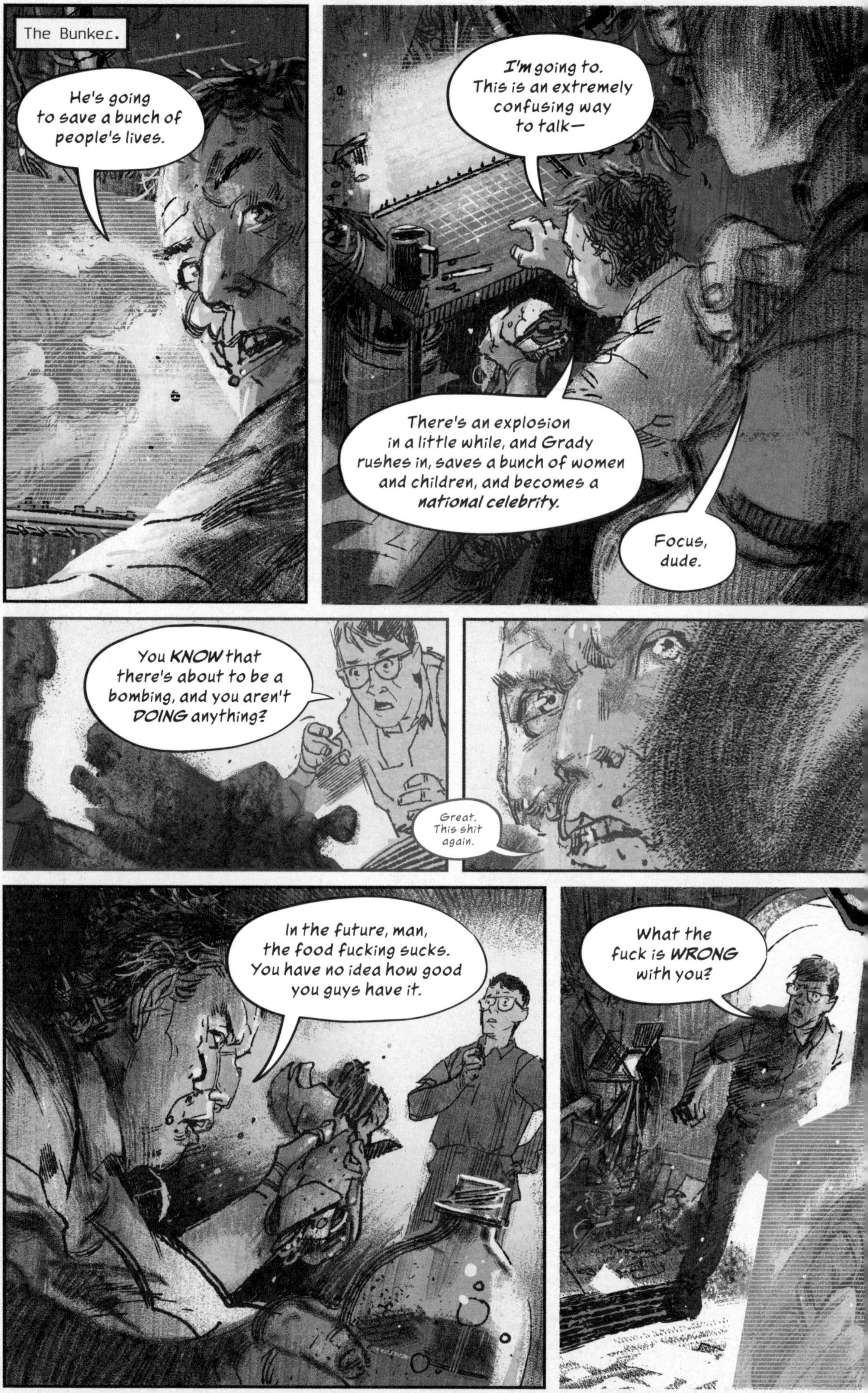
The Bunker.
He's going to save a bunch of people's lives.
I'm going to. This is an extremely confusing way to talk—
There's an explosion in a little while, and Grady rushes in, saves a bunch of women and children, and becomes a national celebrity.
Focus, dude.
You KNOW that there's about to be a bombing, and you aren't DOING anything?
Great. This shit again.
In the future, man, the food fucking sucks. You have no idea how good you guys have it.
What the fuck is WRONG with you?

Goddamn asshole future dickweed.

BEEP

BEEP BEEP

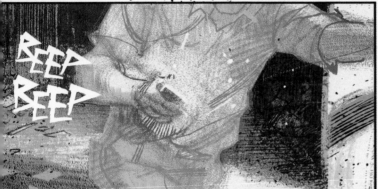

BEEP BEEP

C'mon, c'mon, c'mon, pick up.

Billy Ryder

BEEP

Who was that?

...Nobody.

BRRING!

Hold on, it's Billy—

We've gotta go, Heidi. Right now.

Let me just—

NO.

We have to move.

KLAK!

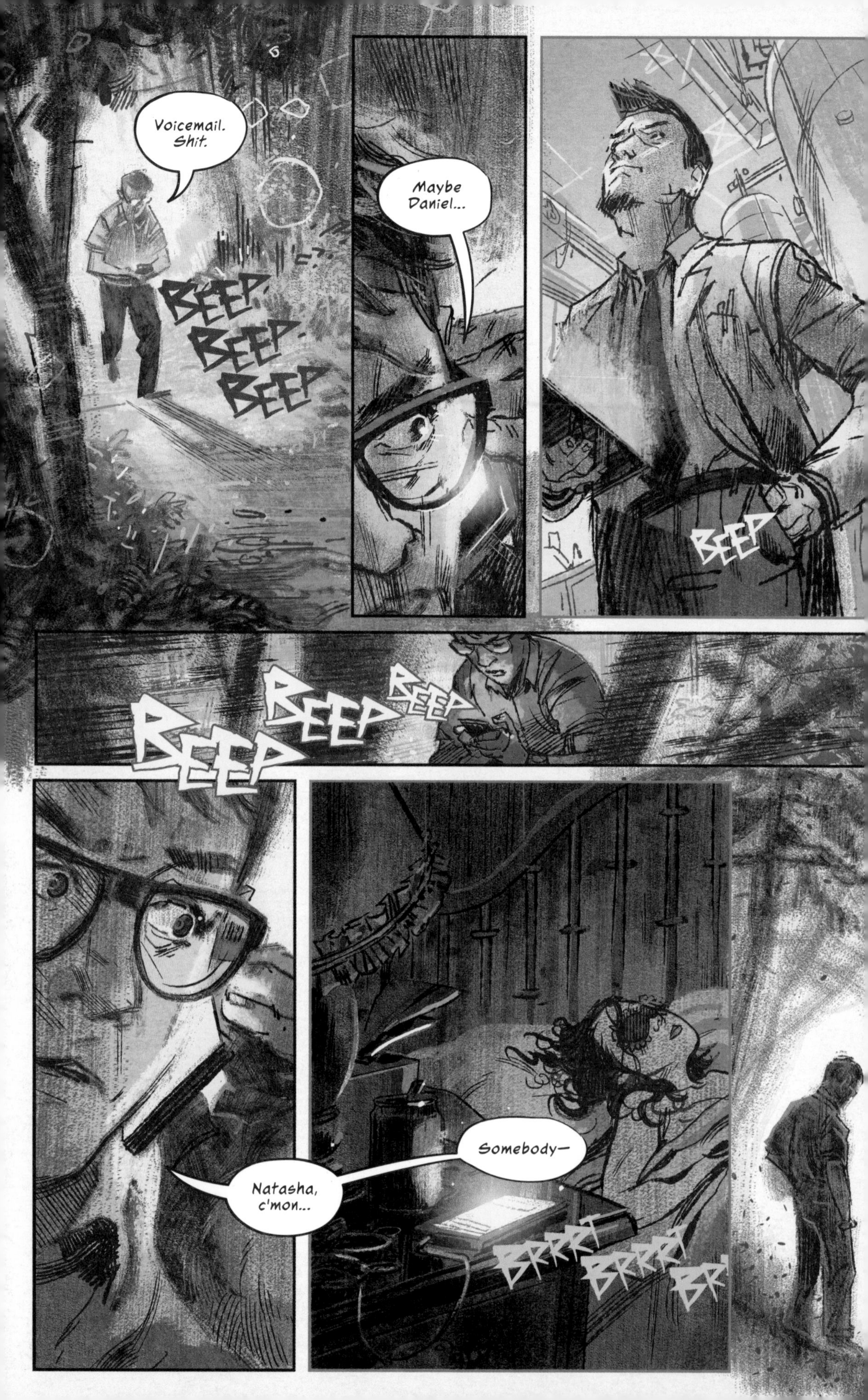
Voicemail. Shit.
BEEP BEEP BEEP
Maybe Daniel...
BEEP
BEEP BEEP BEEP
Natasha, c'mon...
Somebody—
BRRRT BRRRT BR

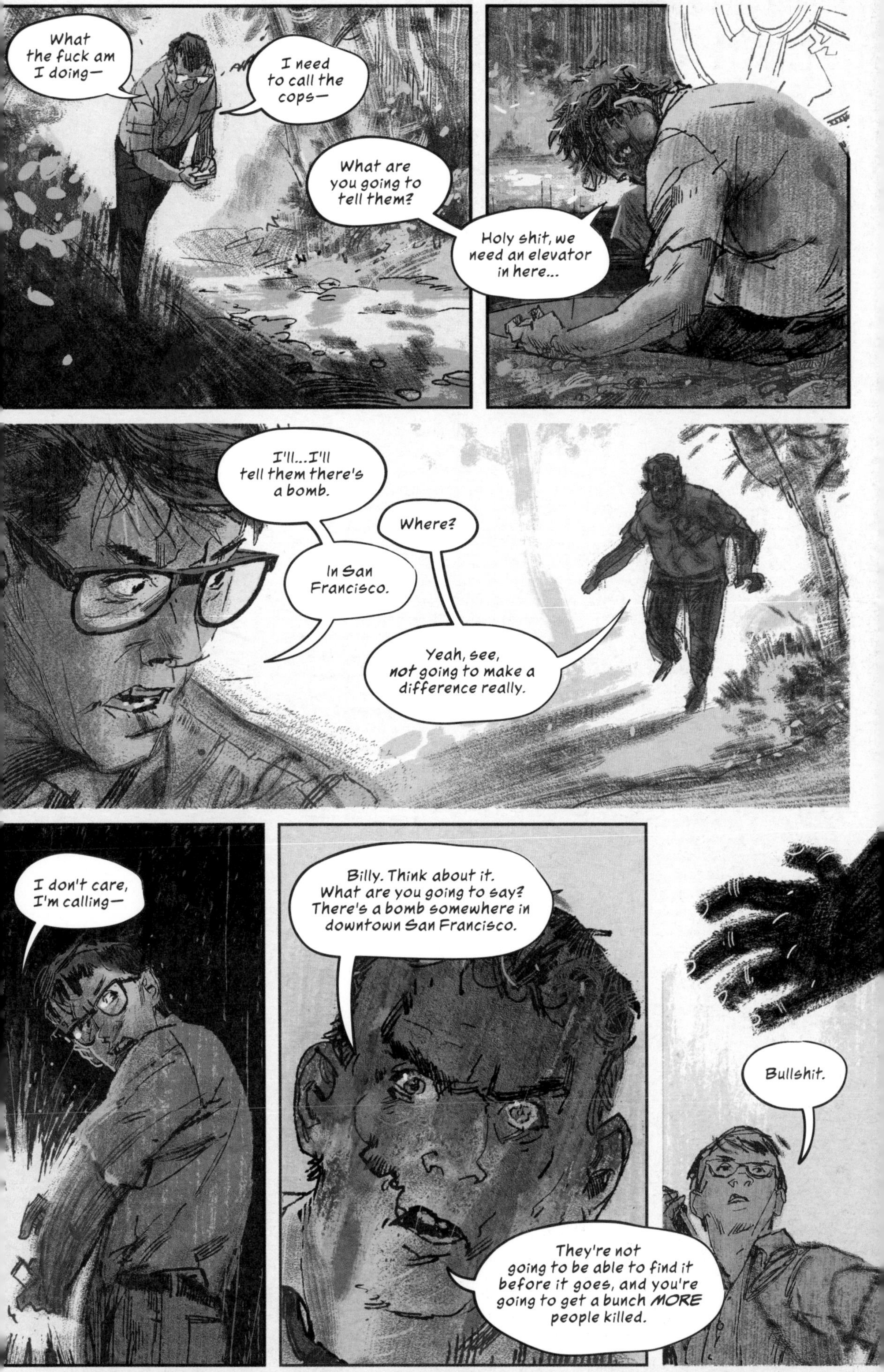
What the fuck am I doing—
I need to call the cops—
What are you going to tell them?
Holy shit, we need an elevator in here...
I'll...I'll tell them there's a bomb.
Where?
In San Francisco.
Yeah, see, *not* going to make a difference really.
I don't care, I'm calling—
Billy. Think about it. What are you going to say? There's a bomb somewhere in downtown San Francisco.
They're not going to be able to find it before it goes, and you're going to get a bunch *MORE* people killed.
Bullshit.

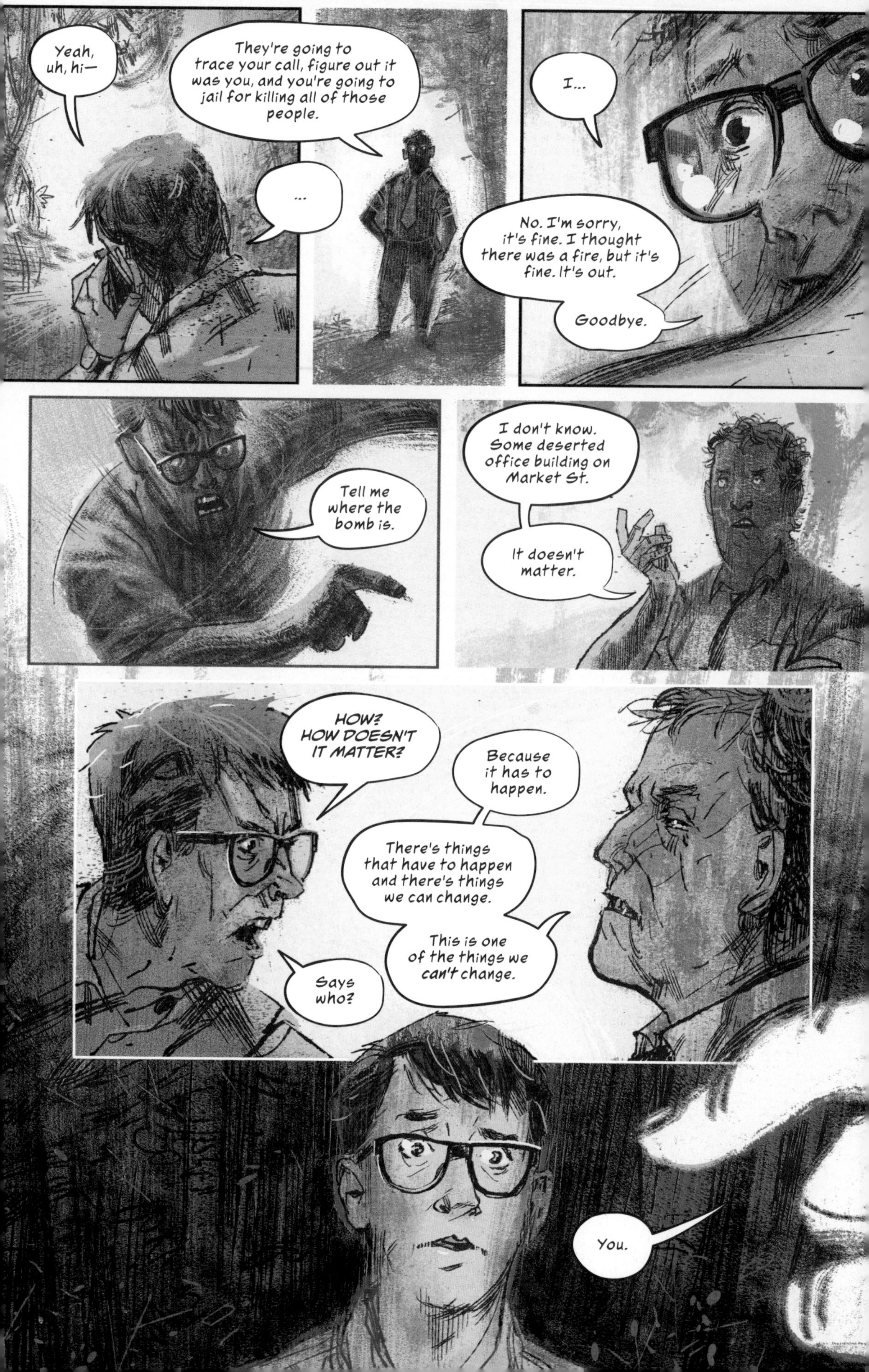
Yeah, uh, hi—
They're going to trace your call, figure out it was you, and you're going to jail for killing all of those people.
...
I...
No. I'm sorry, it's fine. I thought there was a fire, but it's fine. It's out.
Goodbye.
Tell me where the bomb is.
I don't know. Some deserted office building on Market St.
It doesn't matter.
HOW? HOW DOESN'T IT MATTER?
Because it has to happen.
There's things that have to happen and there's things we can change.
This is one of the things we can't change.
Says who?
You.

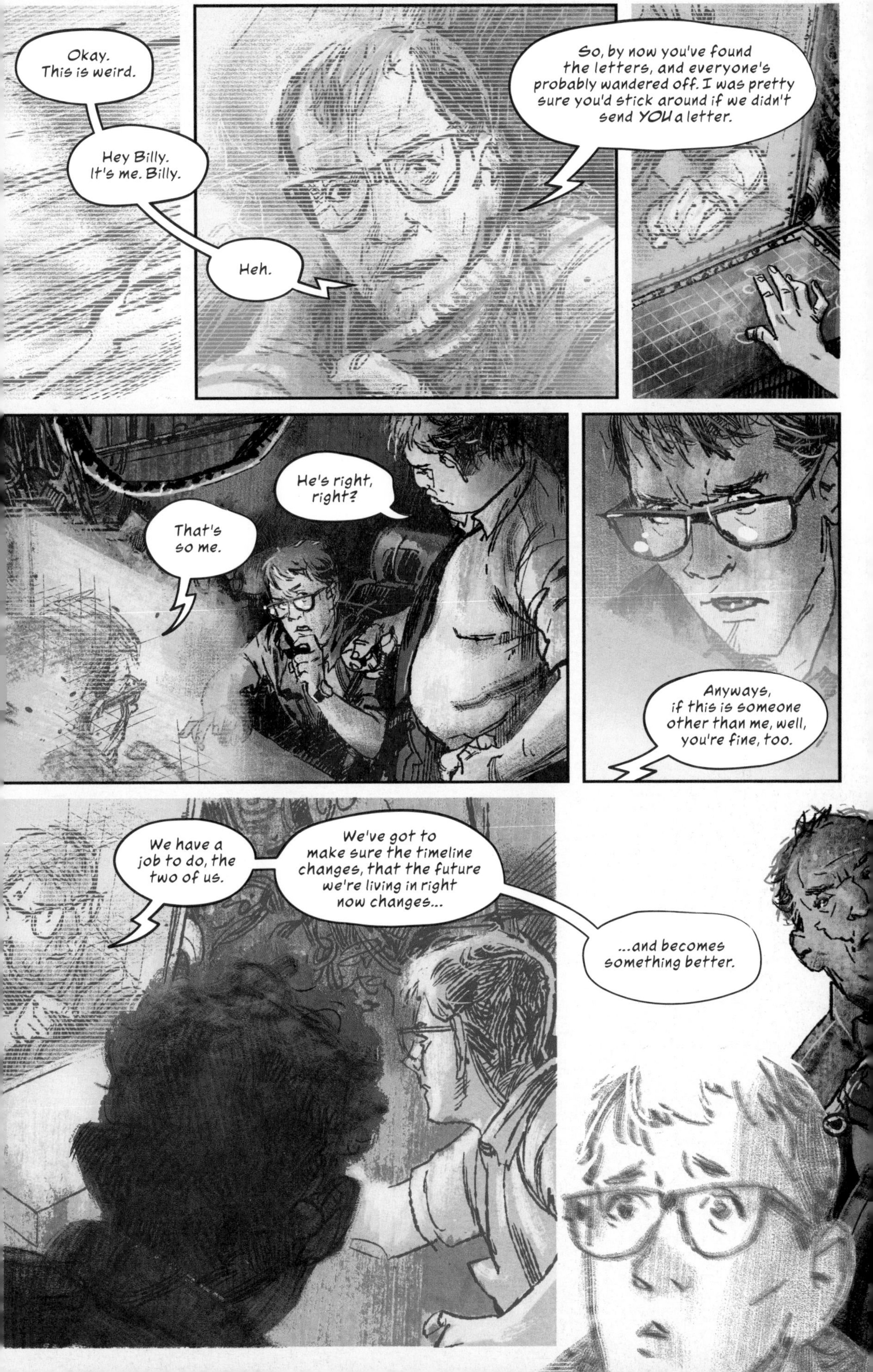
Okay. This is weird.
Hey Billy. It's me. Billy.
Heh.
So, by now you've found the letters, and everyone's probably wandered off. I was pretty sure you'd stick around if we didn't send YOU a letter.
He's right, right?
That's so me.
Anyways, if this is someone other than me, well, you're fine, too.
We have a job to do, the two of us.
We've got to make sure the timeline changes, that the future we're living in right now changes...
...and becomes something better.

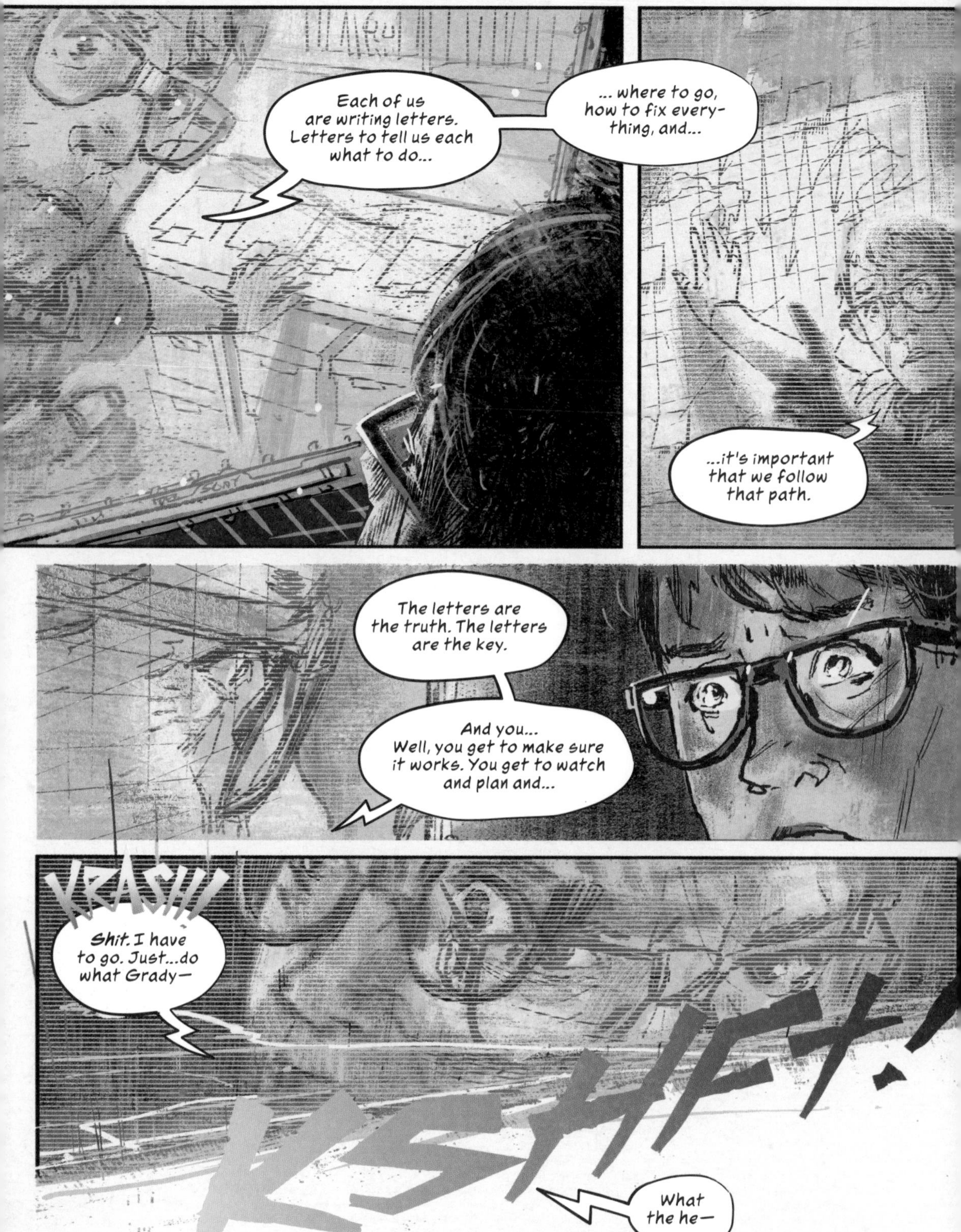
Each of us are writing letters. Letters to tell us each what to do...
... where to go, how to fix everything, and...
...it's important that we follow that path.
The letters are the truth. The letters are the key.
And you... Well, you get to make sure it works. You get to watch and plan and...
KRASH!
Shit. I have to go. Just...do what Grady—
KSHHH!
What the he—

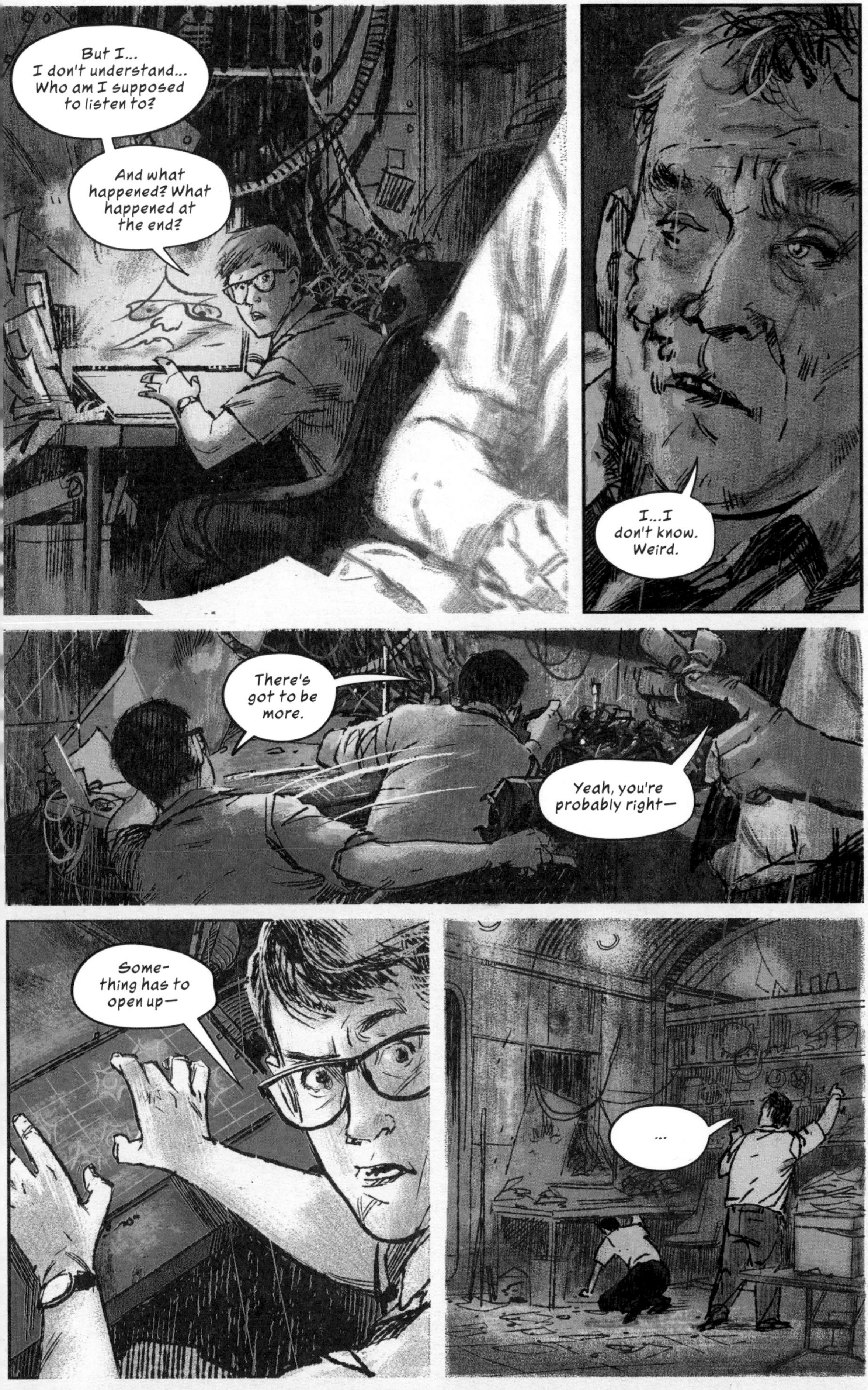
But I... I don't understand... Who am I supposed to listen to?
And what happened? What happened at the end?
I...I don't know. Weird.
There's got to be more.
Yeah, you're probably right—
Some-thing has to open up—
...

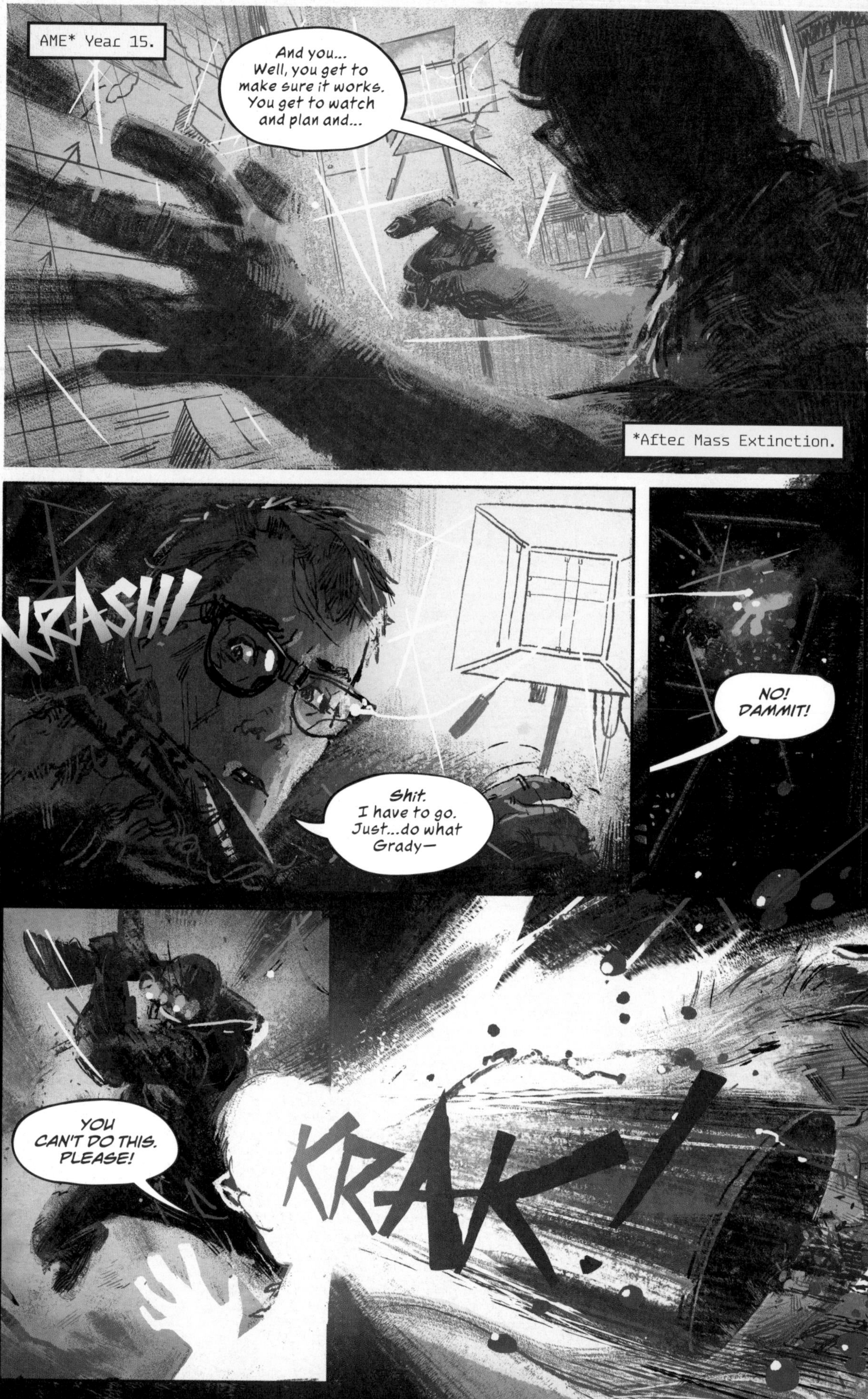
AME* Year 15.
And you... Well, you get to make sure it works. You get to watch and plan and...
*After Mass Extinction.
KRASH!
Shit. I have to go. Just...do what Grady—
NO! DAMMIT!
YOU CAN'T DO THIS. PLEASE!
KRAK-!

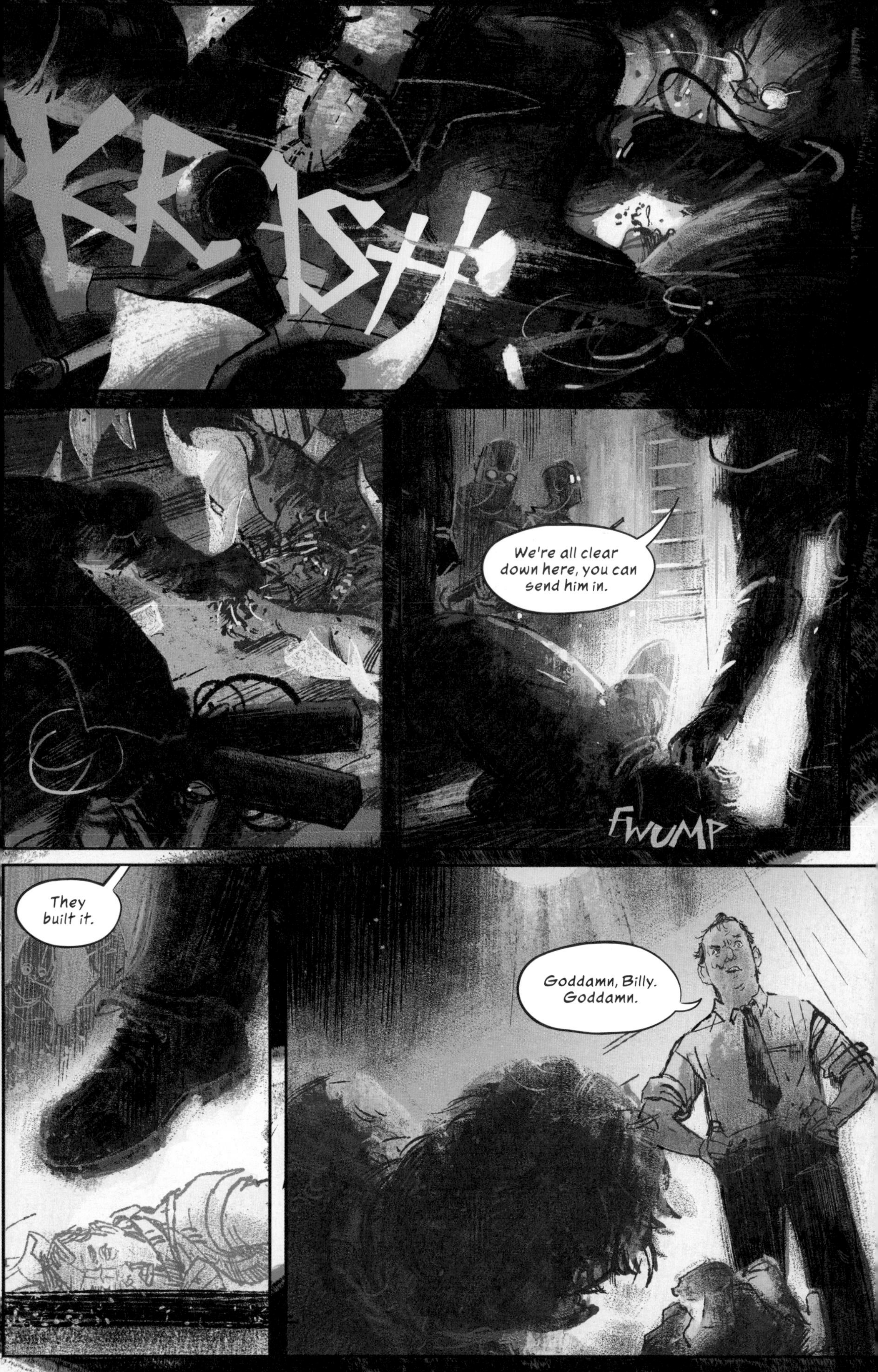
KRASH
We're all clear down here, you can send him in.
FWUMP
They built it.
Goddamn, Billy. Goddamn.

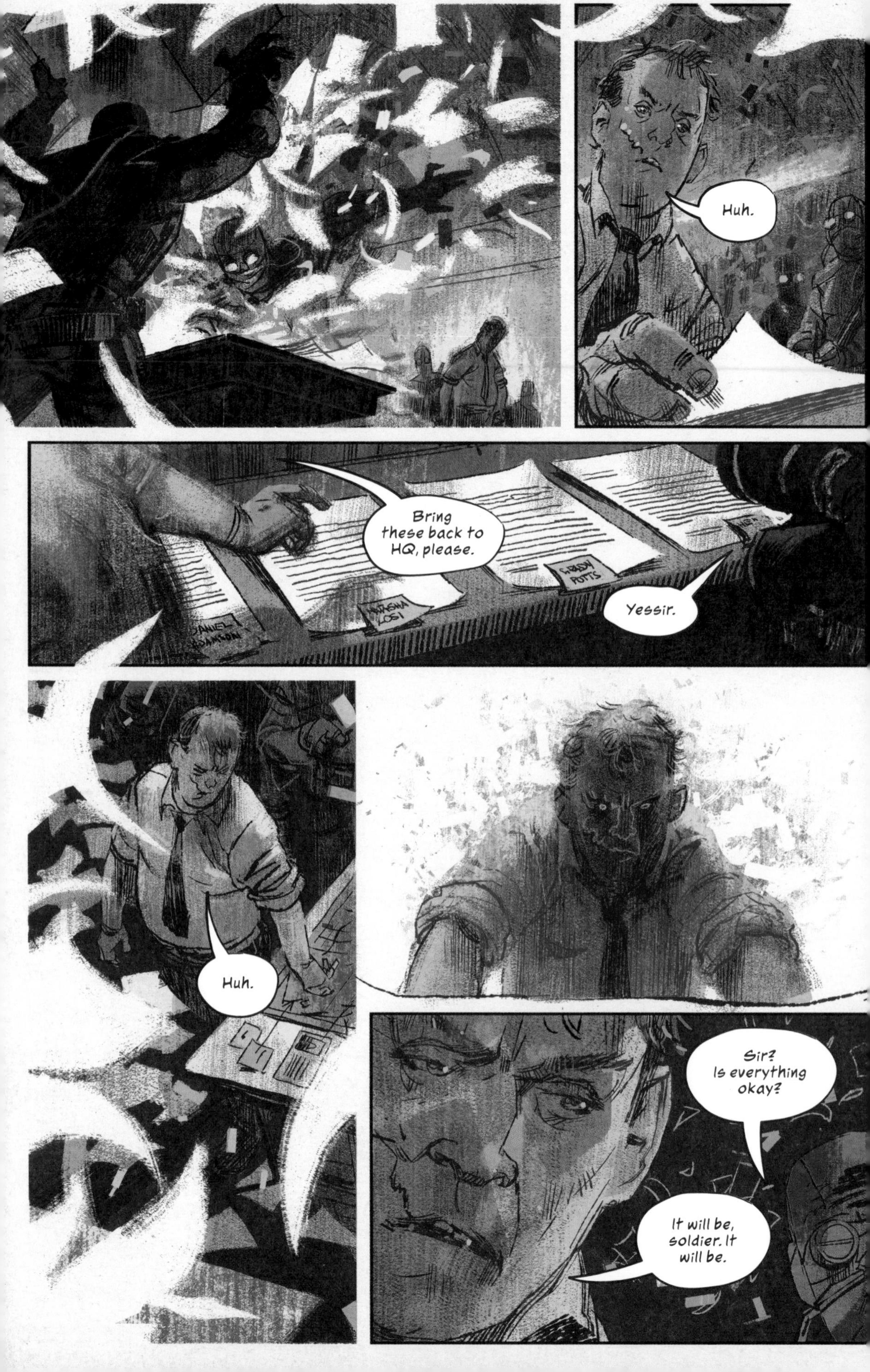
Huh.
Bring these back to HQ, please.
Yessir.
Huh.
Sir? Is everything okay?
It will be, soldier. It will be.

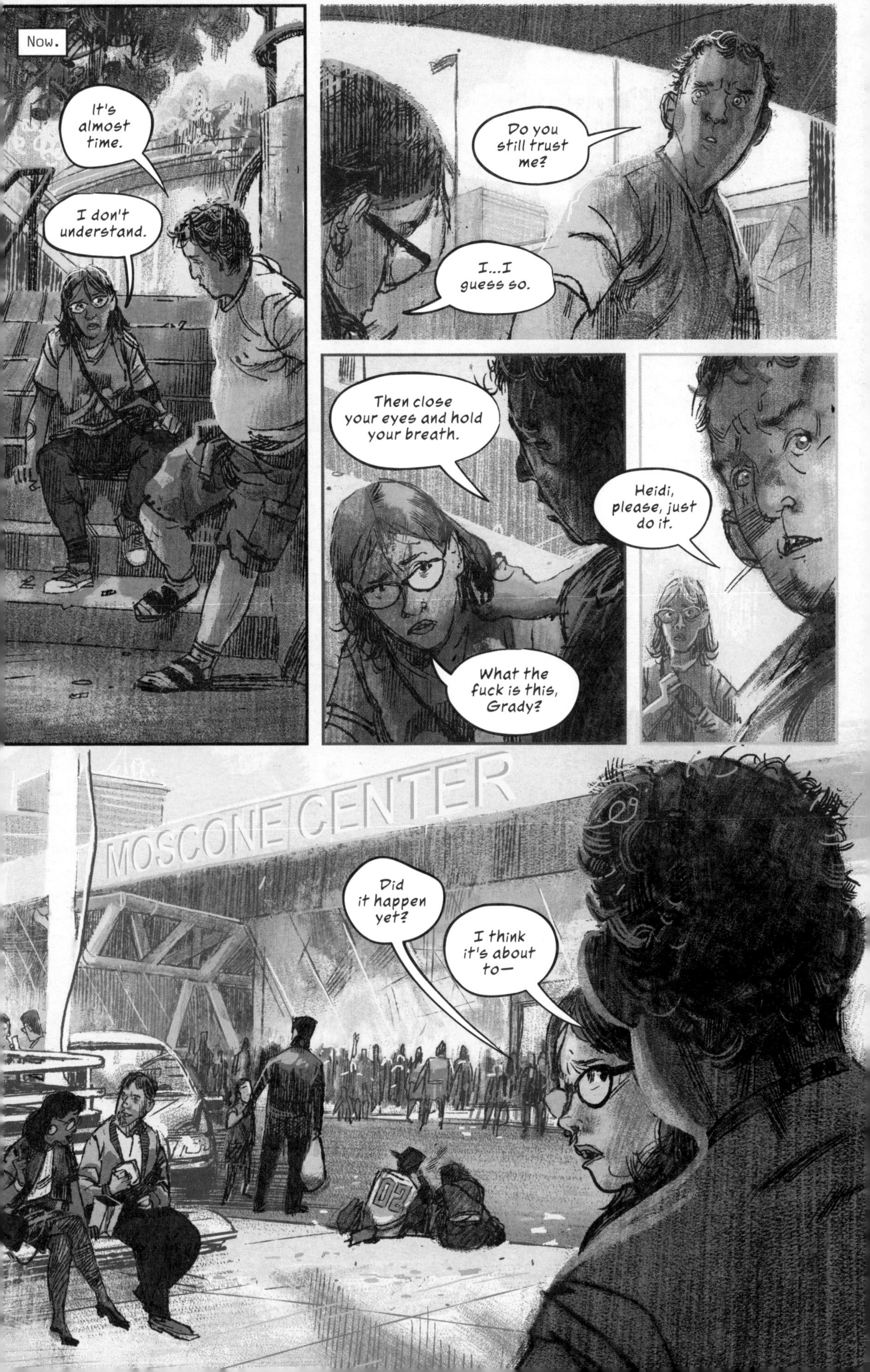
Now.
It's almost time.
I don't understand.
Do you still trust me?
I...I guess so.
Then close your eyes and hold your breath.
What the fuck is this, Grady?
Heidi, please, just do it.
MOSCONE CENTER
Did it happen yet?
I think it's about to—

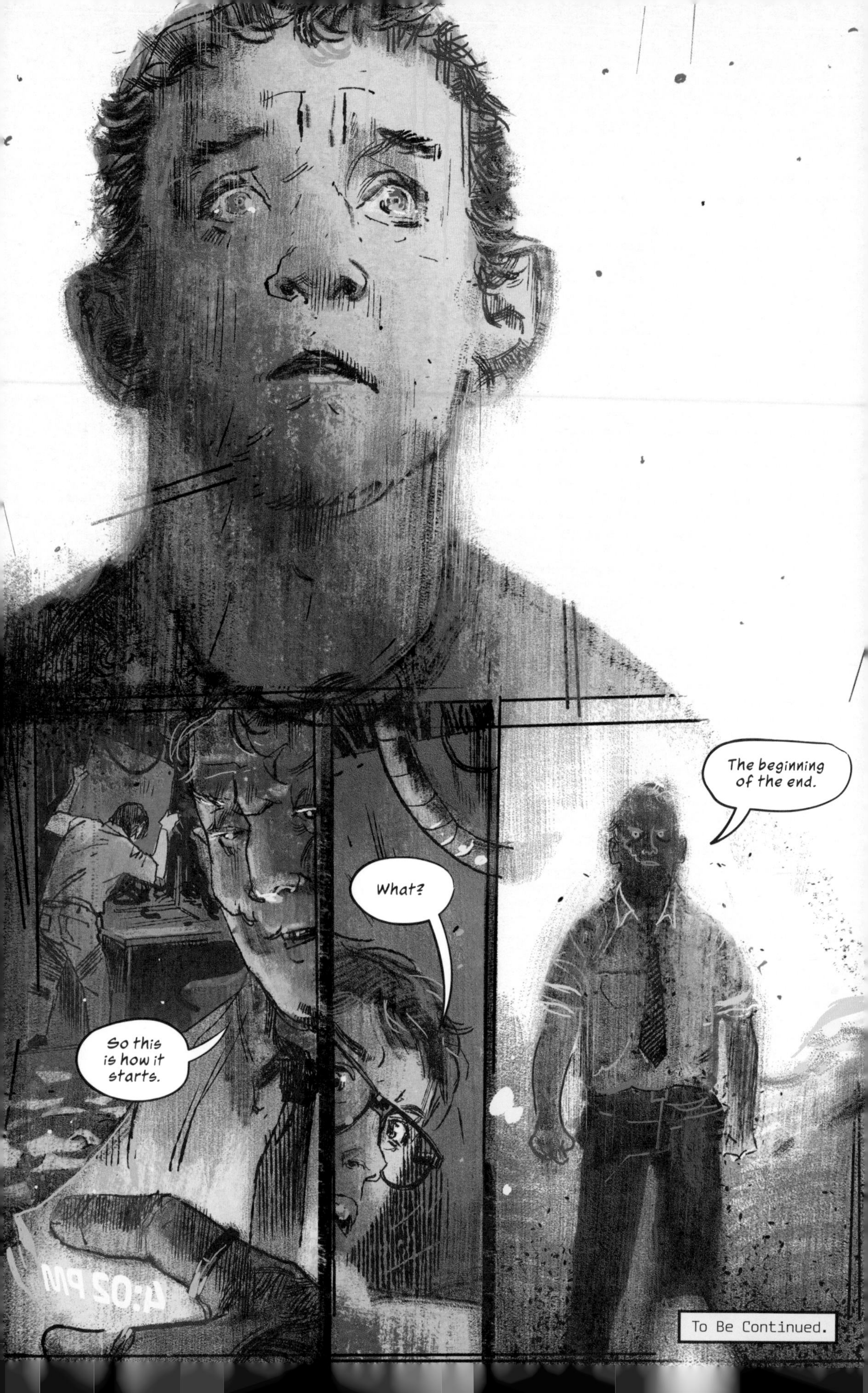
So this is how it starts.
What?
The beginning of the end.
To Be Continued.

# CHAPTER
## 03

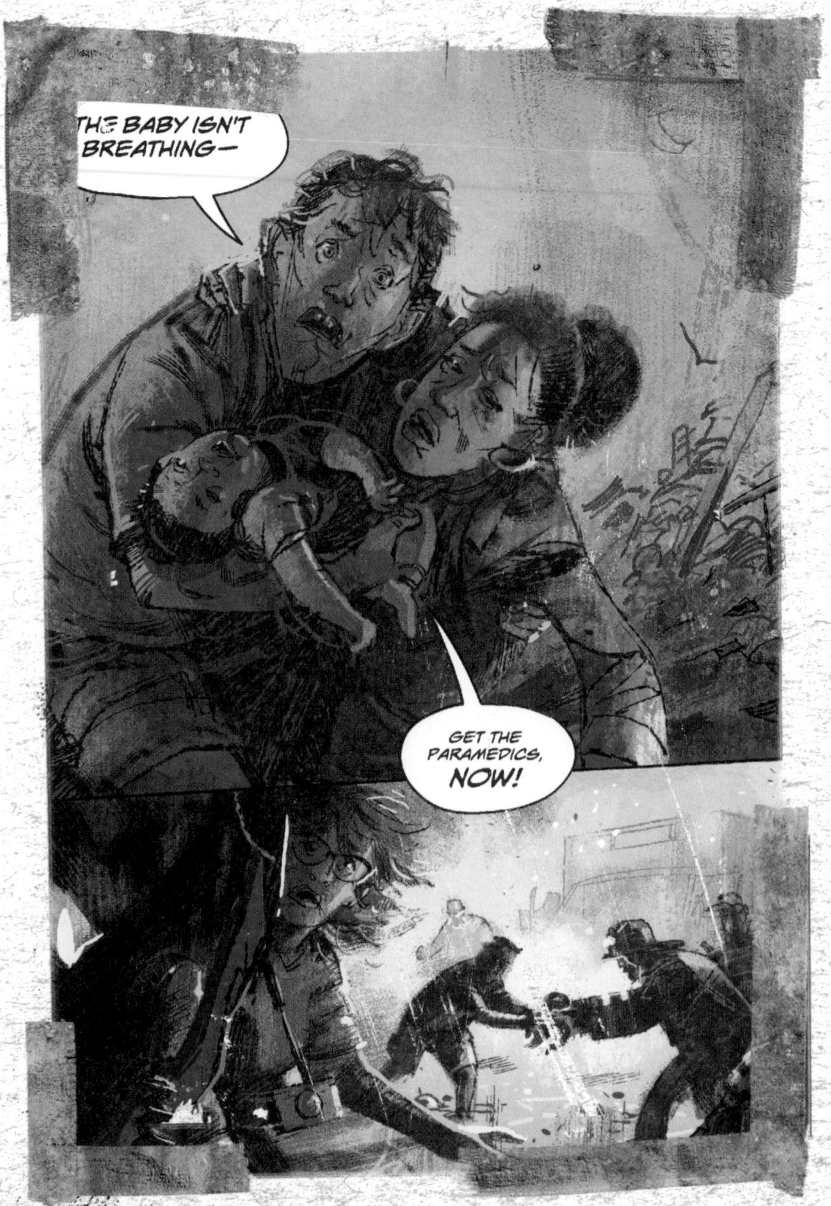
THE BABY ISN'T BREATHING—
GET THE PARAMEDICS, NOW!

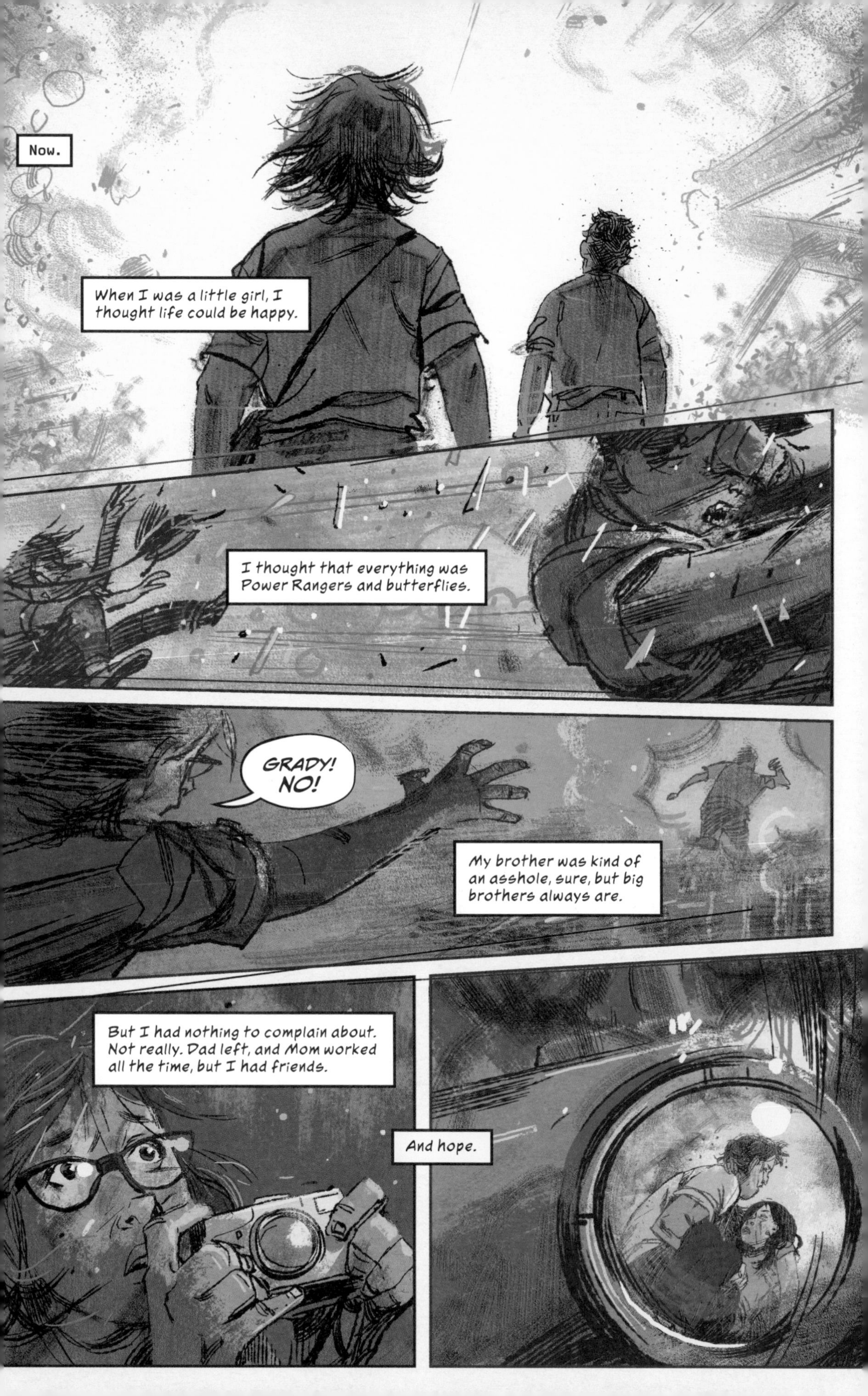
Now.
When I was a little girl, I thought life could be happy.
I thought that everything was Power Rangers and butterflies.
GRADY! NO!
My brother was kind of an asshole, sure, but big brothers always are.
But I had nothing to complain about. Not really. Dad left, and Mom worked all the time, but I had friends.
And hope.

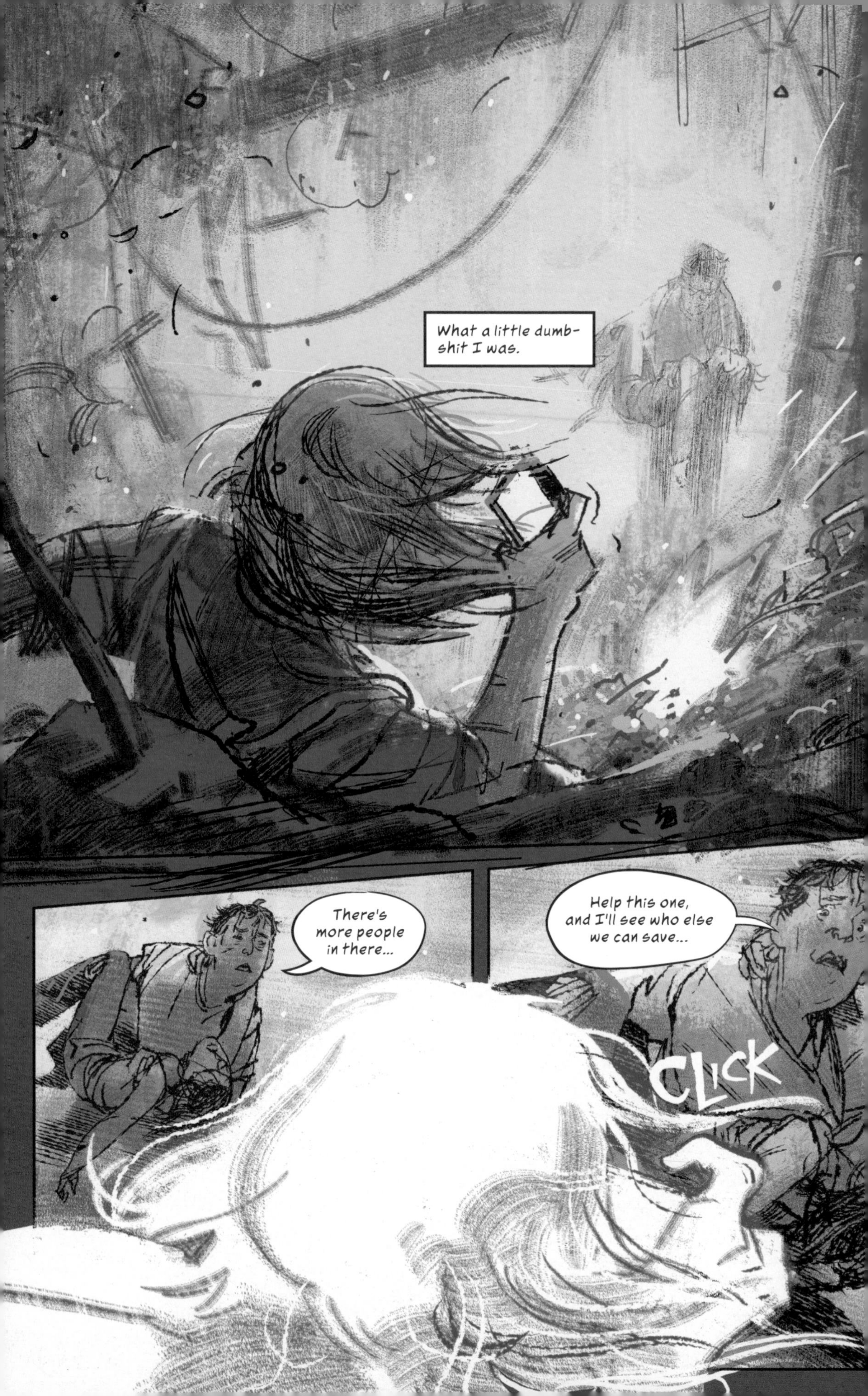
What a little dumb-shit I was.
There's more people in there...
Help this one, and I'll see who else we can save...
CLICK

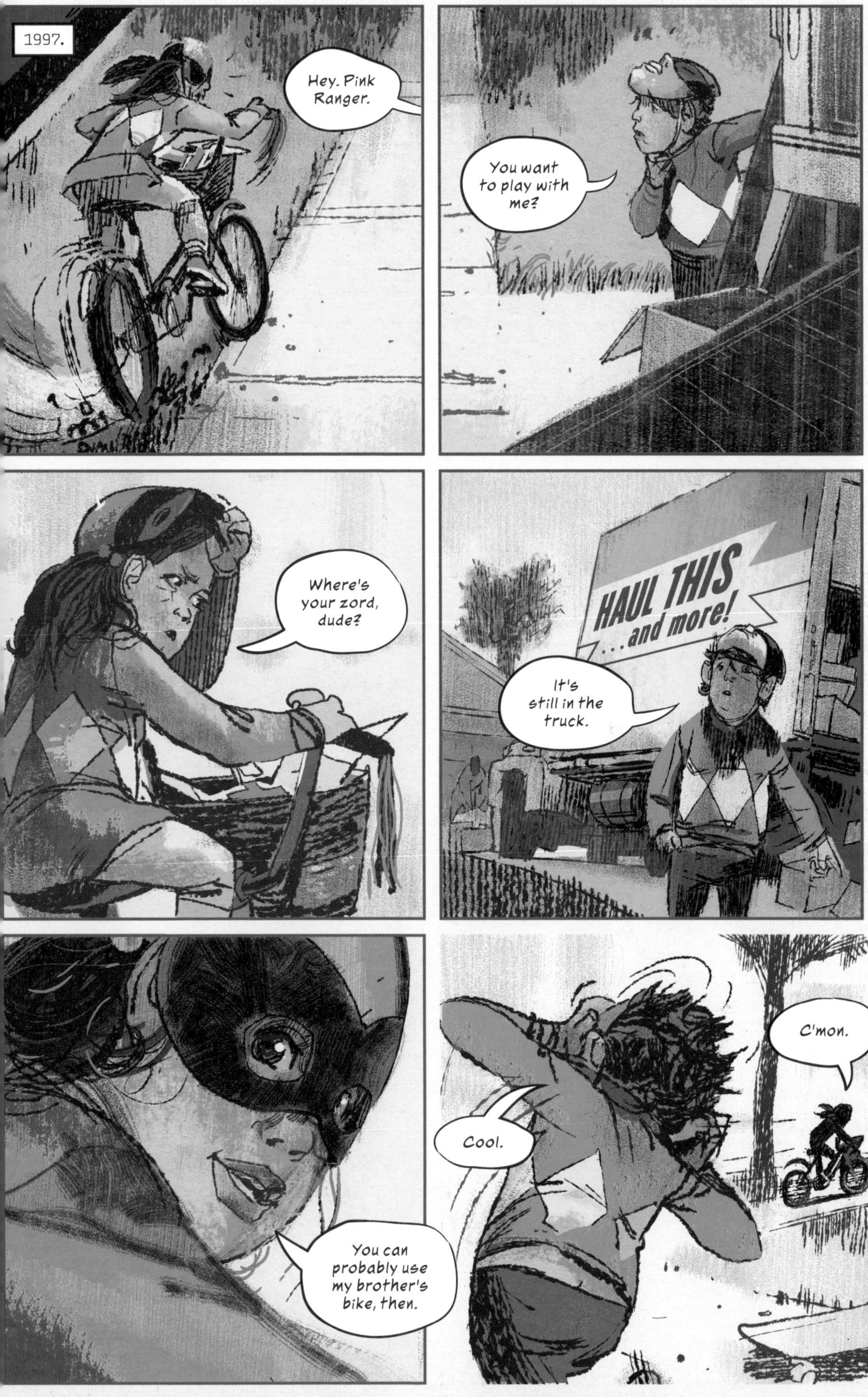
1997.
Hey. Pink Ranger.
You want to play with me?
Where's your zord, dude?
HAUL THIS ...and more!
It's still in the truck.
You can probably use my brother's bike, then.
Cool.
C'mon.

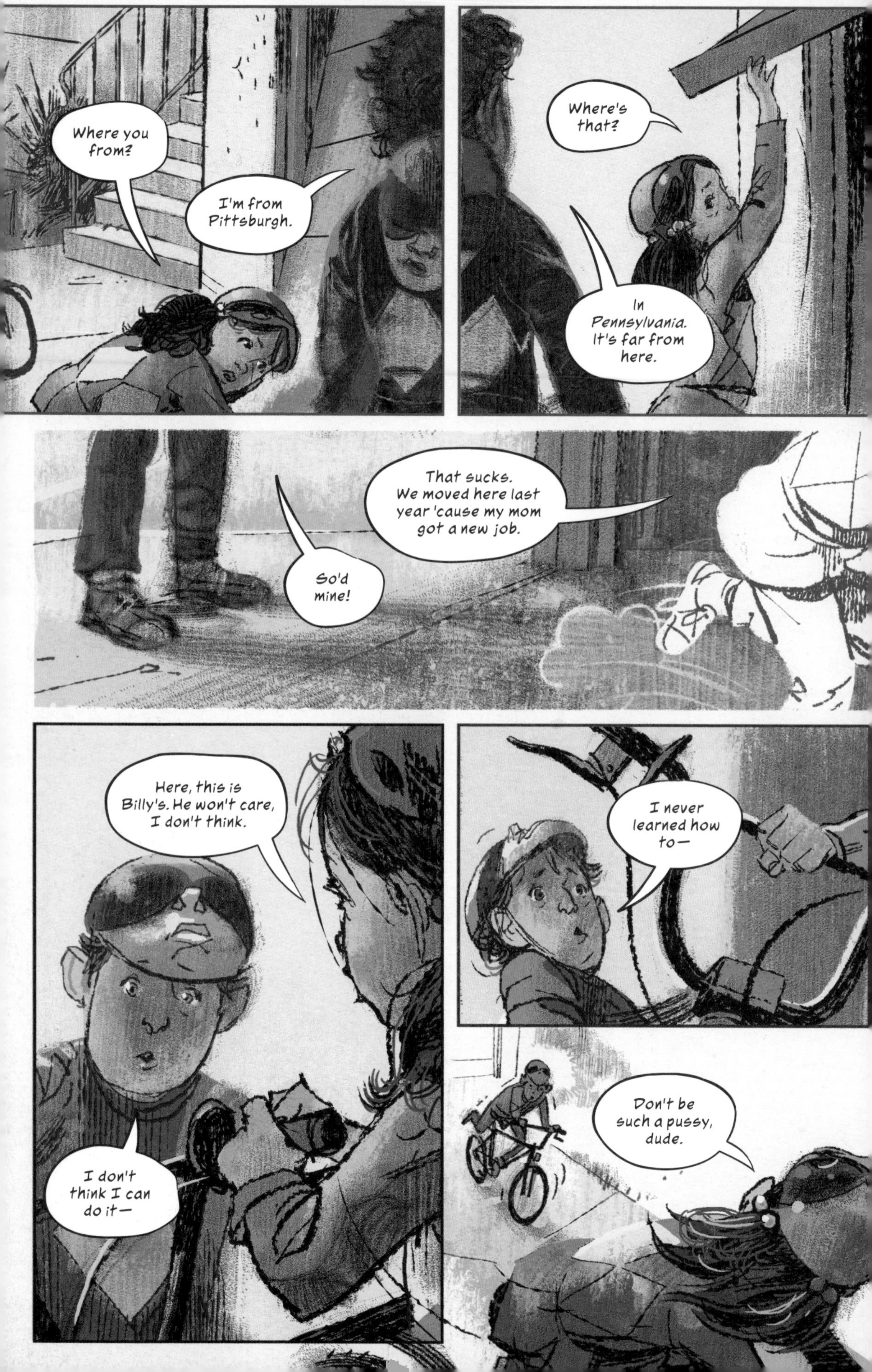
Where you from?
I'm from Pittsburgh.
Where's that?
In Pennsylvania. It's far from here.
That sucks. We moved here last year 'cause my mom got a new job.
So'd mine!
Here, this is Billy's. He won't care, I don't think.
I don't think I can do it—
I never learned how to—
Don't be such a pussy, dude.

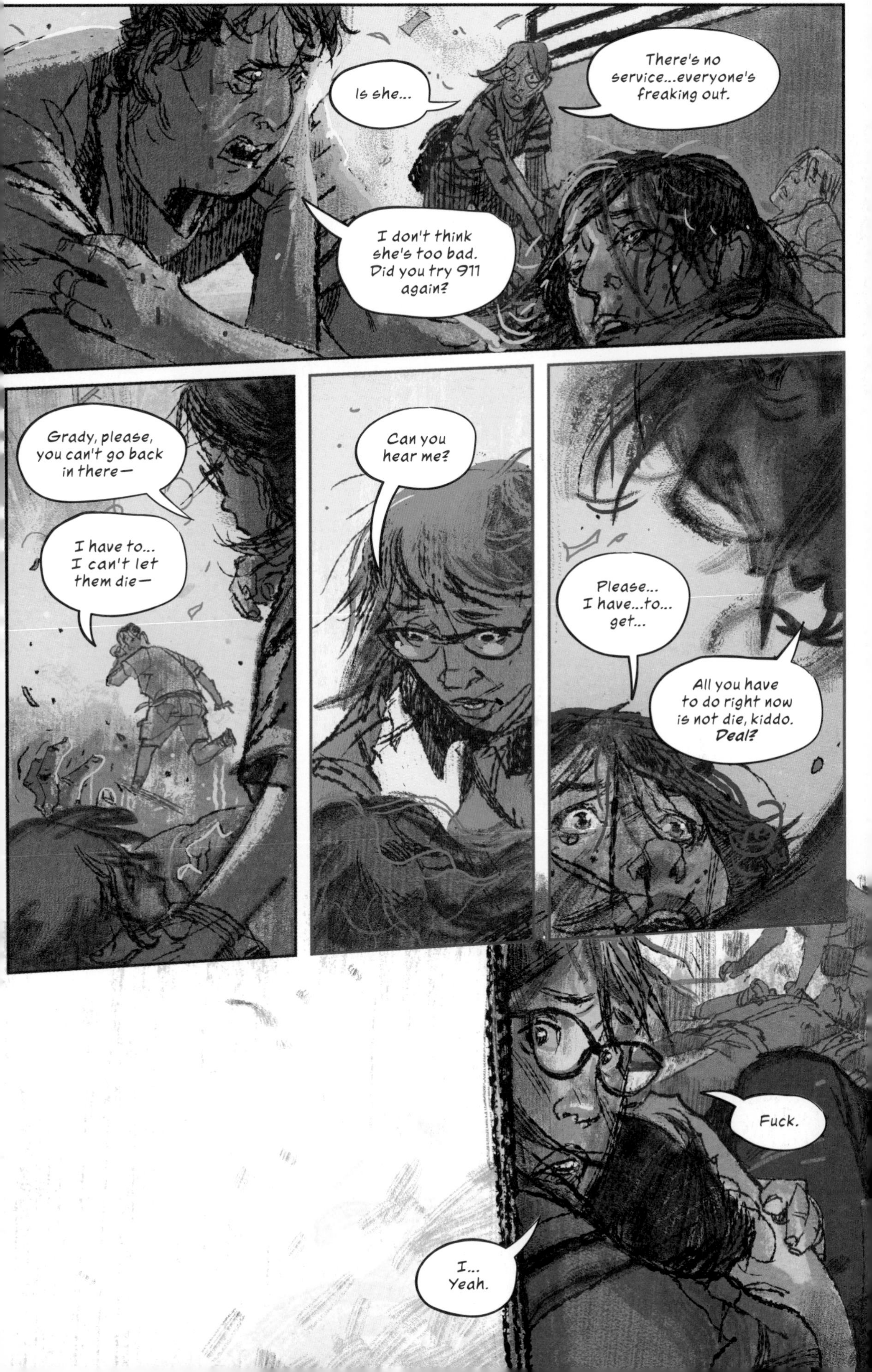
Is she...
There's no service...everyone's freaking out.
I don't think she's too bad. Did you try 911 again?
Grady, please, you can't go back in there—
I have to... I can't let them die—
Can you hear me?
Please... I have...to... get...
All you have to do right now is not die, kiddo. *Deal?*
Fuck.
I... Yeah.

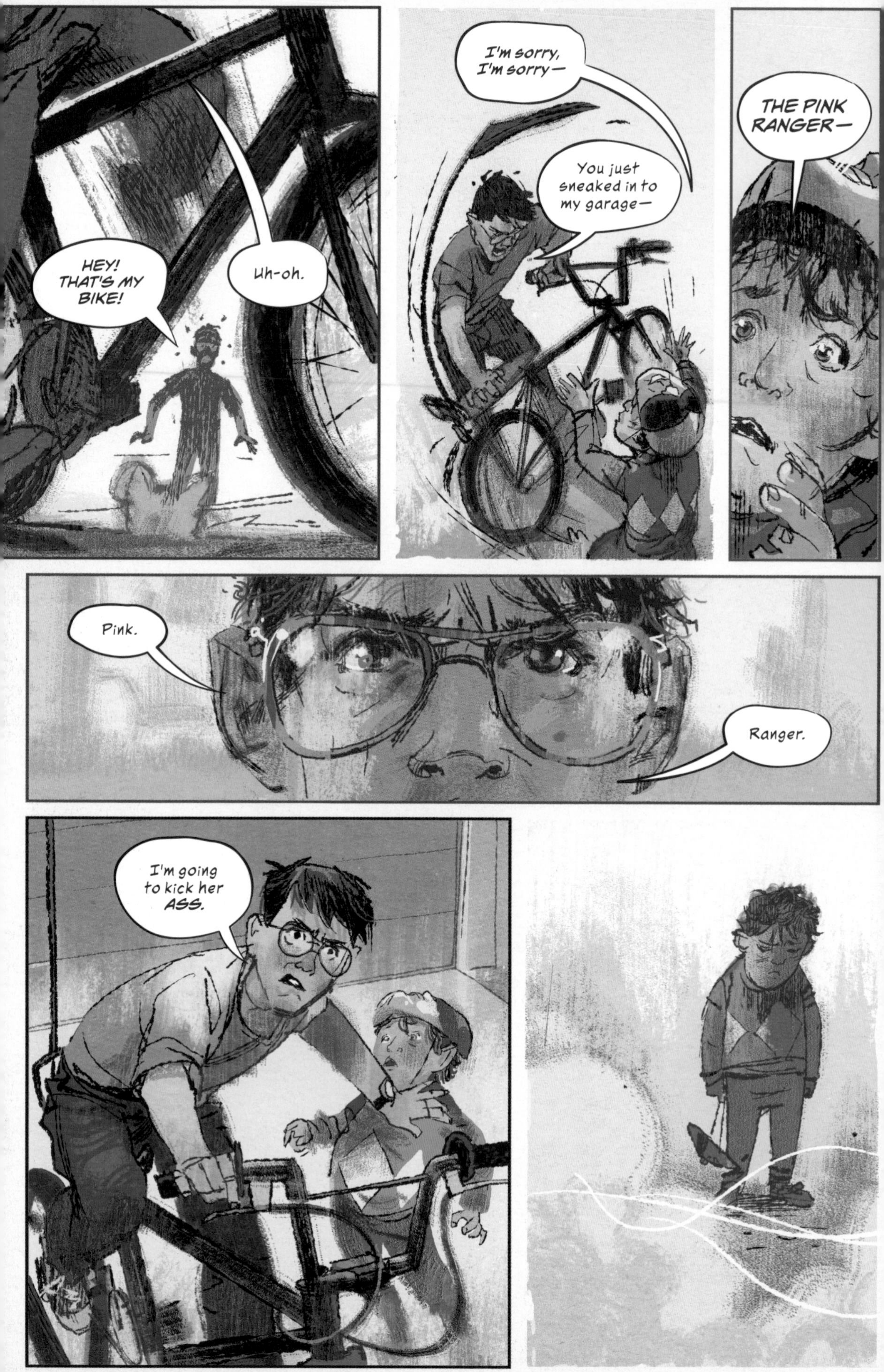
HEY! THAT'S MY BIKE!
Uh-oh.
I'm sorry, I'm sorry—
You just sneaked in to my garage—
THE PINK RANGER—
Pink.
Ranger.
I'm going to kick her ASS.

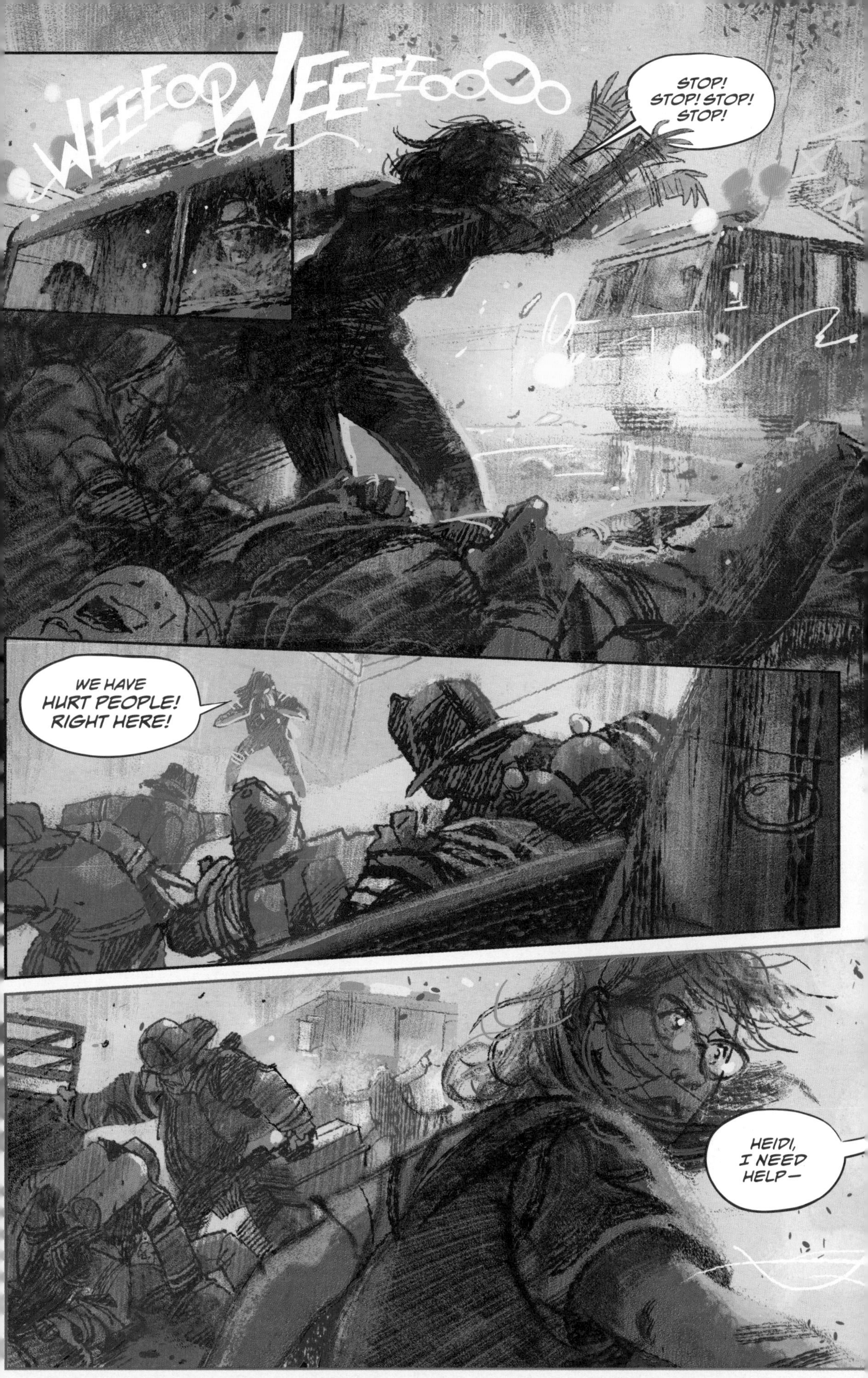
WEEEOO WEEEEEOOOOO
STOP! STOP! STOP! STOP!
WE HAVE HURT PEOPLE! RIGHT HERE!
HEIDI, I NEED HELP—

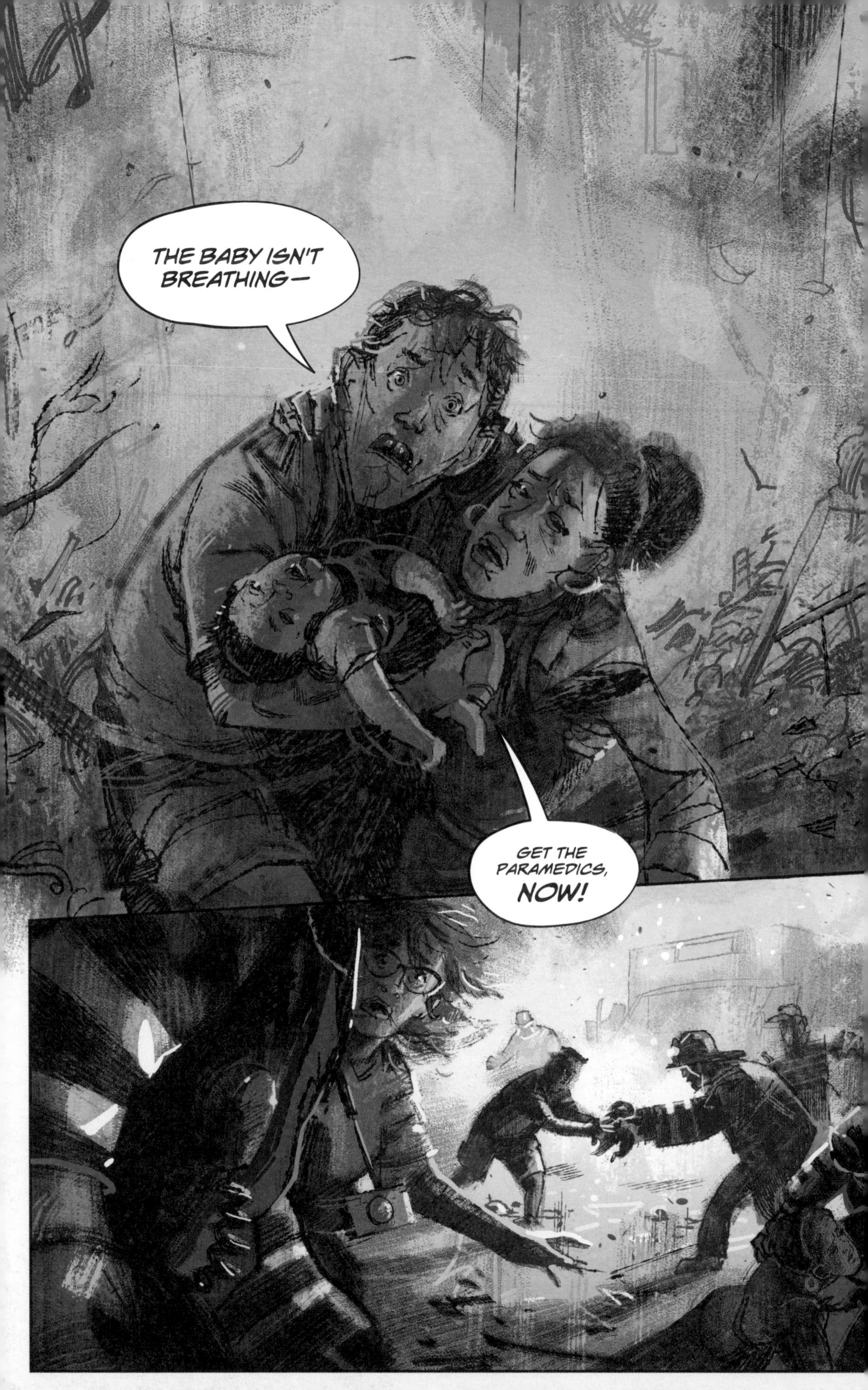
THE BABY ISN'T BREATHING—
GET THE PARAMEDICS, NOW!

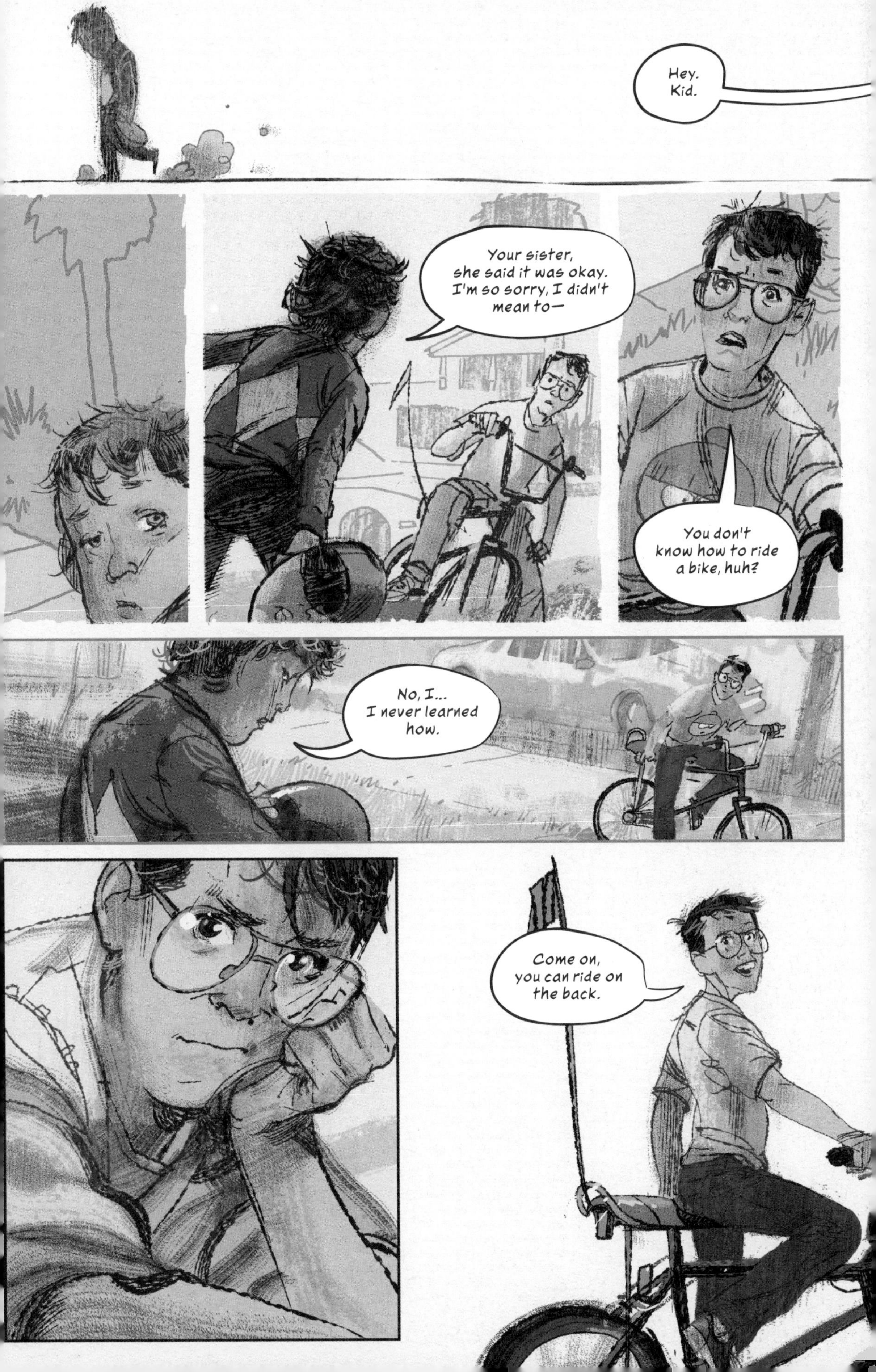
Hey.
Kid.
Your sister, she said it was okay. I'm so sorry, I didn't mean to—
You don't know how to ride a bike, huh?
No, I... I never learned how.
Come on, you can ride on the back.

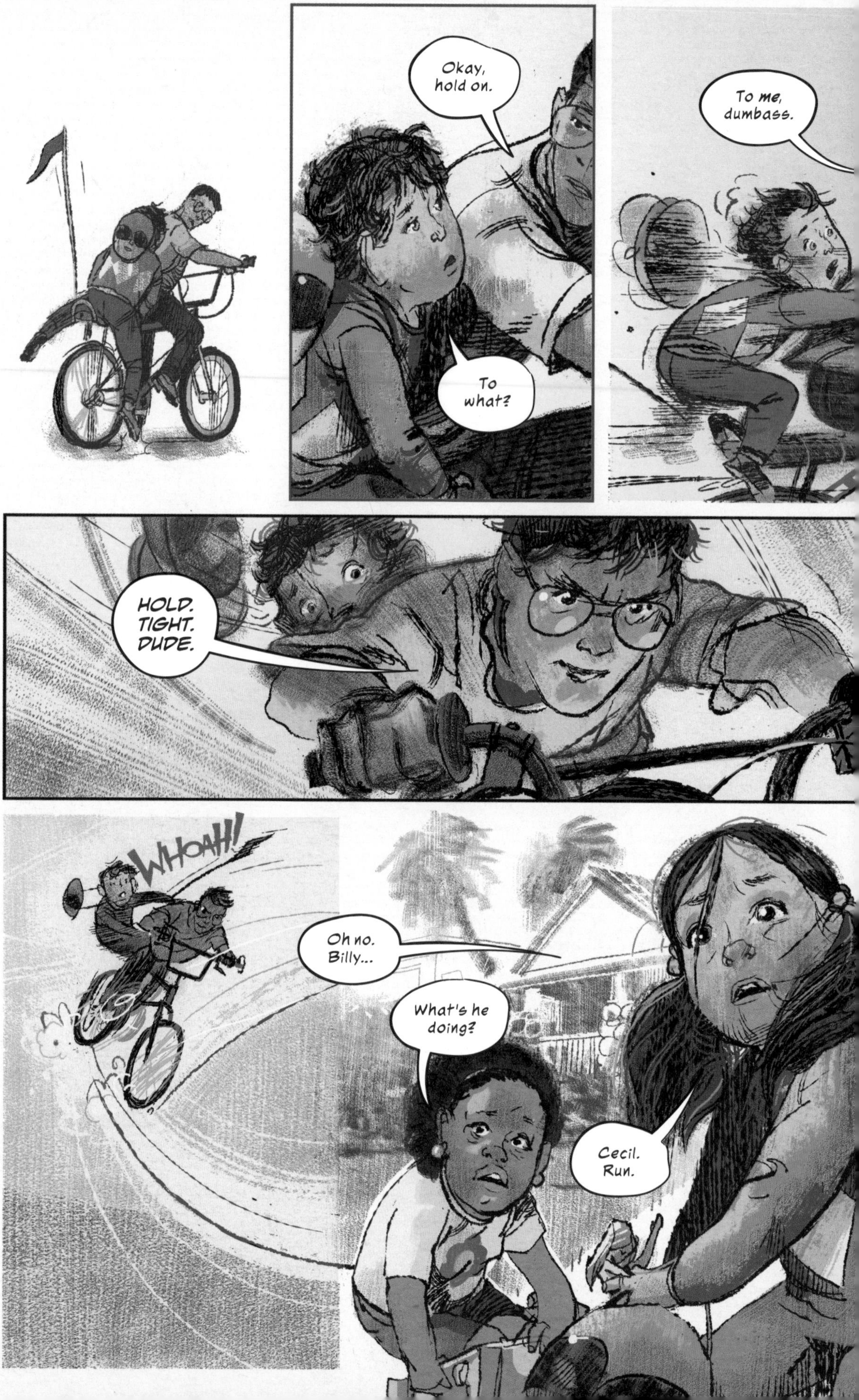
Okay, hold on.
To what?
To me, dumbass.
HOLD. TIGHT. DUDE.
WHOAH!
Oh no. Billy...
What's he doing?
Cecil. Run.

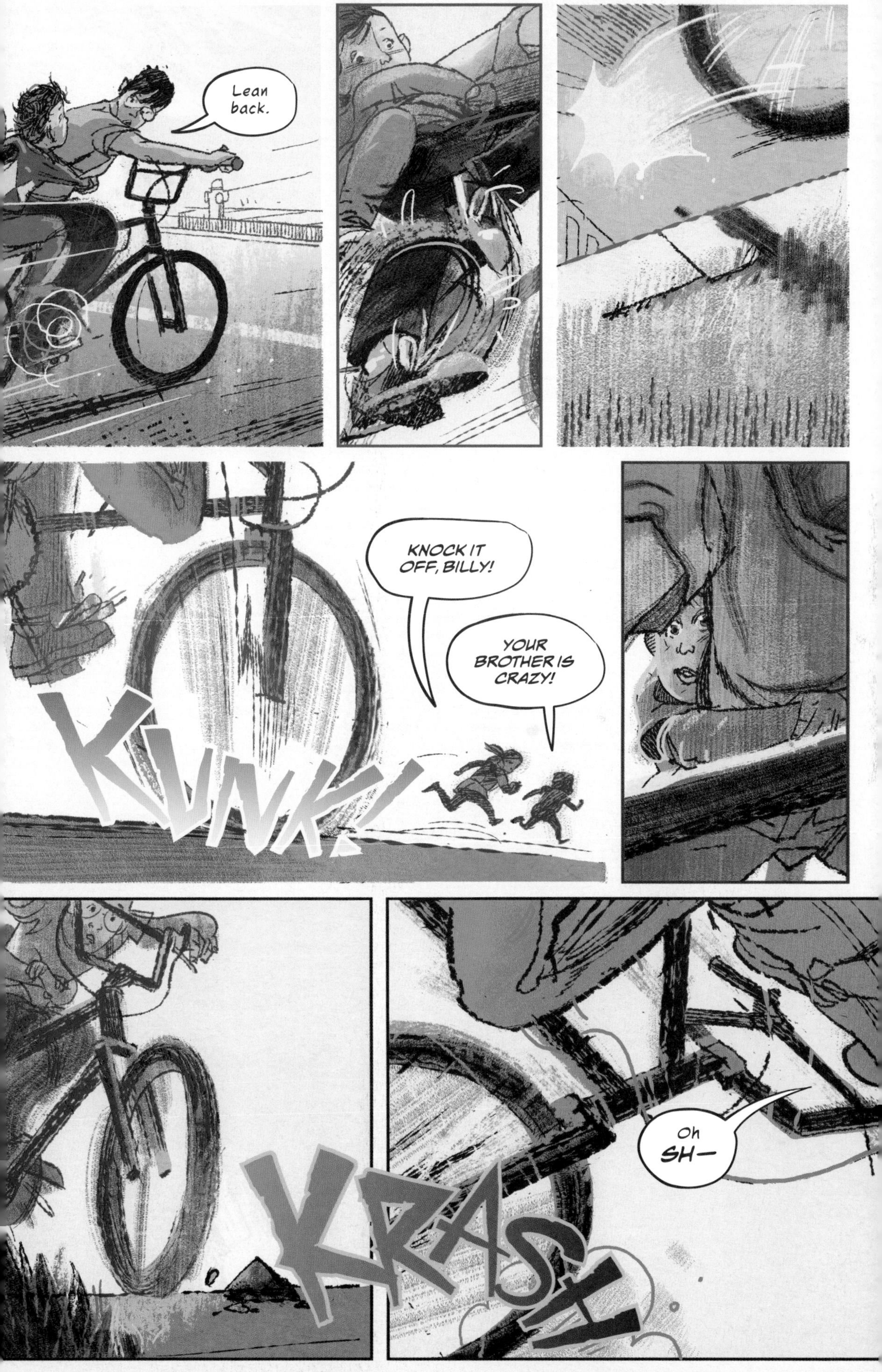
Lean back.
KNOCK IT OFF, BILLY!
YOUR BROTHER IS CRAZY!
KLUNK!
KRASH
Oh SH—

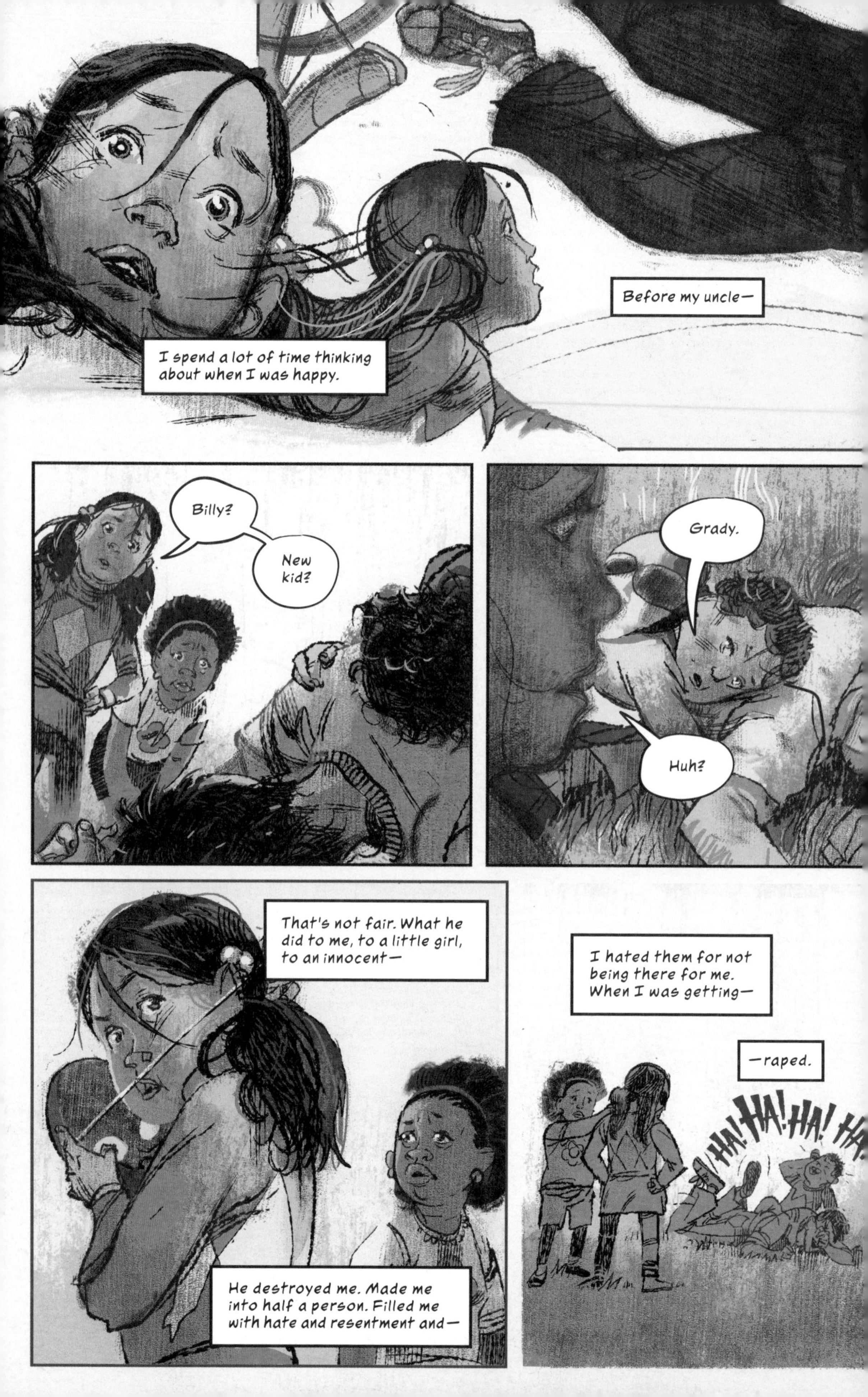
I spend a lot of time thinking about when I was happy.
Before my uncle—
Billy?
New kid?
Grady.
Huh?
That's not fair. What he did to me, to a little girl, to an innocent—
He destroyed me. Made me into half a person. Filled me with hate and resentment and—
I hated them for not being there for me. When I was getting—
—raped.
HA! HA! HA! HA!

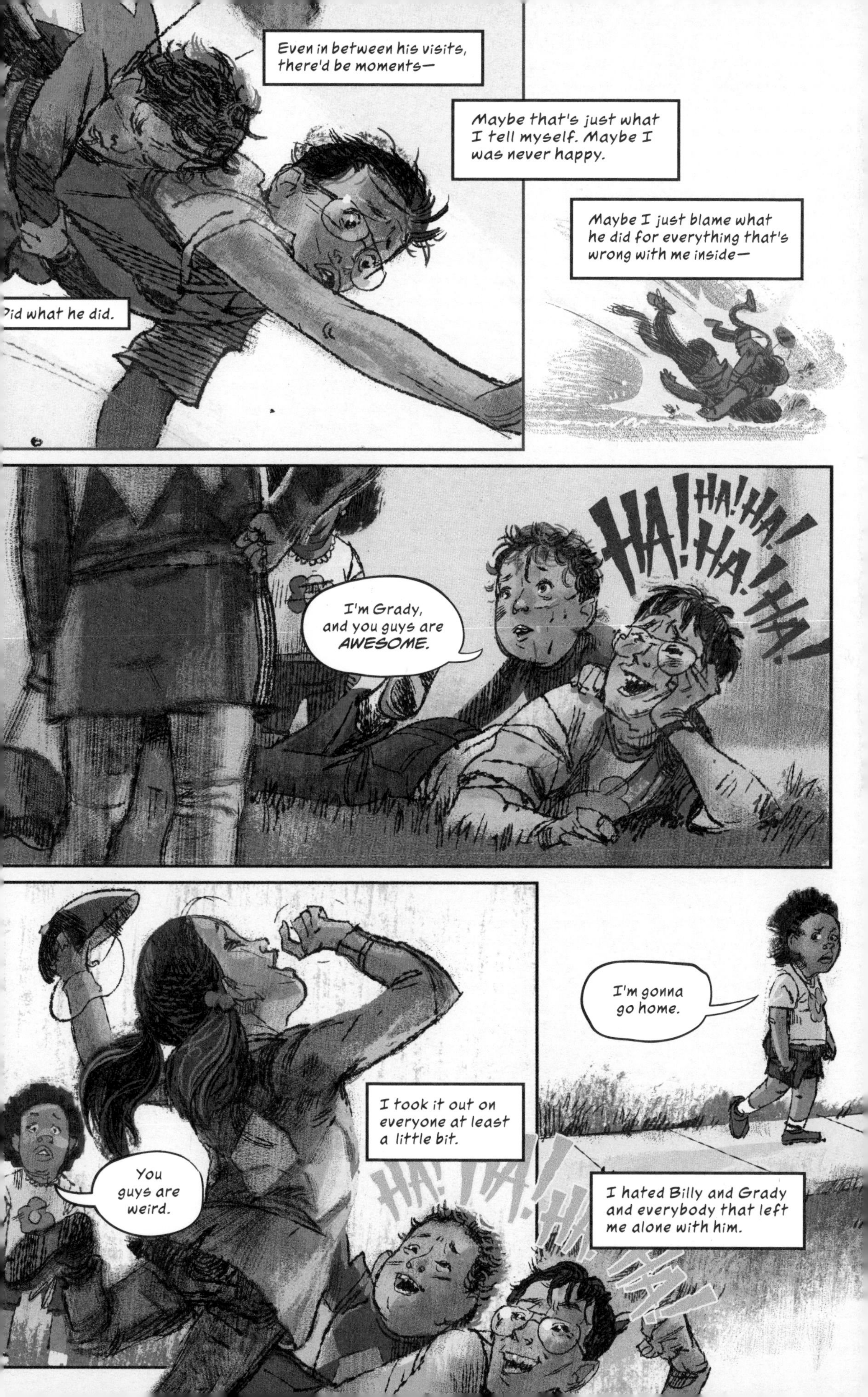

Even in between his visits, there'd be moments—
Did what he did.
Maybe that's just what I tell myself. Maybe I was never happy.
Maybe I just blame what he did for everything that's wrong with me inside—
I'm Grady, and you guys are AWESOME.
HA! HA! HA! HA! HA! HA!
I took it out on everyone at least a little bit.
You guys are weird.
HA! HA!
I'm gonna go home.
I hated Billy and Grady and everybody that left me alone with him.

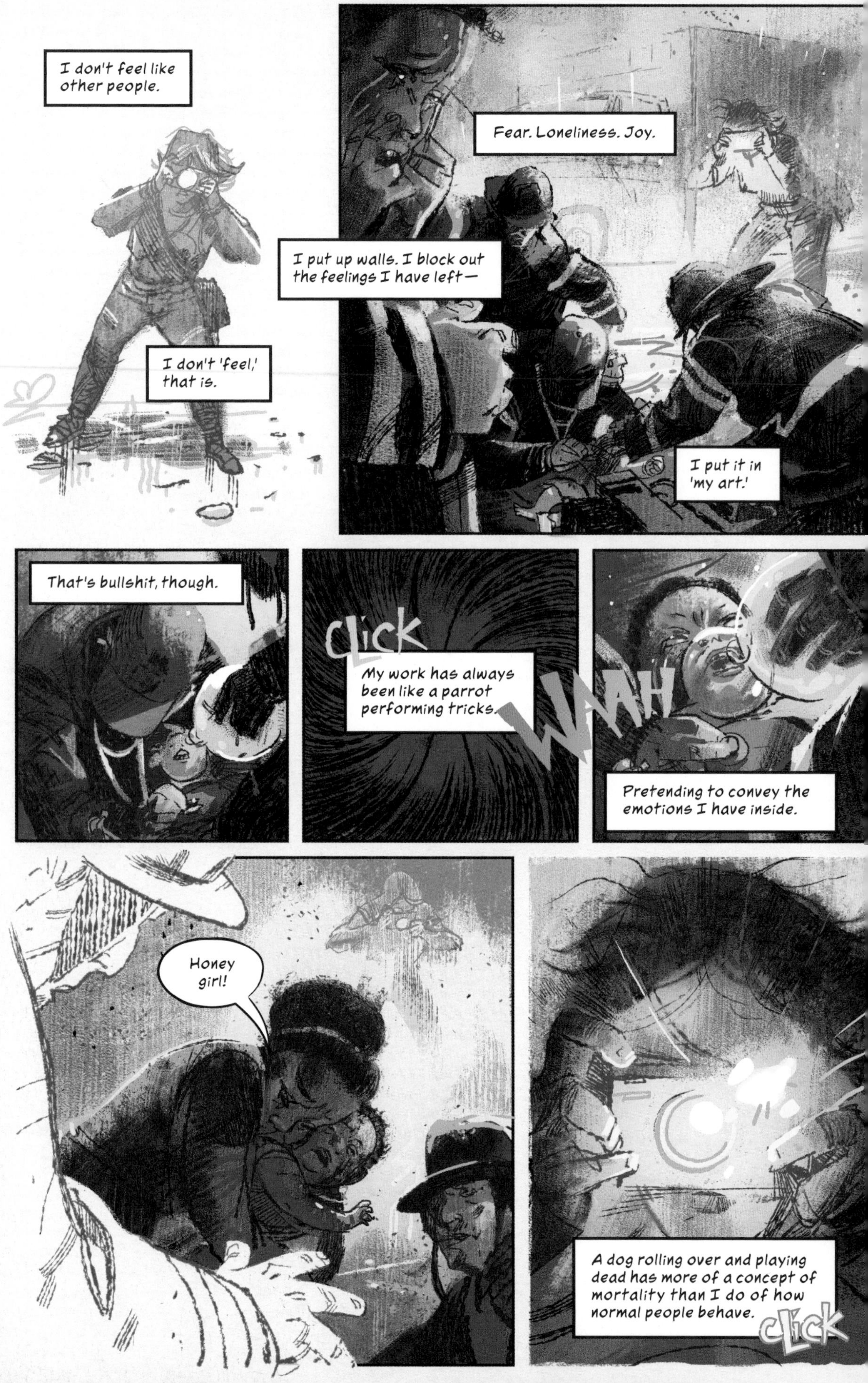
I don't feel like other people.
Fear. Loneliness. Joy.
I put up walls. I block out the feelings I have left—
I don't 'feel,' that is.
I put it in 'my art.'
That's bullshit, though.
CLICK
My work has always been like a parrot performing tricks.
WAAH
Pretending to convey the emotions I have inside.
Honey girl!
A dog rolling over and playing dead has more of a concept of mortality than I do of how normal people behave.
CLICK

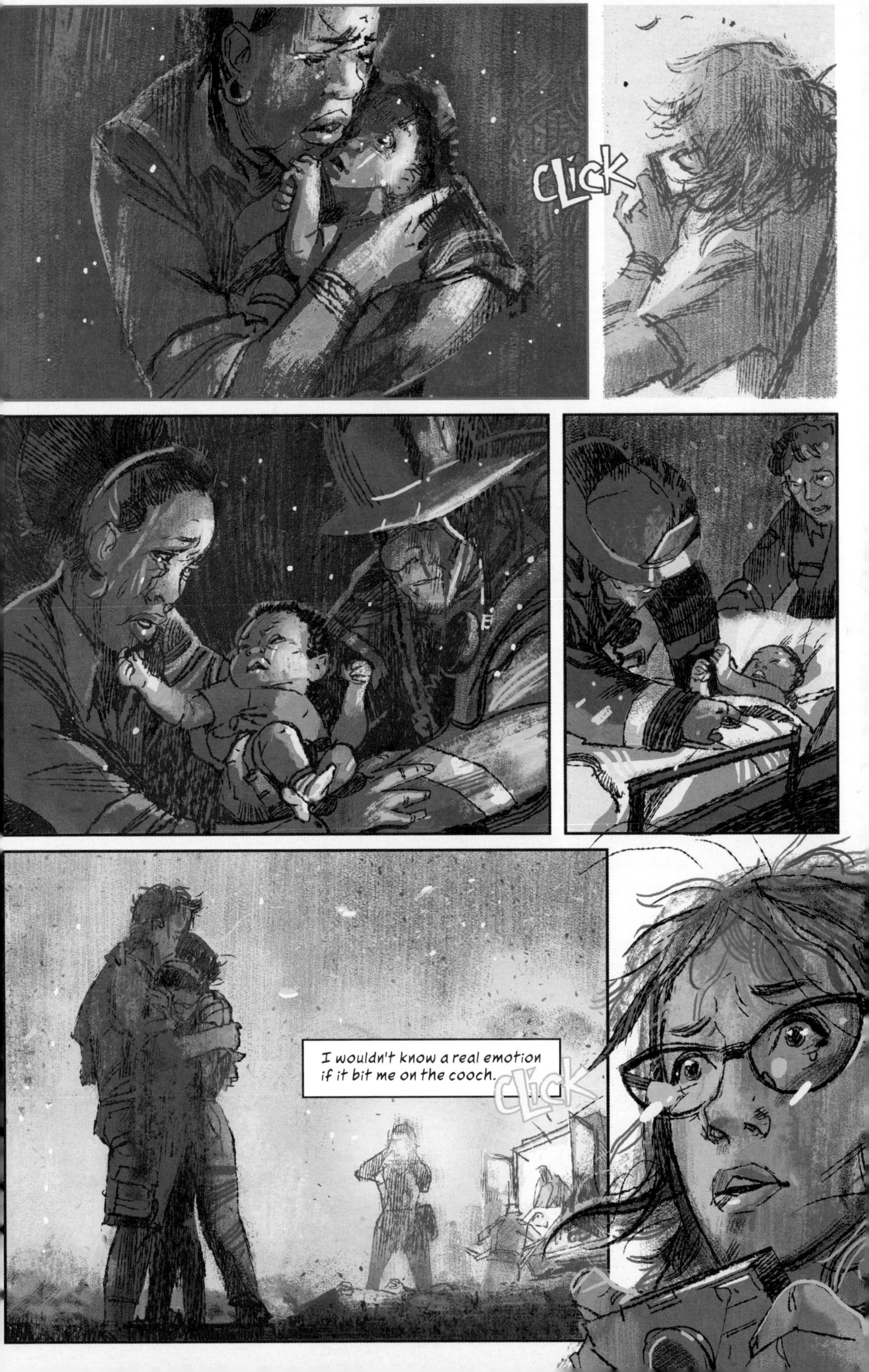
CLICK
I wouldn't know a real emotion if it bit me on the cooch.
CLICK

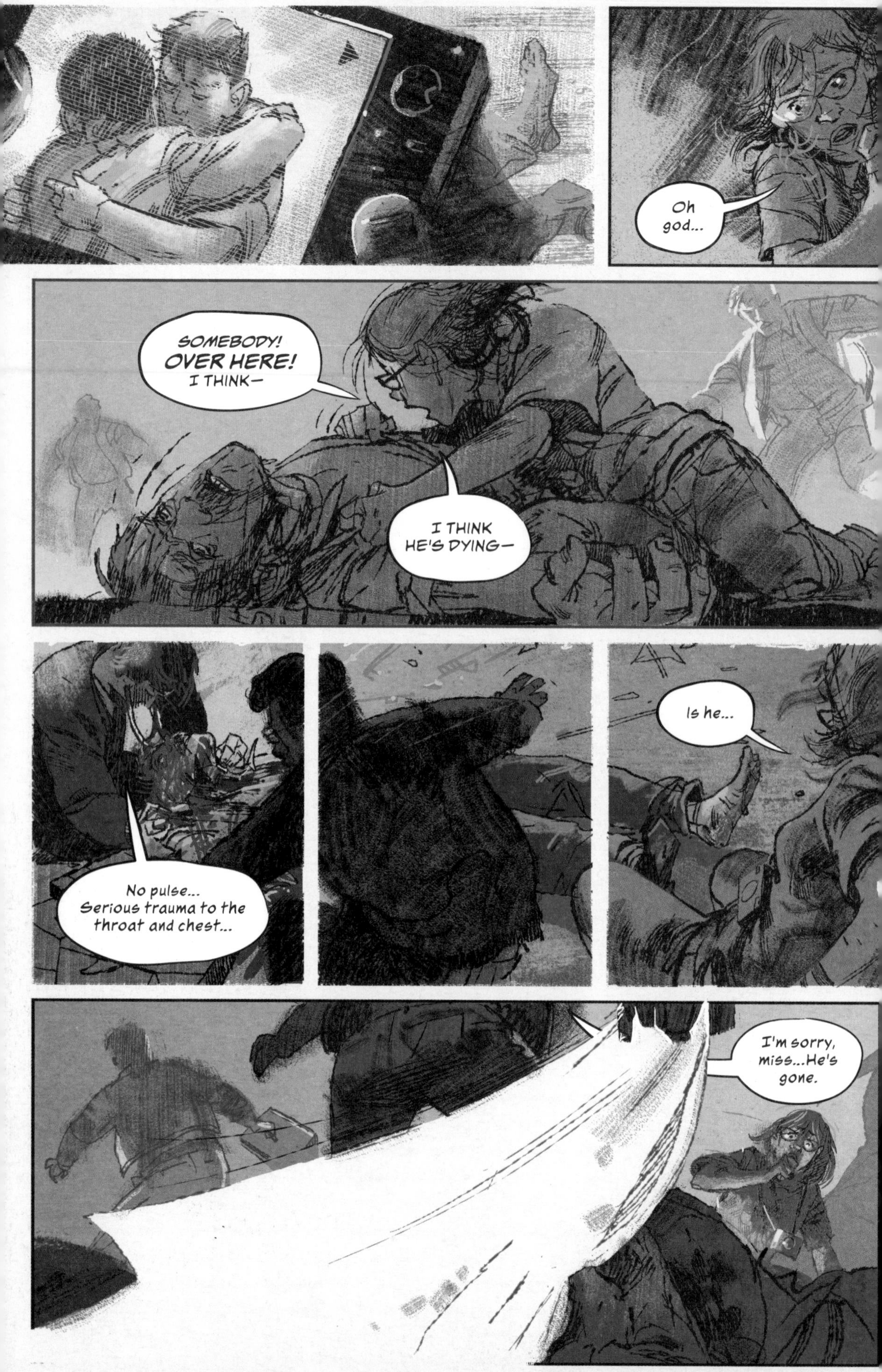
Oh god...
SOMEBODY! OVER HERE! I THINK—
I THINK HE'S DYING—
No pulse... Serious trauma to the throat and chest...
Is he...
I'm sorry, miss...He's gone.

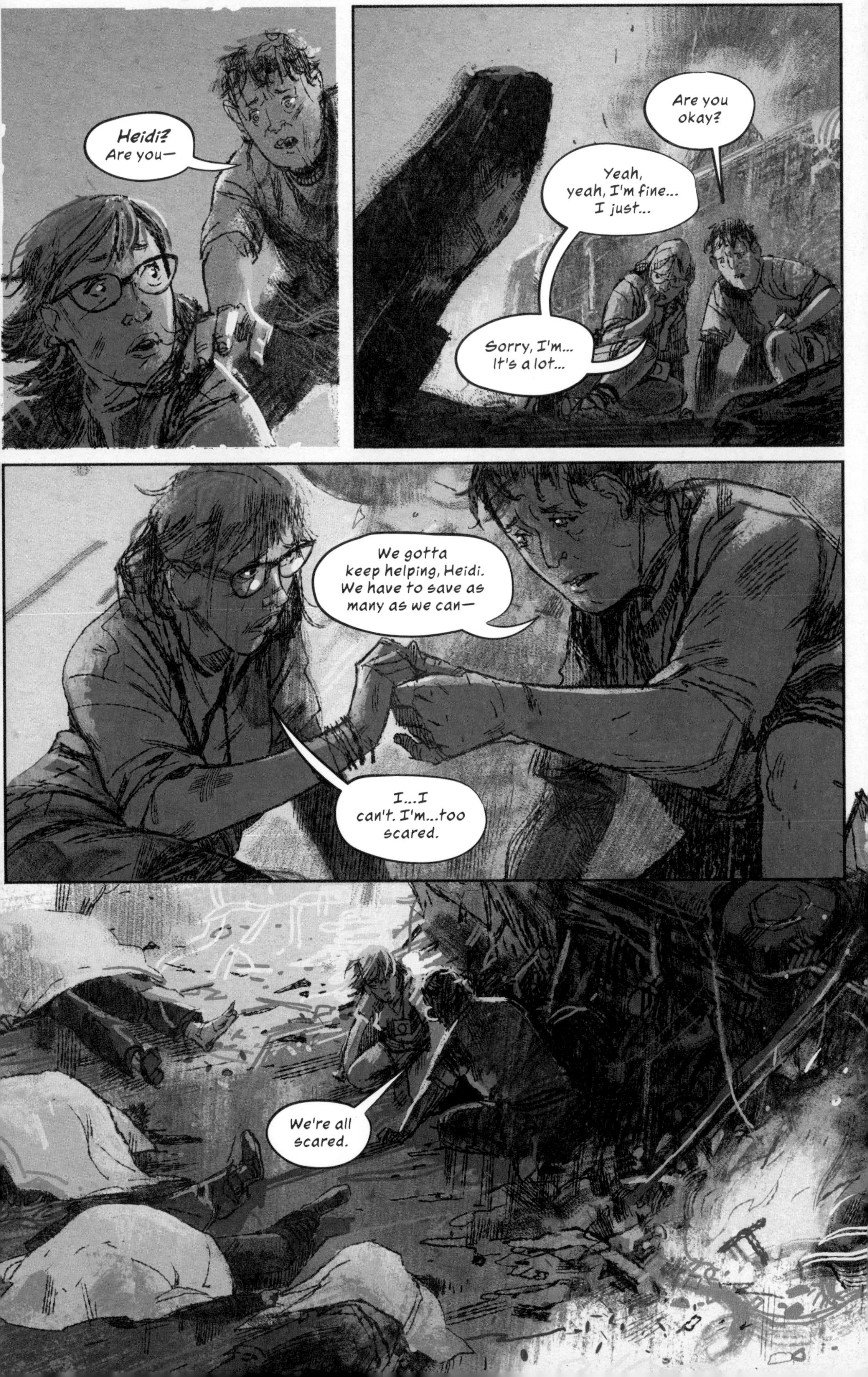
Heidi? Are you—
Are you okay?
Yeah, yeah, I'm fine... I just...
Sorry, I'm... It's a lot...
We gotta keep helping, Heidi. We have to save as many as we can—
I...I can't. I'm...too scared.
We're all scared.

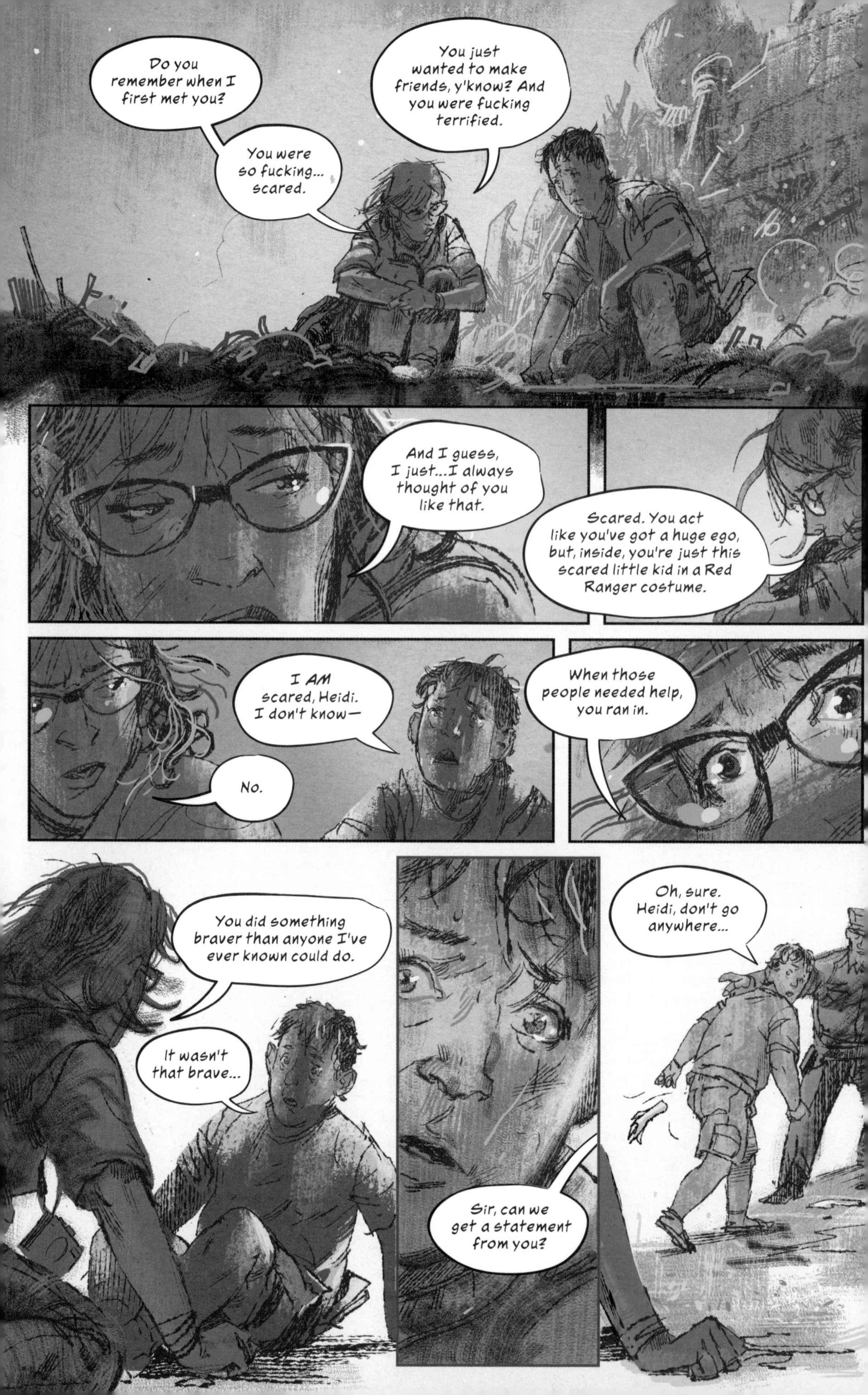

Do you remember when I first met you?
You were so fucking... scared.
You just wanted to make friends, y'know? And you were fucking terrified.
And I guess, I just...I always thought of you like that.
Scared. You act like you've got a huge ego, but, inside, you're just this scared little kid in a Red Ranger costume.
I AM scared, Heidi. I don't know—
No.
When those people needed help, you ran in.
You did something braver than anyone I've ever known could do.
It wasn't that brave...
Sir, can we get a statement from you?
Oh, sure. Heidi, don't go anywhere...

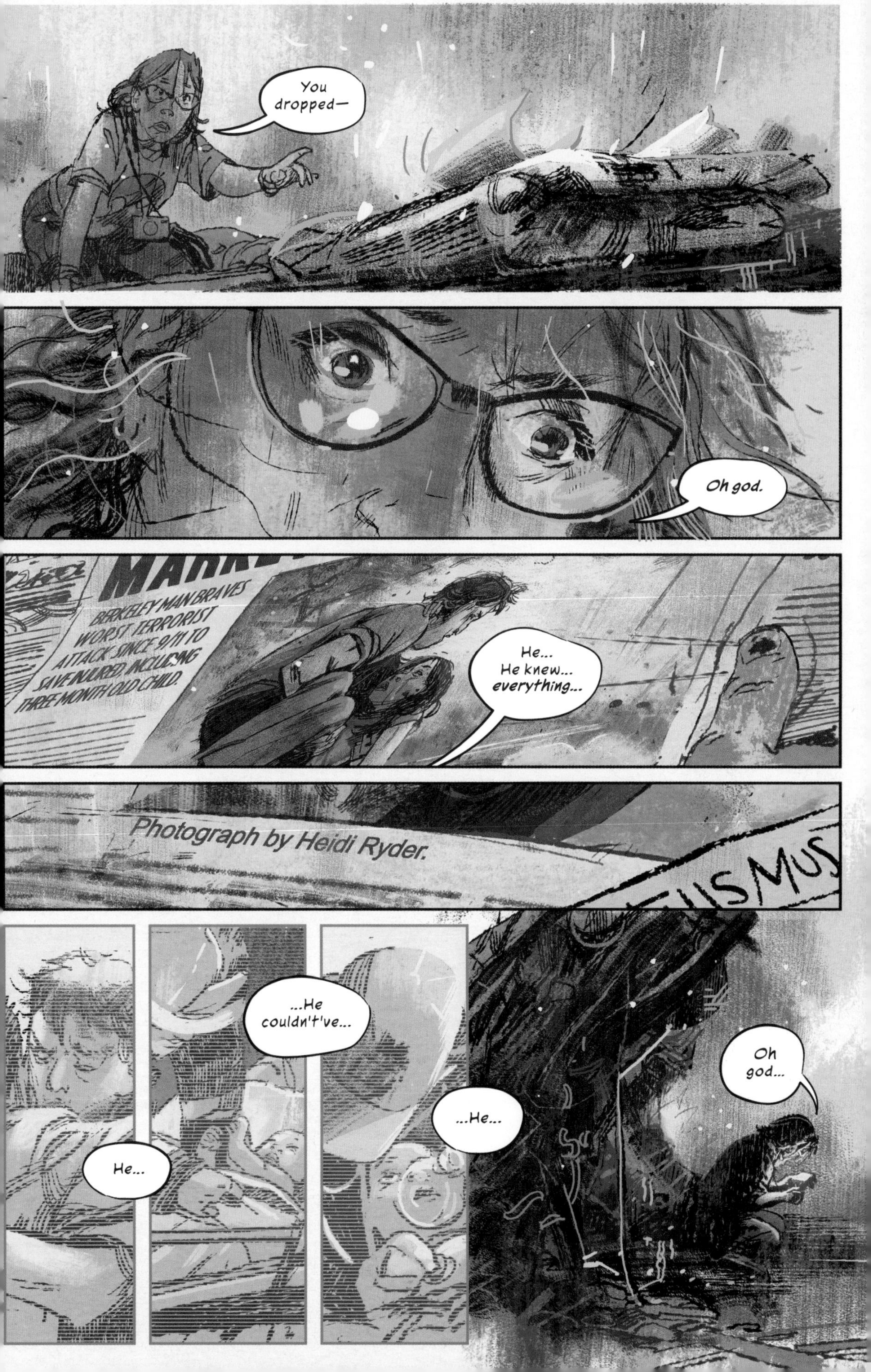
You dropped—
Oh god.
BERKELEY MAN BRAVES WORST TERRORIST ATTACK SINCE 9/11 TO SAVE INJURED, INCLUDING THREE MONTH OLD CHILD.
He... He knew... everything...
Photograph by Heidi Ryder.
He...
...He couldn't've...
...He...
Oh god...

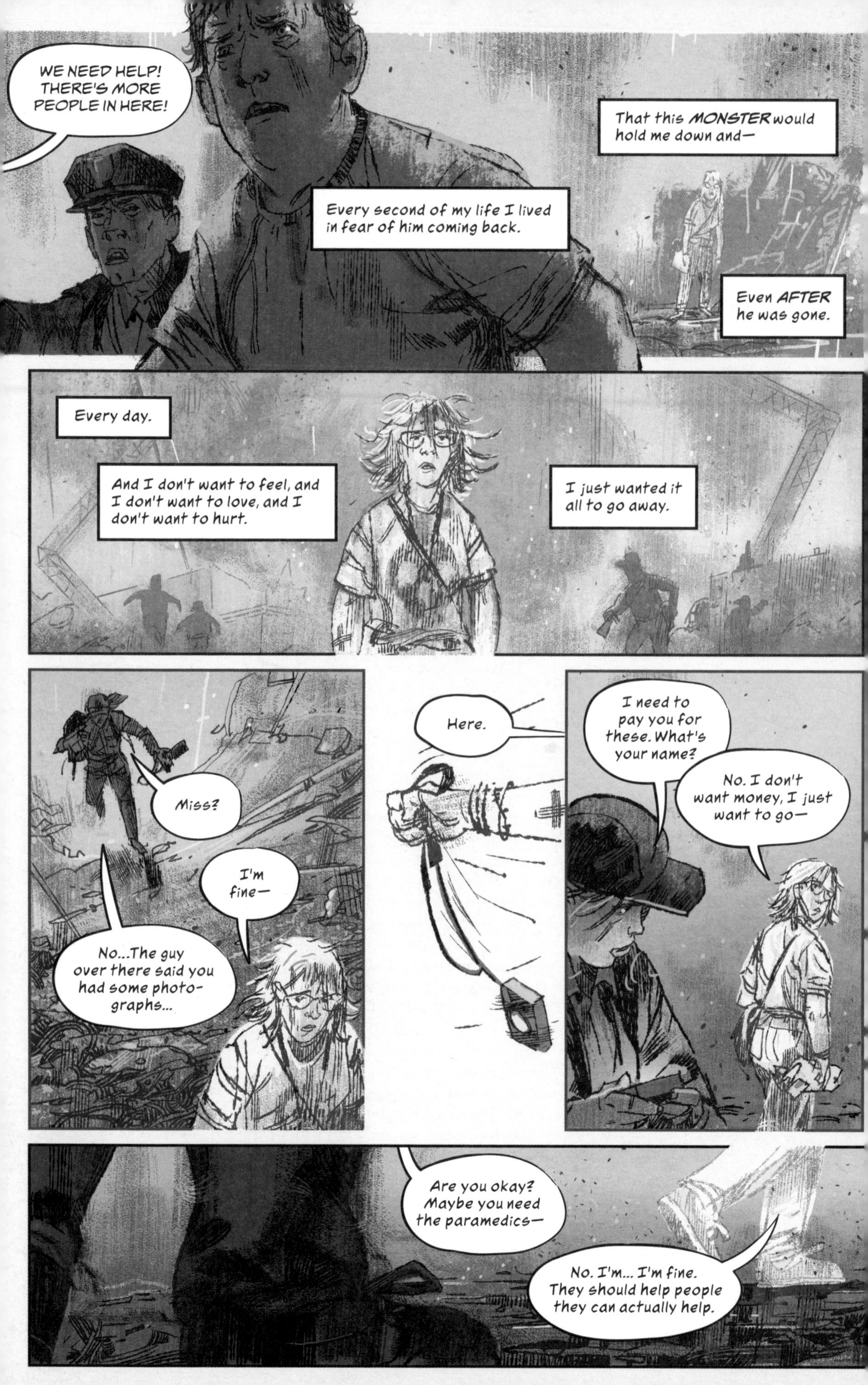
WE NEED HELP! THERE'S MORE PEOPLE IN HERE!
Every second of my life I lived in fear of him coming back.
That this MONSTER would hold me down and—
Even AFTER he was gone.
Every day.
And I don't want to feel, and I don't want to love, and I don't want to hurt.
I just wanted it all to go away.
Miss?
No...The guy over there said you had some photo-graphs...
I'm fine—
Here.
I need to pay you for these. What's your name?
No. I don't want money, I just want to go—
Are you okay? Maybe you need the paramedics—
No. I'm... I'm fine. They should help people they can actually help.

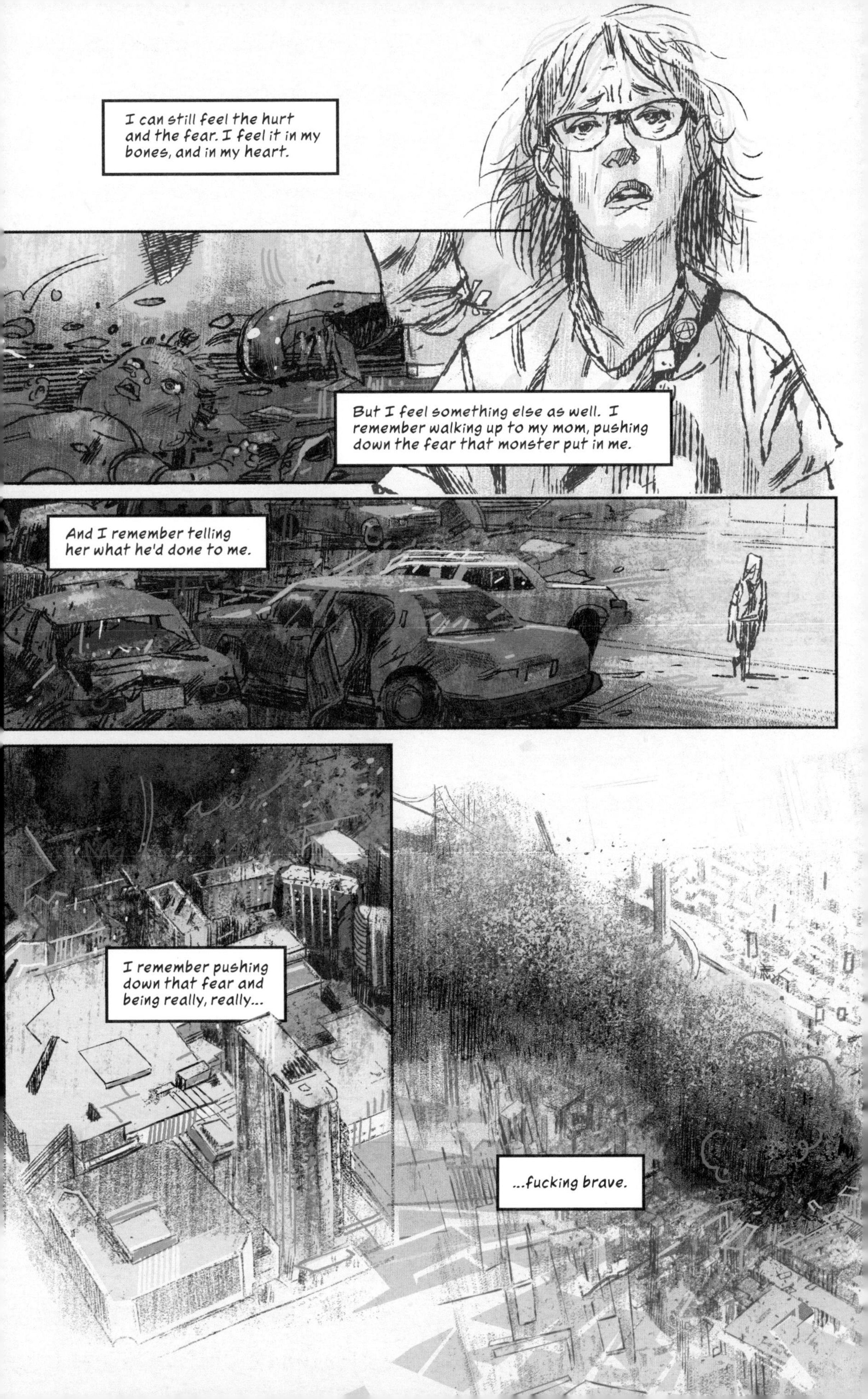
I can still feel the hurt and the fear. I feel it in my bones, and in my heart.
But I feel something else as well. I remember walking up to my mom, pushing down the fear that monster put in me.
And I remember telling her what he'd done to me.
I remember pushing down that fear and being really, really...
...fucking brave.

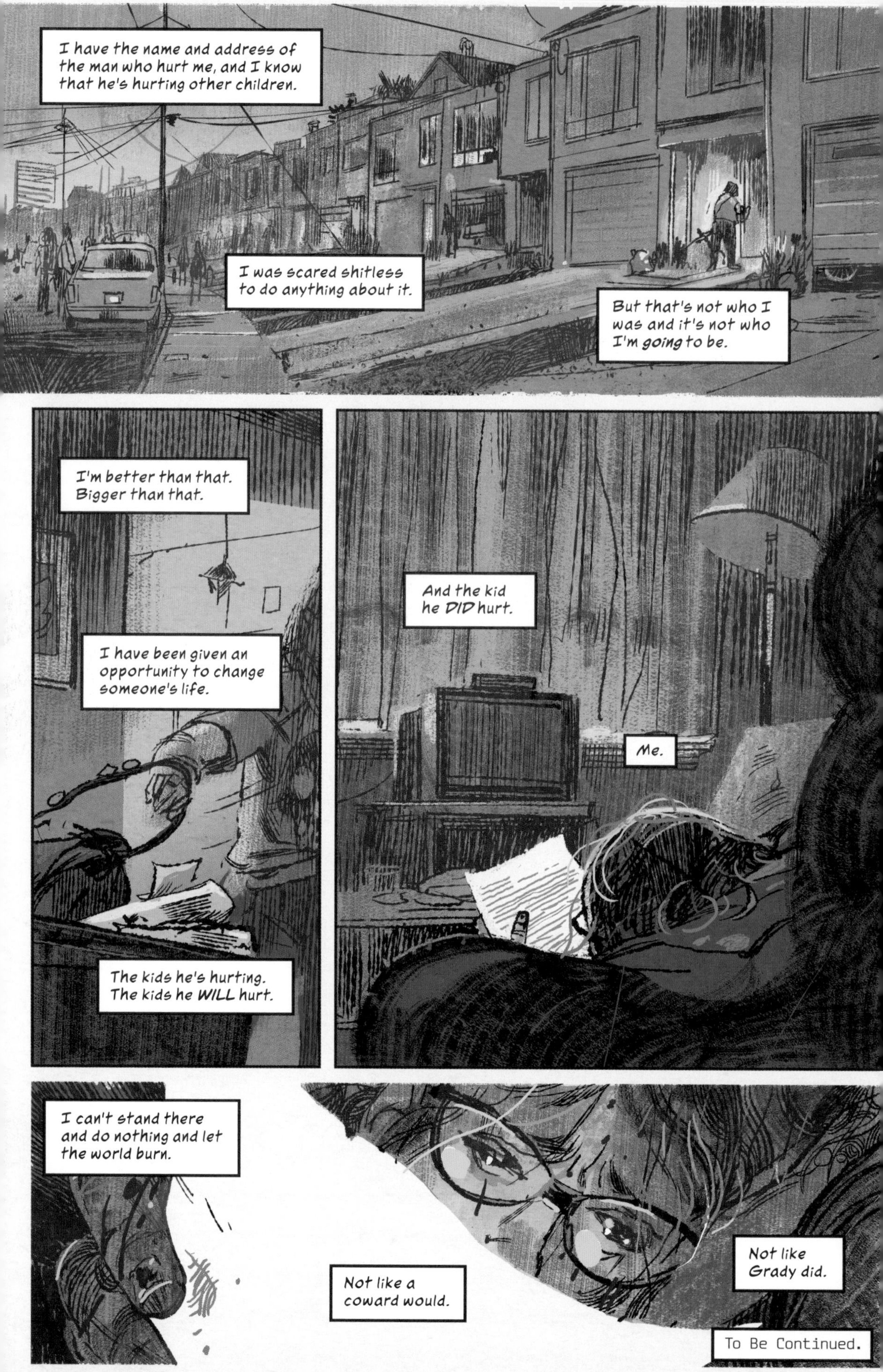
I have the name and address of the man who hurt me, and I know that he's hurting other children.
I was scared shitless to do anything about it.
But that's not who I was and it's not who I'm *going* to be.
I'm better than that. Bigger than that.
I have been given an opportunity to change someone's life.
The kids he's hurting. The kids he **WILL** hurt.
And the kid he **DID** hurt.
Me.
I can't stand there and do nothing and let the world burn.
Not like a coward would.
Not like Grady did.
To Be Continued.

CHAPTER
04

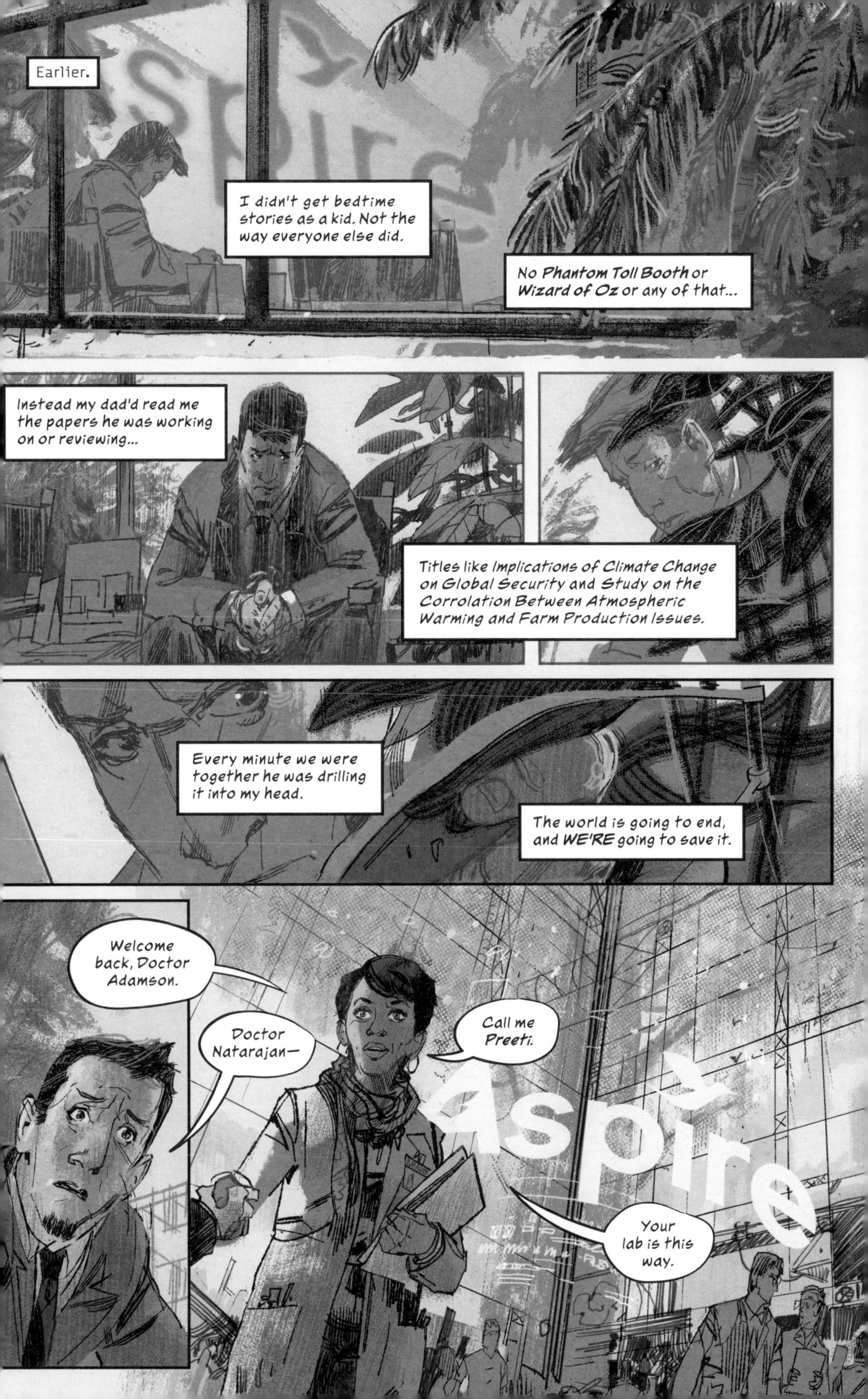

Earlier.
I didn't get bedtime stories as a kid. Not the way everyone else did.
No *Phantom Toll Booth* or *Wizard of Oz* or any of that...
Instead my dad'd read me the papers he was working on or reviewing...
Titles like *Implications of Climate Change on Global Security* and *Study on the Corrolation Between Atmospheric Warming and Farm Production Issues.*
Every minute we were together he was drilling it into my head.
The world is going to end, and **WE'RE** going to save it.
Welcome back, Doctor Adamson.
Doctor Natarajan—
Call me *Preeti.*
aspire
Your lab is this way.

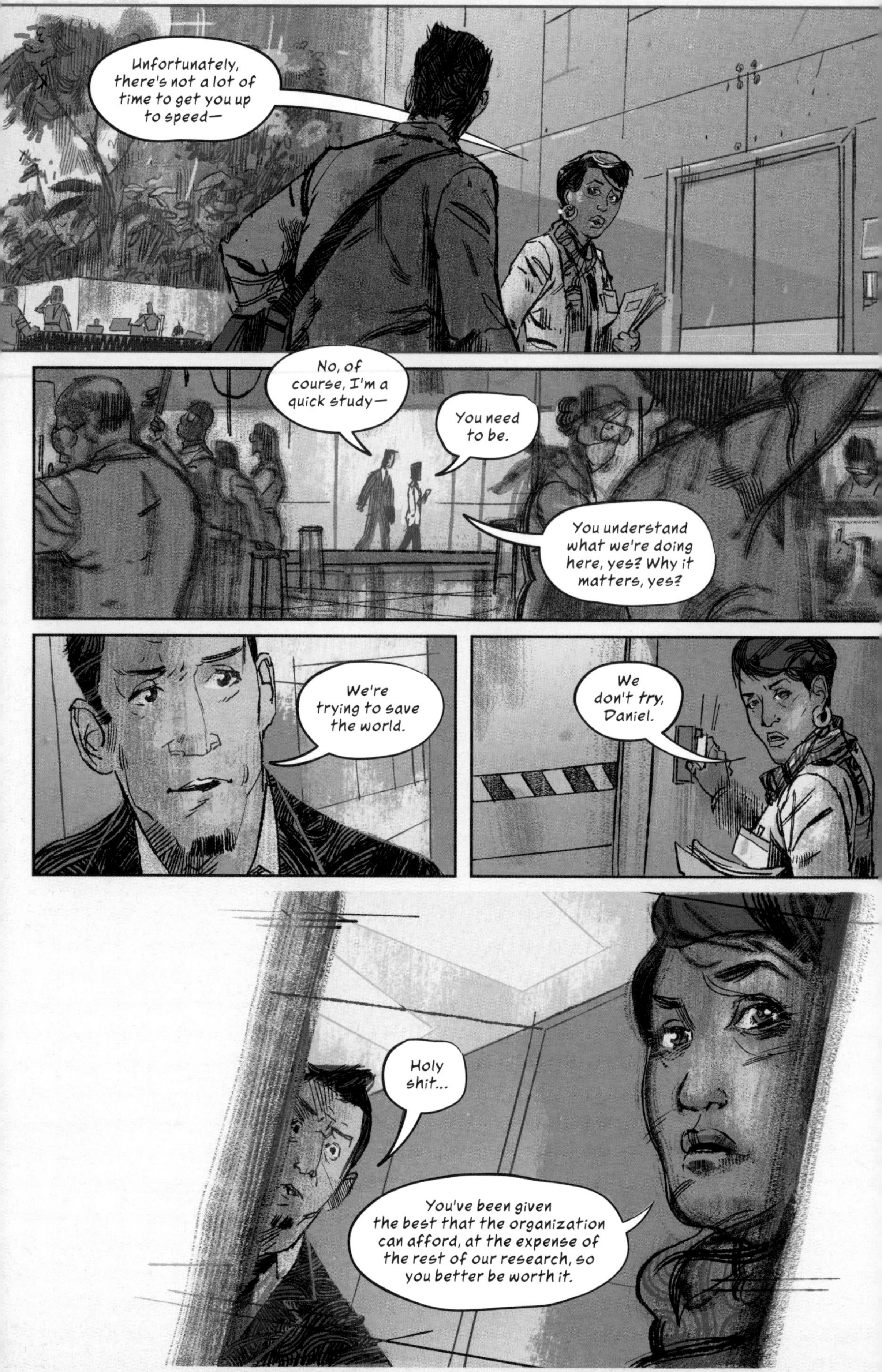
Unfortunately, there's not a lot of time to get you up to speed—
No, of course, I'm a quick study—
You need to be.
You understand what we're doing here, yes? Why it matters, yes?
We're trying to save the world.
We don't *try*, Daniel.
Holy shit...
You've been given the best that the organization can afford, at the expense of the rest of our research, so you better be worth it.

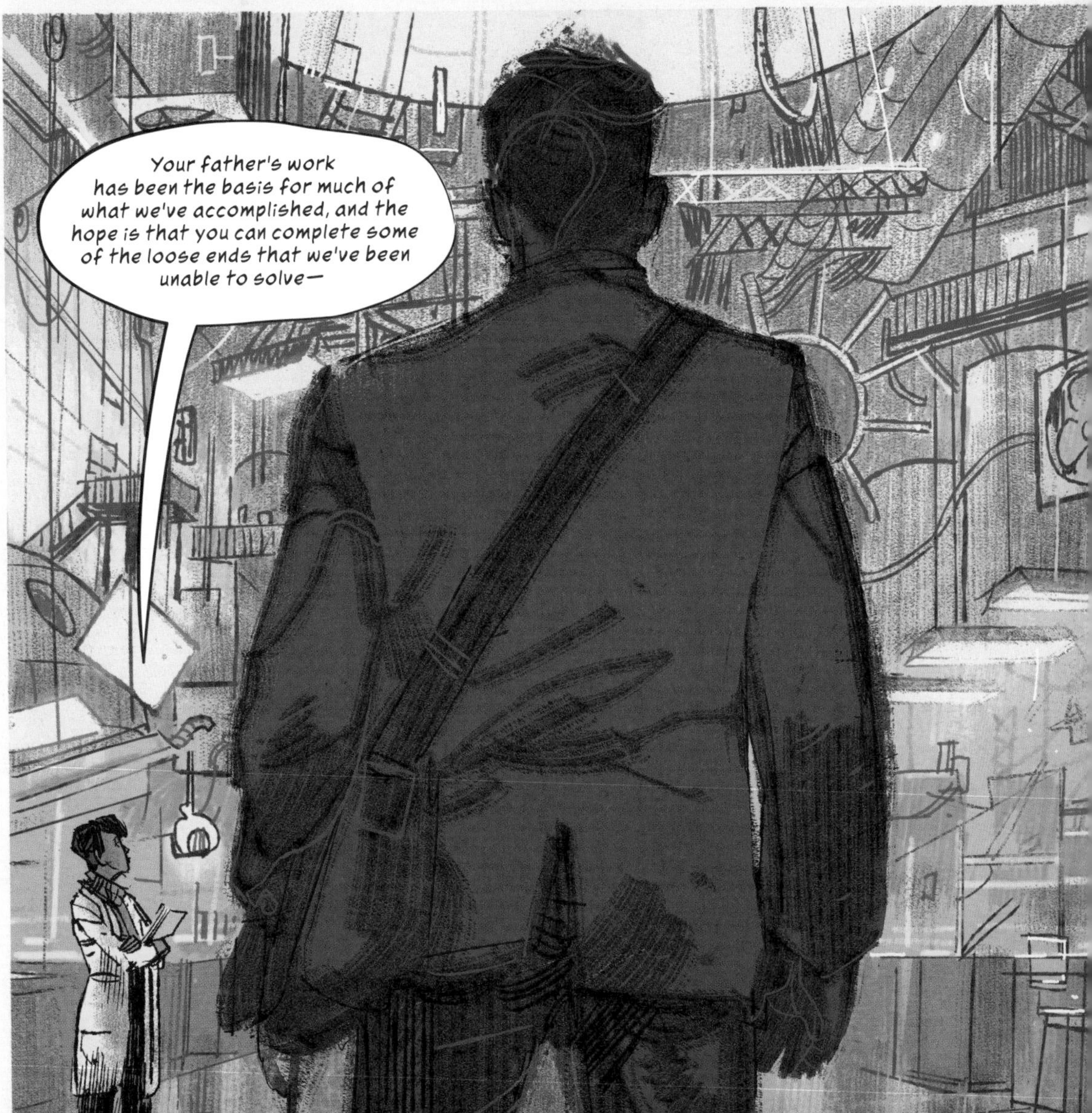
Your father's work has been the basis for much of what we've accomplished, and the hope is that you can complete some of the loose ends that we've been unable to solve—

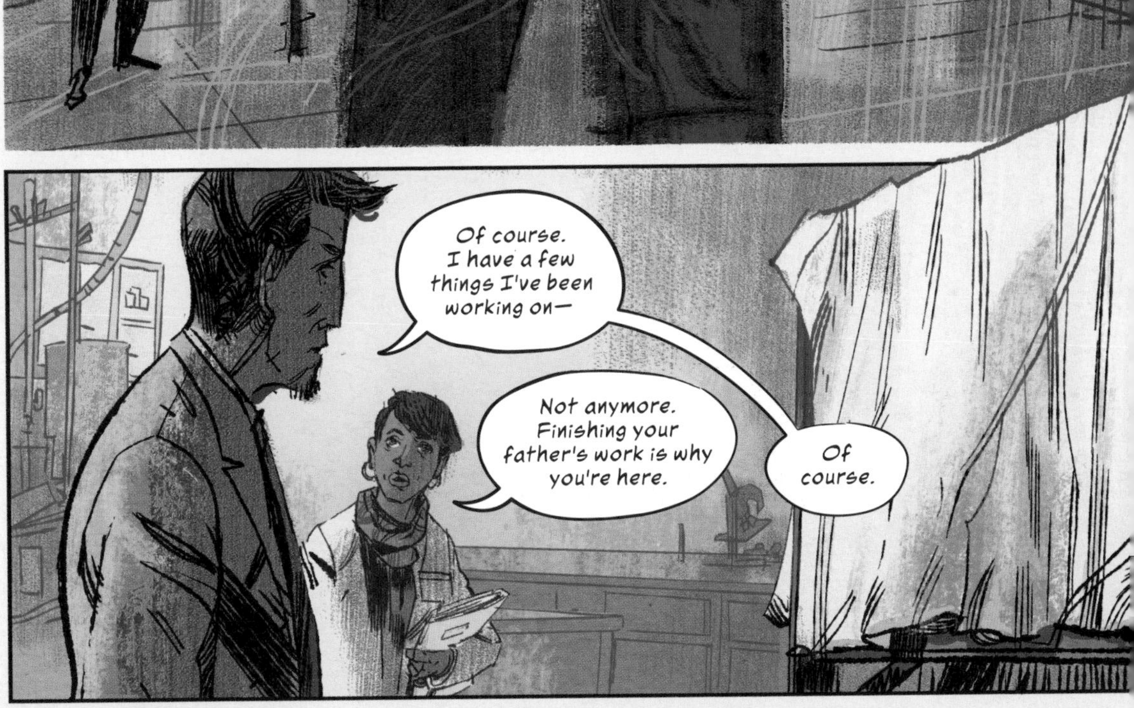
Of course. I have a few things I've been working on—
Not anymore. Finishing your father's work is why you're here.
Of course.

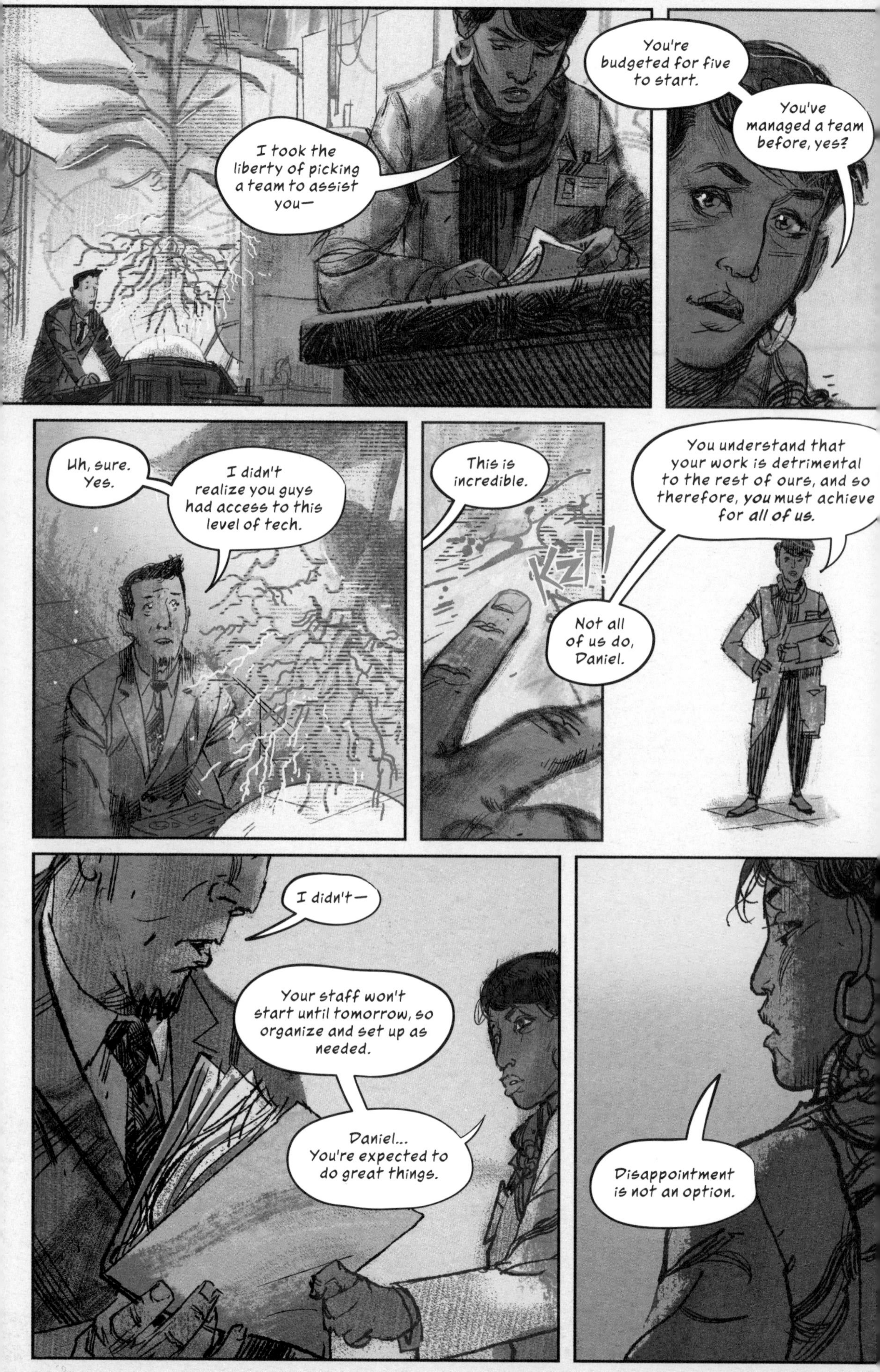
I took the liberty of picking a team to assist you—
You're budgeted for five to start.
You've managed a team before, yes?
Uh, sure. Yes.
I didn't realize you guys had access to this level of tech.
This is incredible.
KZT!
You understand that your work is detrimental to the rest of ours, and so therefore, you must achieve for all of us.
Not all of us do, Daniel.
I didn't—
Your staff won't start until tomorrow, so organize and set up as needed.
Daniel... You're expected to do great things.
Disappointment is not an option.

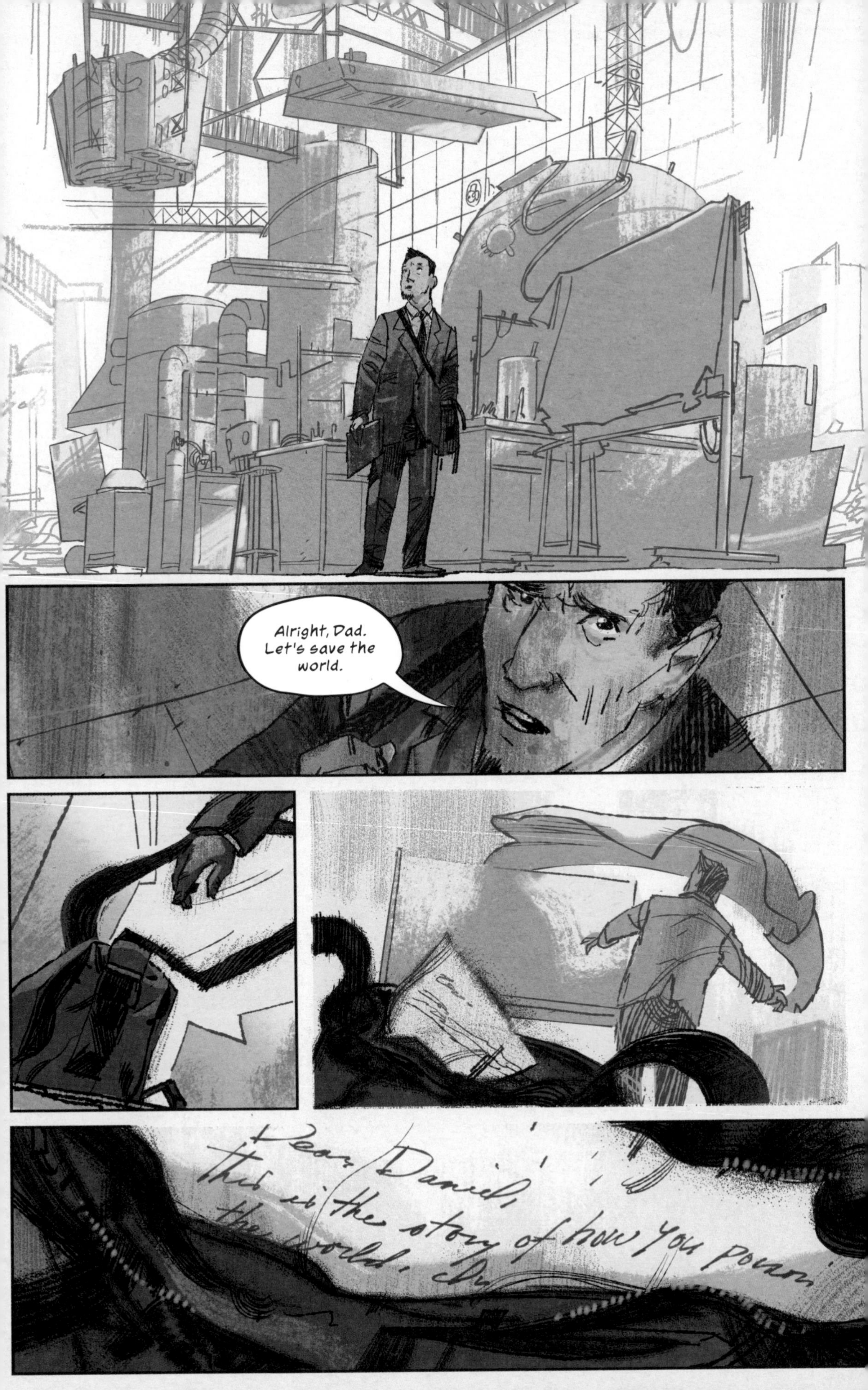

Alright, Dad. Let's save the world.
Dear Daniel,
this is the story of how you poison
the world.

YAWN!

SKRTCH

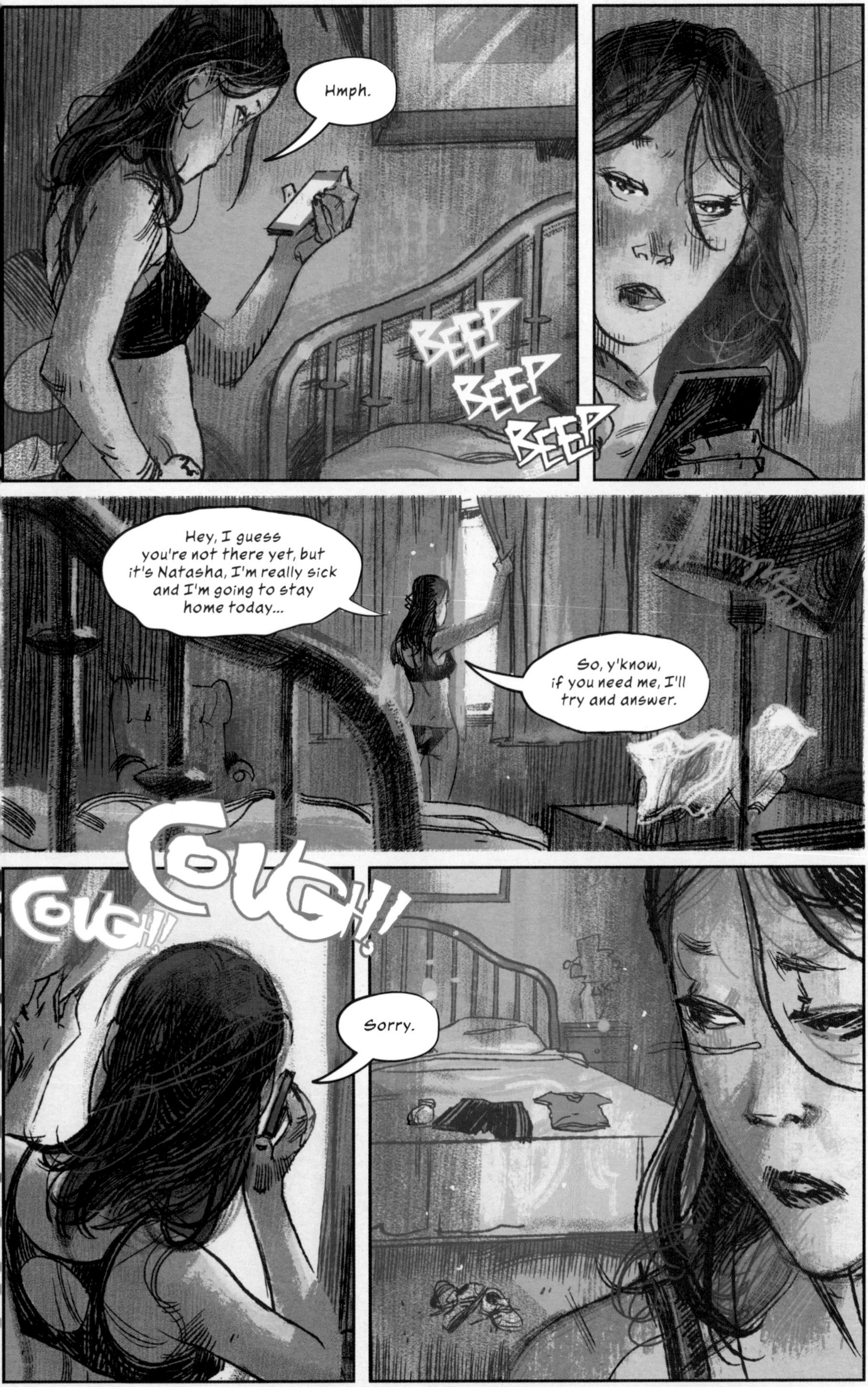
Hmph.
BEEP BEEP BEEP
Hey, I guess you're not there yet, but it's Natasha, I'm really sick and I'm going to stay home today...
So, y'know, if you need me, I'll try and answer.
COUGH!!
COUGH!!
Sorry.

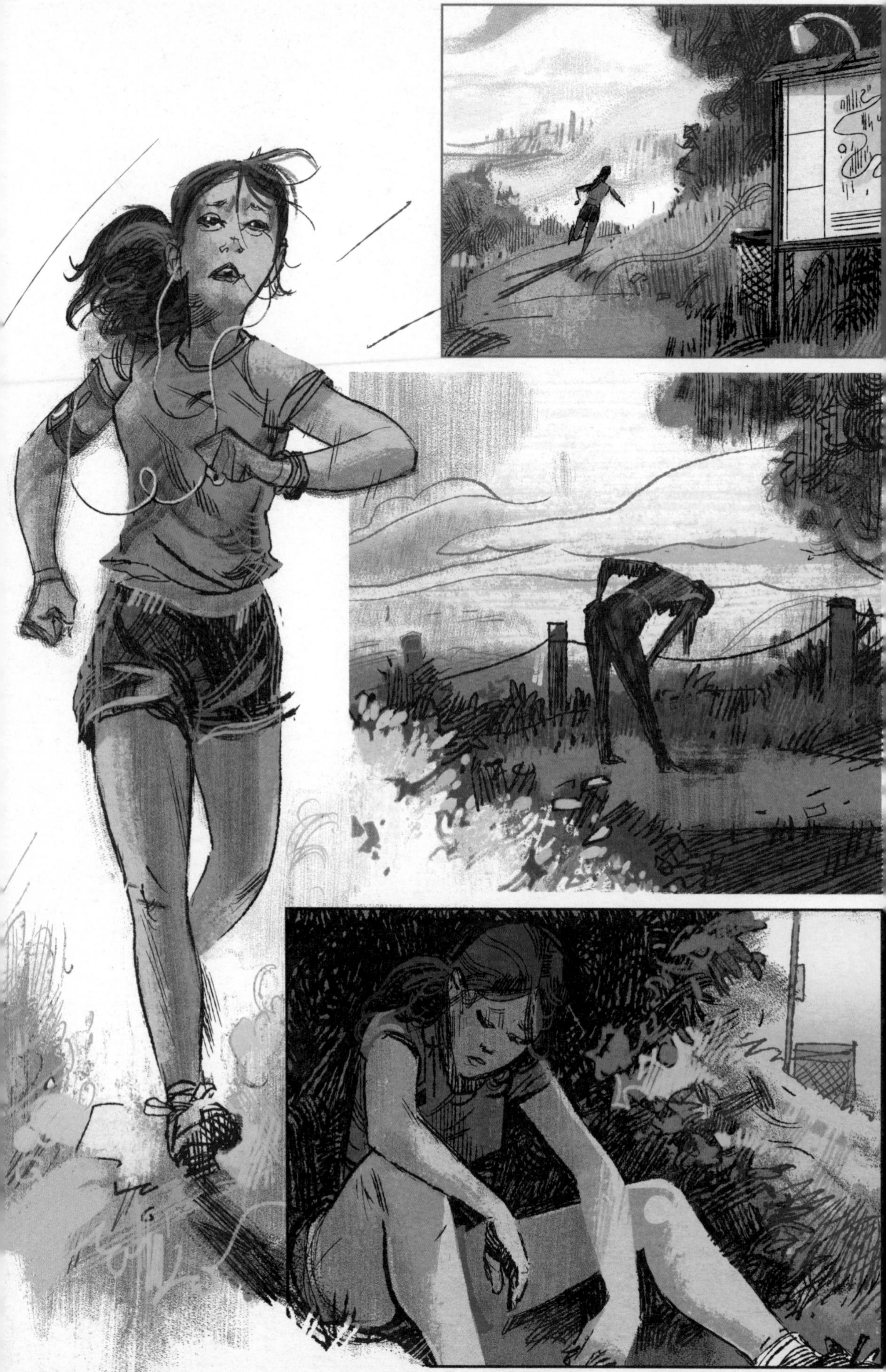

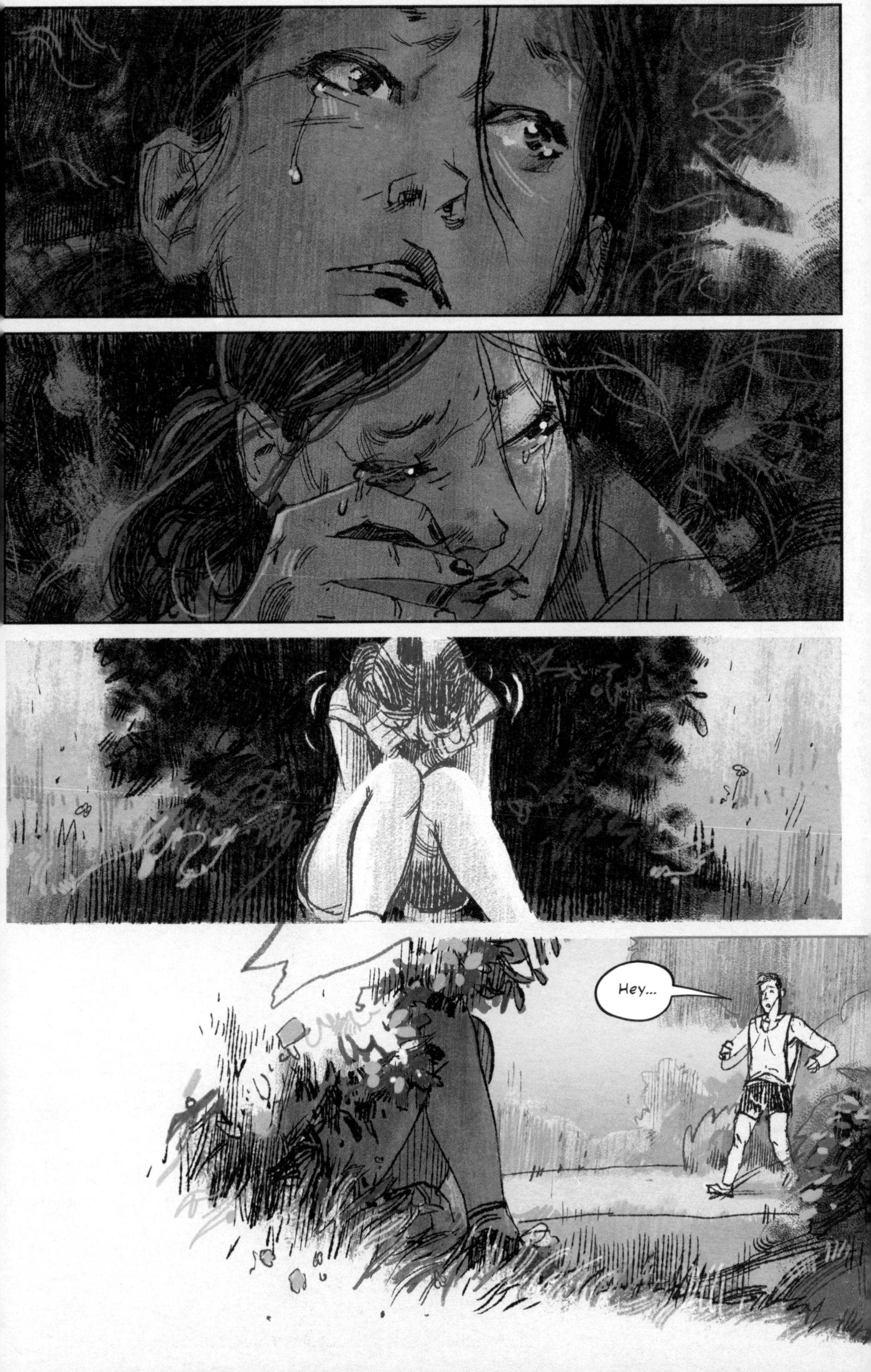
Hey...

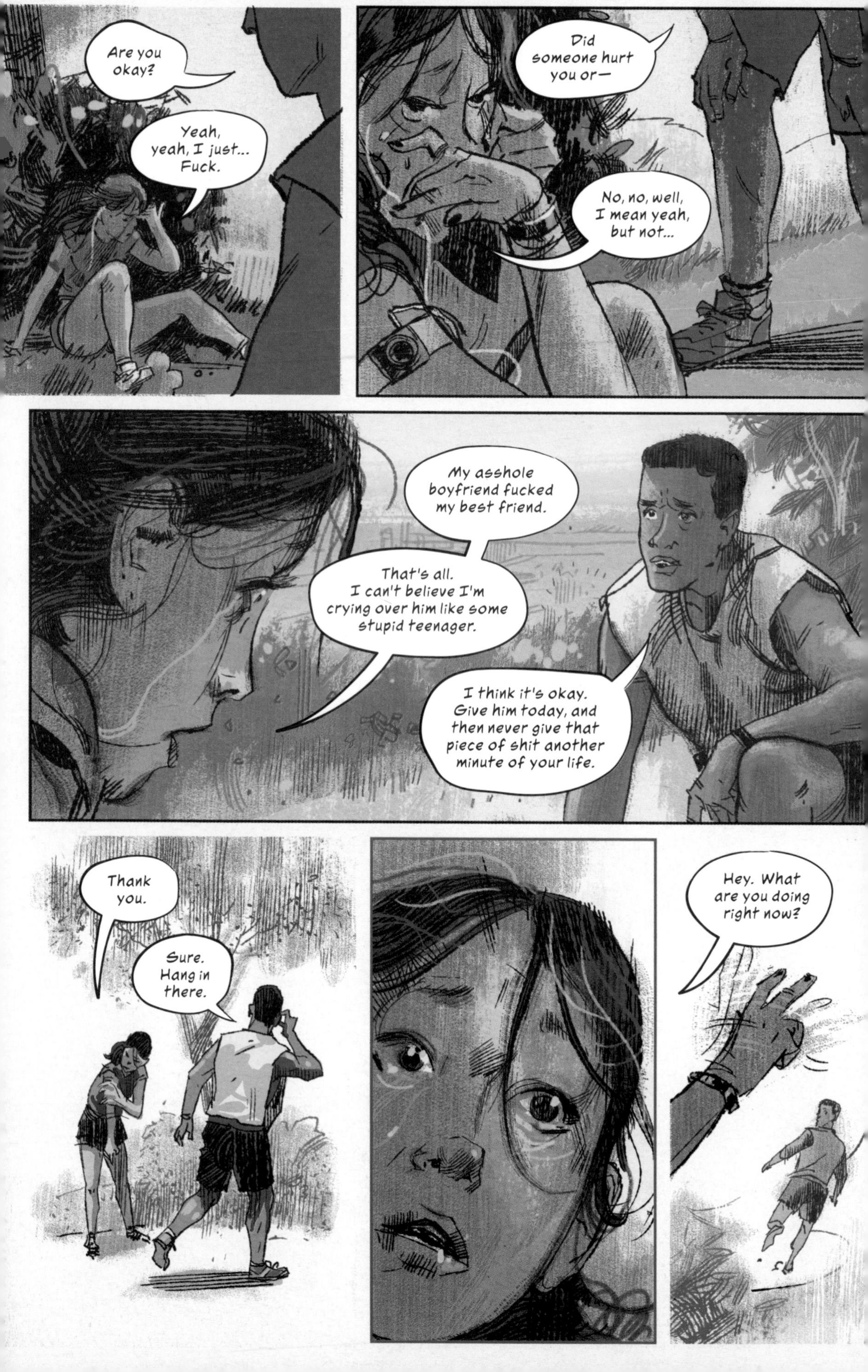
Are you okay?
Yeah, yeah, I just... Fuck.
Did someone hurt you or—
No, no, well, I mean yeah, but not...
My asshole boyfriend fucked my best friend.
That's all. I can't believe I'm crying over him like some stupid teenager.
I think it's okay. Give him today, and then never give that piece of shit another minute of your life.
Thank you.
Sure. Hang in there.
Hey. What are you doing right now?

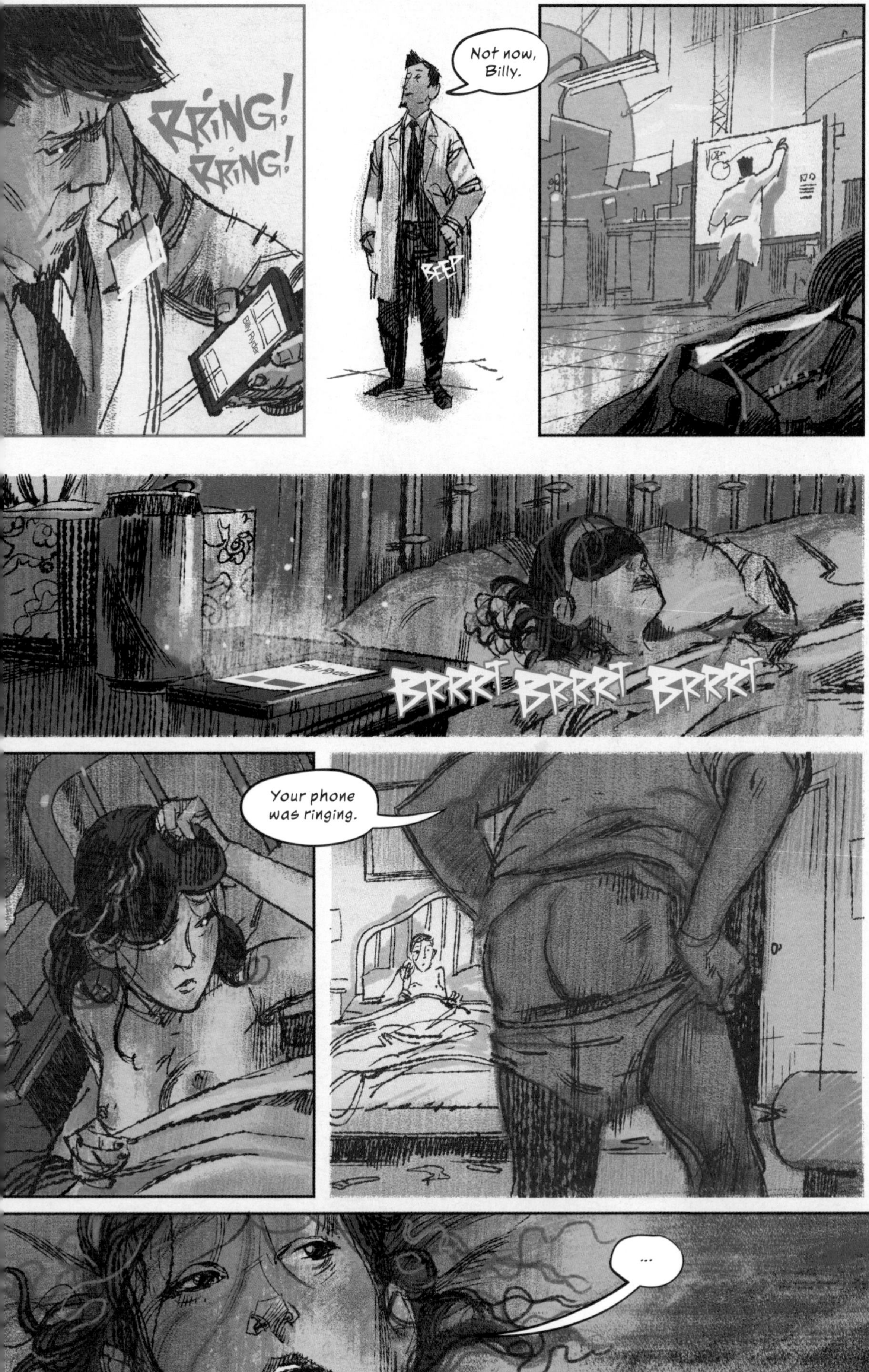
RRING!
RRING!
Billy Ryder
Not now,
Billy.
BEEP
Billy Ryder
BRRRT BRRRT BRRRT
Your phone
was ringing.
...

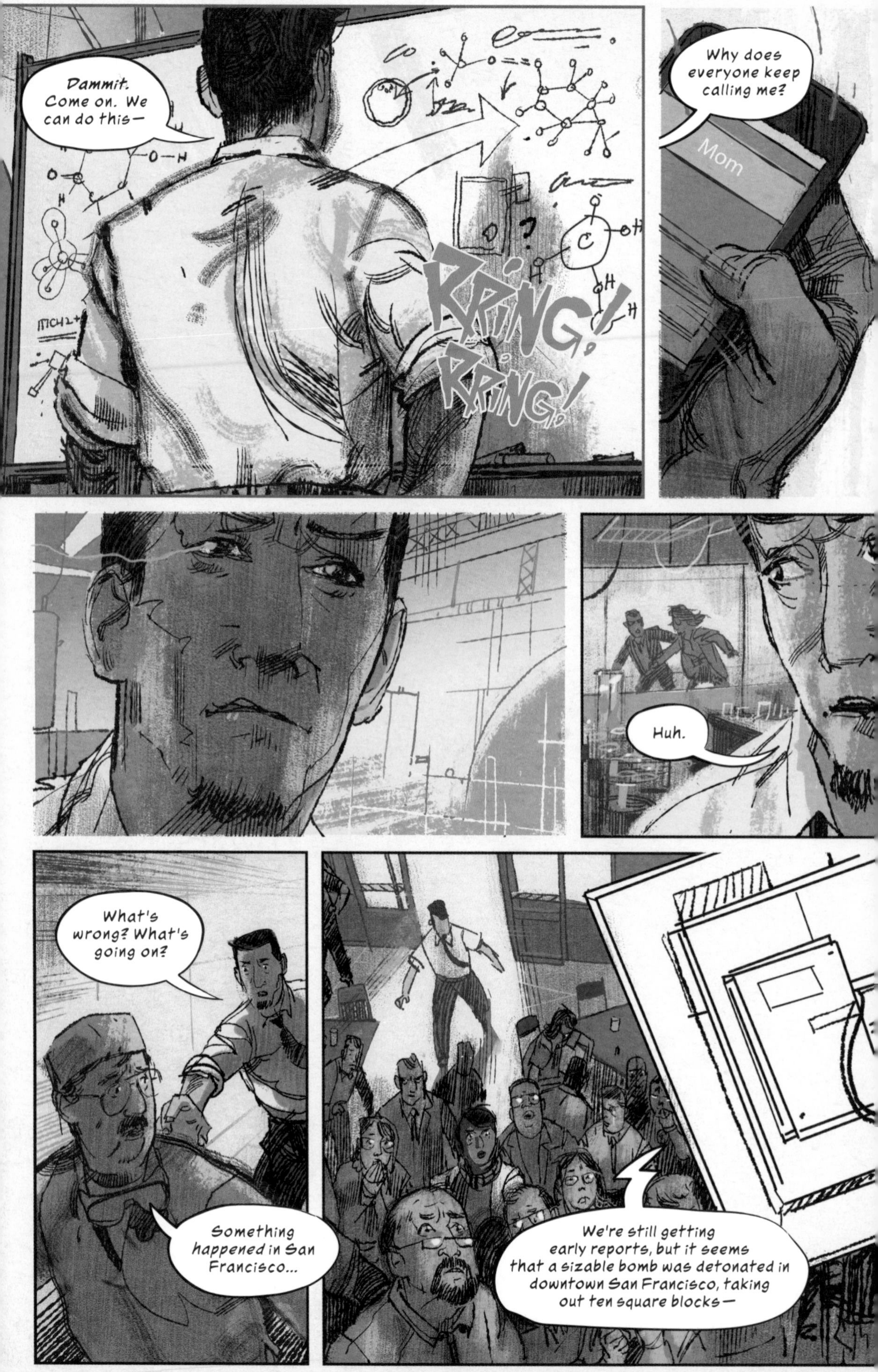
Dammit. Come on. We can do this—
RRING! RRING!
Why does everyone keep calling me?
Mom
Huh.
What's wrong? What's going on?
Something happened in San Francisco...
We're still getting early reports, but it seems that a sizable bomb was detonated in downtown San Francisco, taking out ten square blocks—

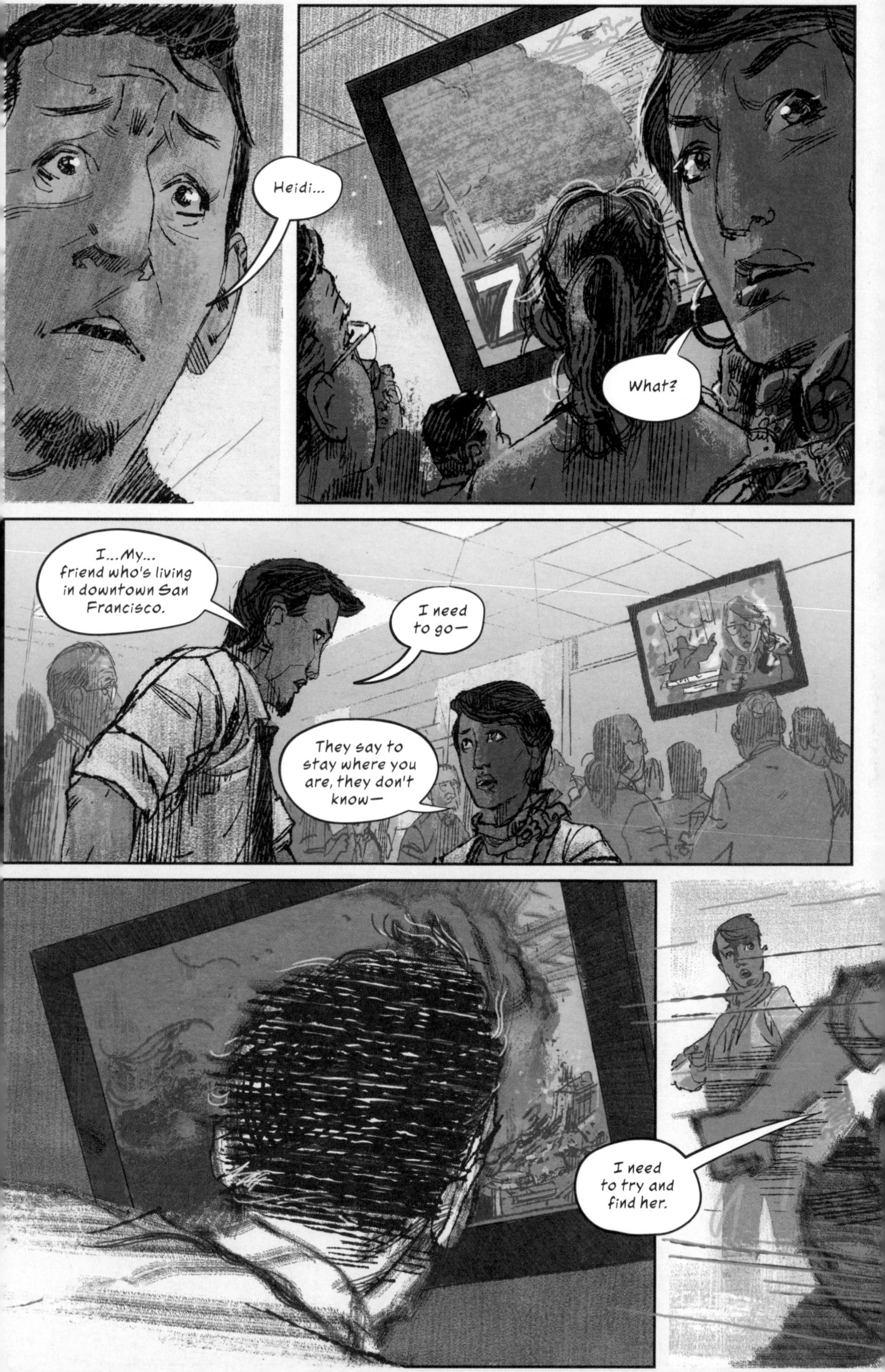
Heidi...
What?
I...My... friend who's living in downtown San Francisco.
I need to go—
They say to stay where you are, they don't know—
I need to try and find her.

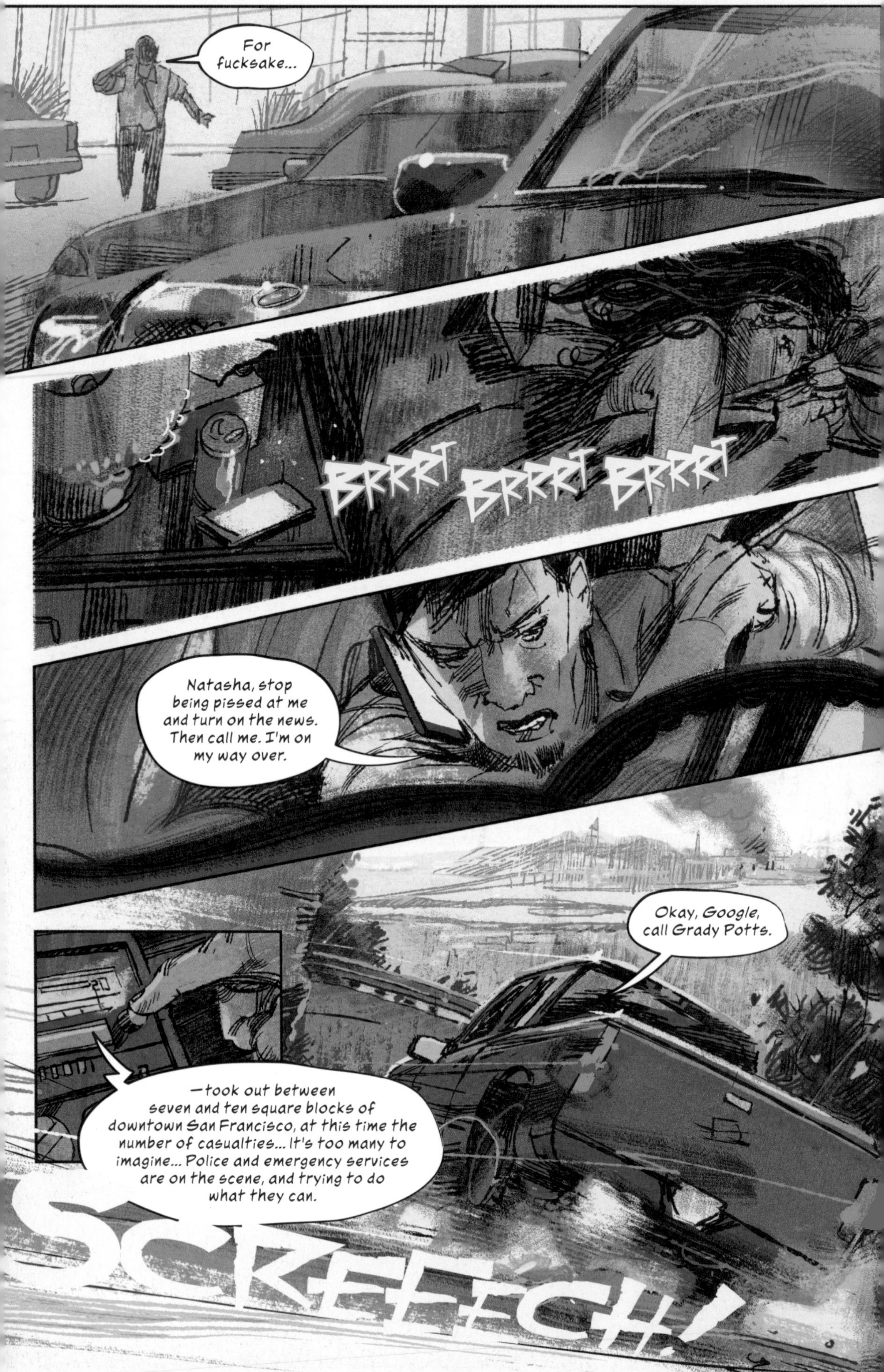
For fucksake...
BRRRT BRRRT BRRRT
Natasha, stop being pissed at me and turn on the news. Then call me. I'm on my way over.
Okay, Google, call Grady Potts.
—took out between seven and ten square blocks of downtown San Francisco, at this time the number of casualties... It's too many to imagine... Police and emergency services are on the scene, and trying to do what they can.
SCREEECH!

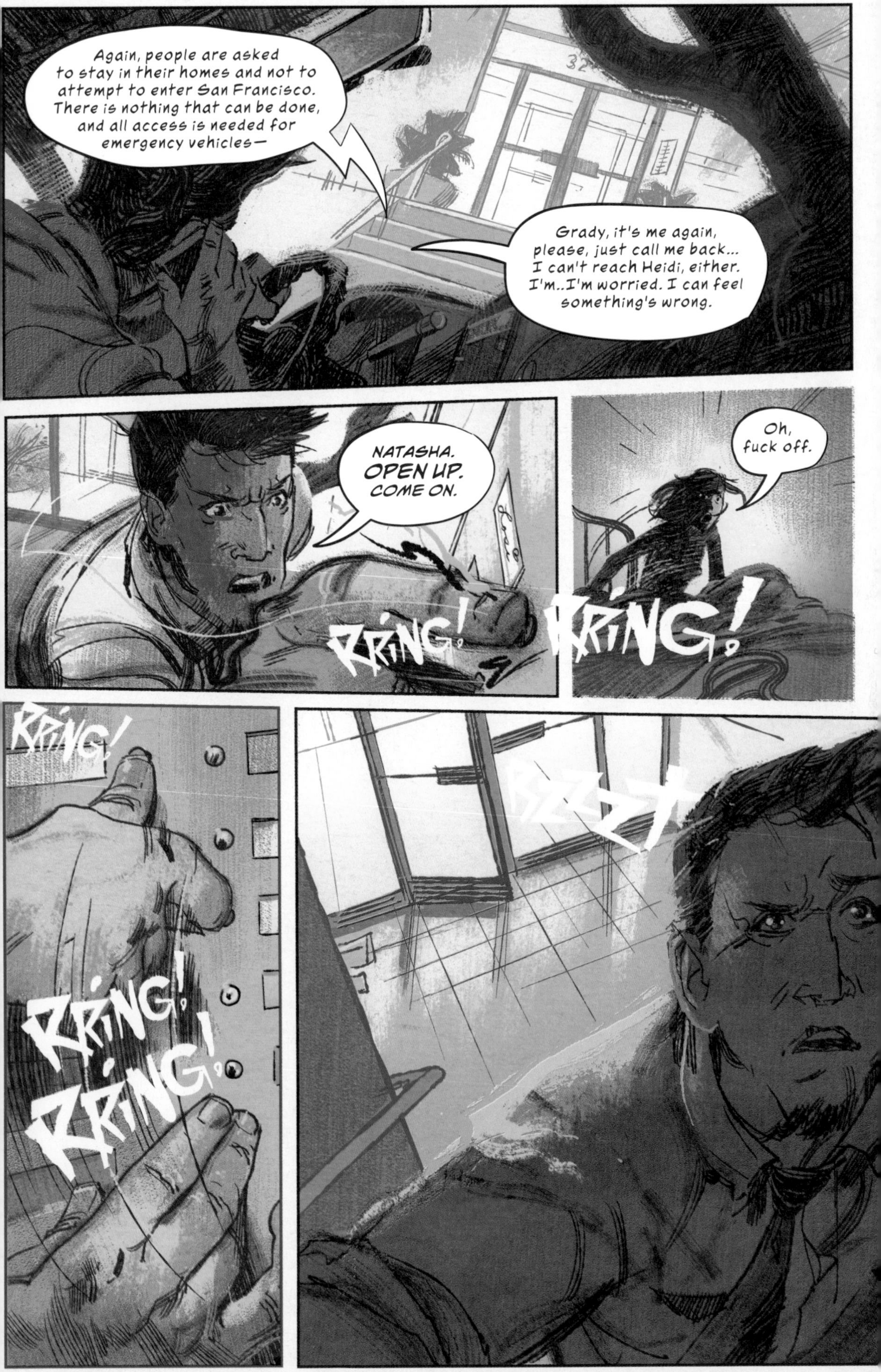
Again, people are asked to stay in their homes and not to attempt to enter San Francisco. There is nothing that can be done, and all access is needed for emergency vehicles—
Grady, it's me again, please, just call me back... I can't reach Heidi, either. I'm..I'm worried. I can feel something's wrong.
NATASHA. OPEN UP. COME ON.
Oh, fuck off.
RRING!
RRING!
RRING!
RRING!
RRING!
BZZZT

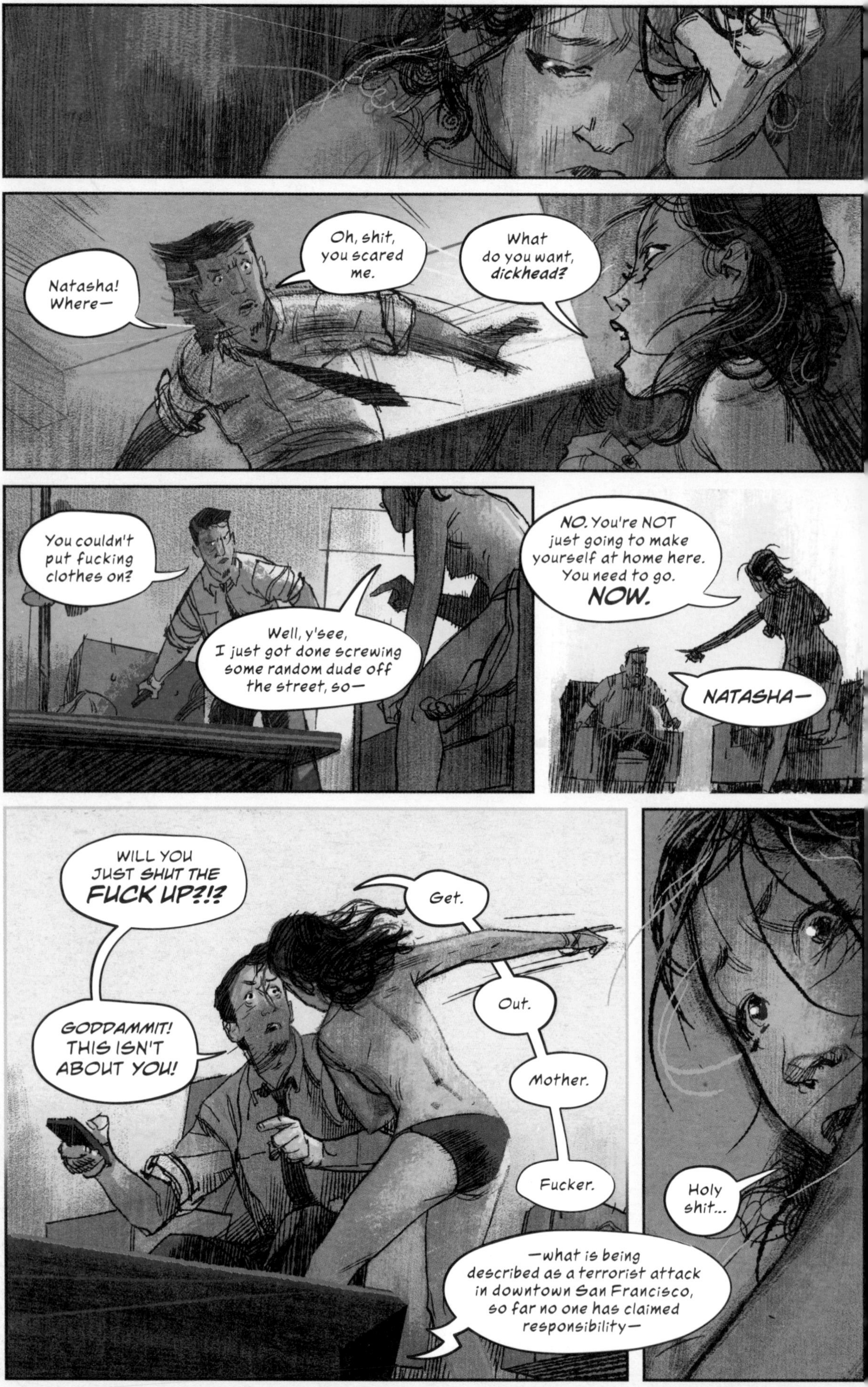
Natasha! Where—
Oh, shit, you scared me.
What do you want, dickhead?
You couldn't put fucking clothes on?
Well, y'see, I just got done screwing some random dude off the street, so—
NO. You're NOT just going to make yourself at home here. You need to go. NOW.
NATASHA—
WILL YOU JUST SHUT THE FUCK UP?!?
GODDAMMIT! THIS ISN'T ABOUT YOU!
Get.
Out.
Mother.
Fucker.
Holy shit...
—what is being described as a terrorist attack in downtown San Francisco, so far no one has claimed responsibility—

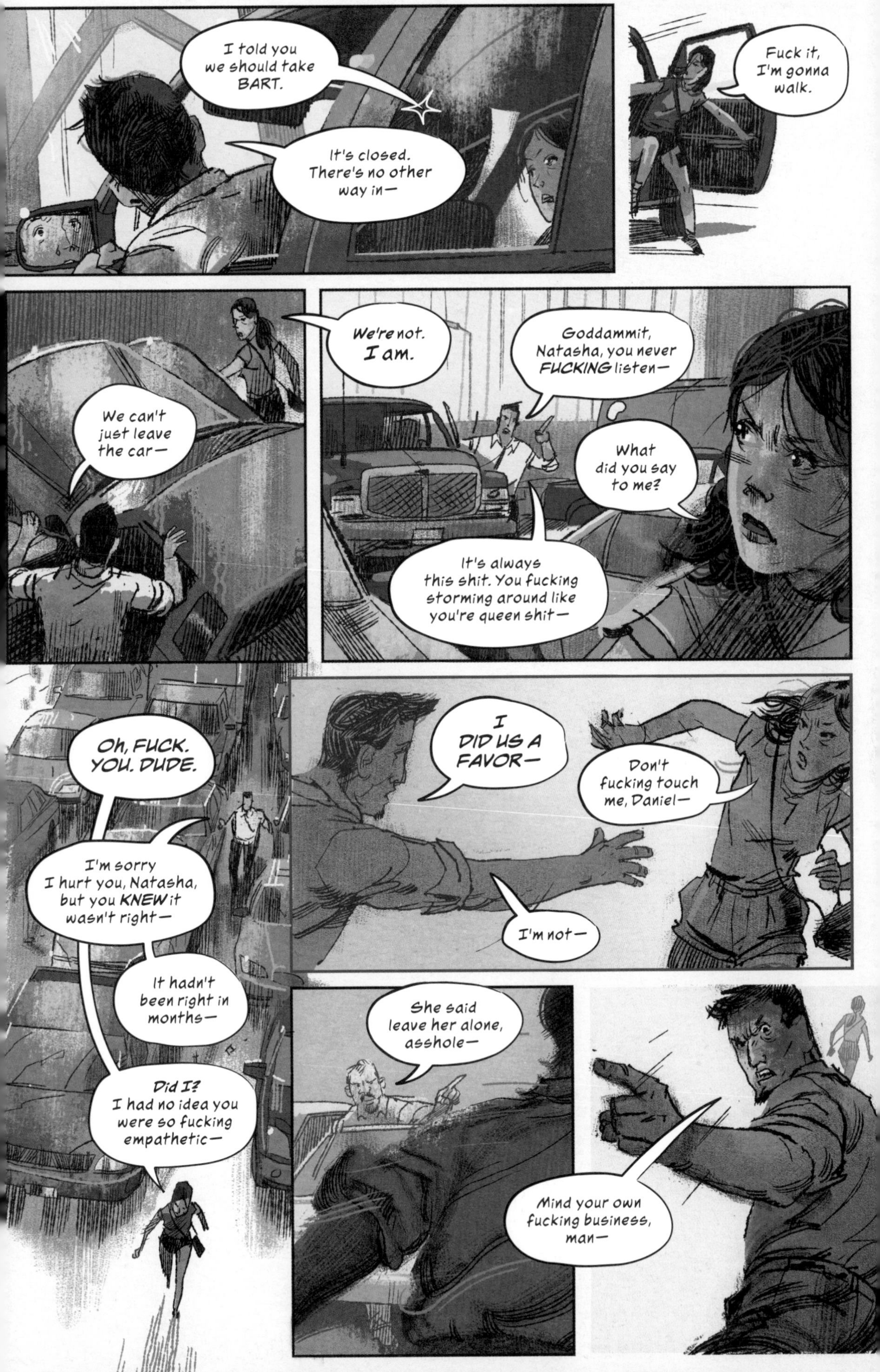
I told you we should take BART.
It's closed. There's no other way in—
Fuck it, I'm gonna walk.
We can't just leave the car—
We're not. I am.
Goddammit, Natasha, you never FUCKING listen—
What did you say to me?
It's always this shit. You fucking storming around like you're queen shit—
Oh, FUCK. YOU. DUDE.
I'm sorry I hurt you, Natasha, but you KNEW it wasn't right—
It hadn't been right in months—
Did I? I had no idea you were so fucking empathetic—
I DID US A FAVOR—
Don't fucking touch me, Daniel—
I'm not—
She said leave her alone, asshole—
Mind your own fucking business, man—

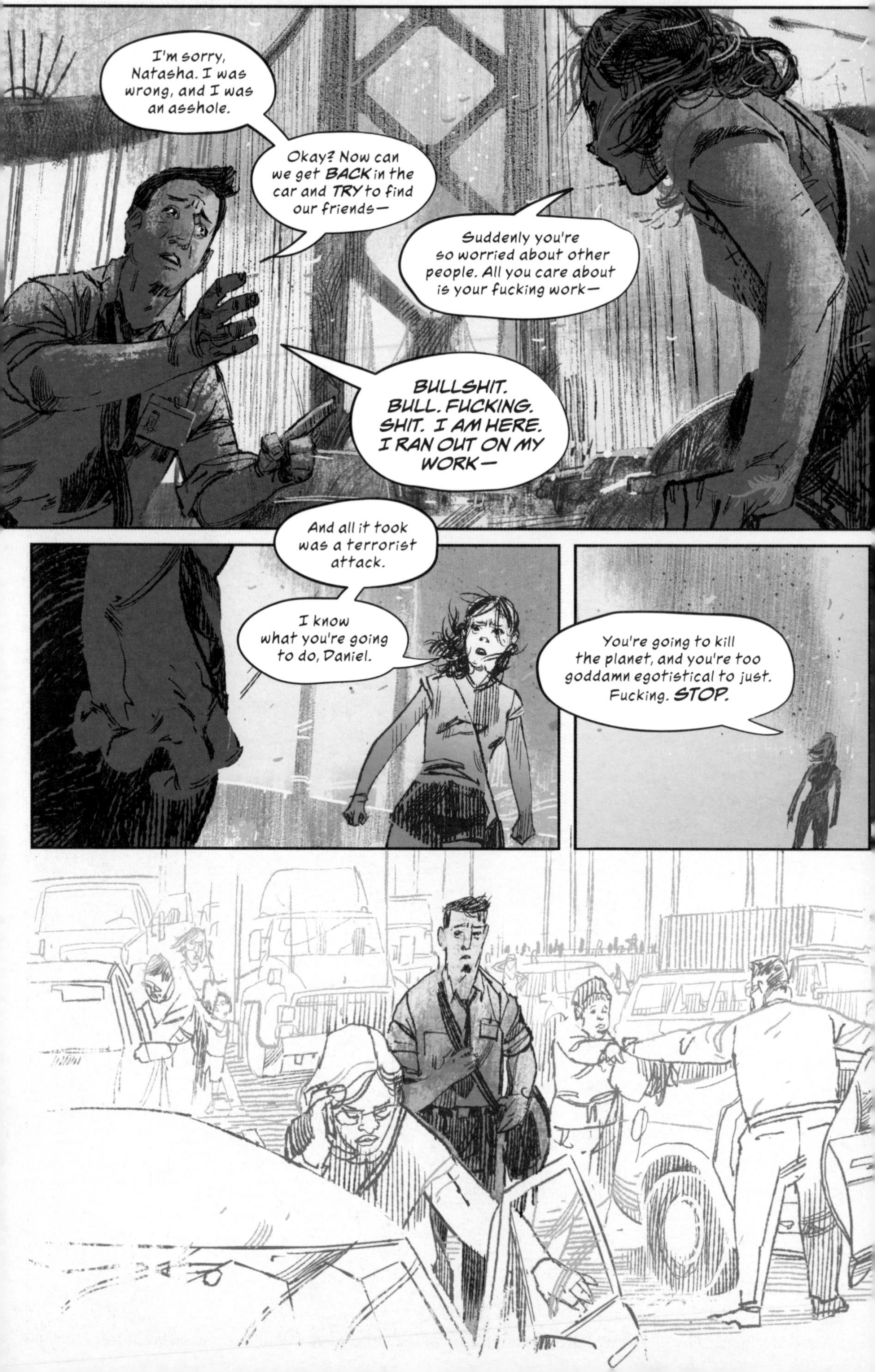

I'm sorry, Natasha. I was wrong, and I was an asshole.
Okay? Now can we get BACK in the car and TRY to find our friends—
Suddenly you're so worried about other people. All you care about is your fucking work—
BULLSHIT. BULL. FUCKING. SHIT. I AM HERE. I RAN OUT ON MY WORK—
And all it took was a terrorist attack.
I know what you're going to do, Daniel.
You're going to kill the planet, and you're too goddamn egotistical to just. Fucking. STOP.

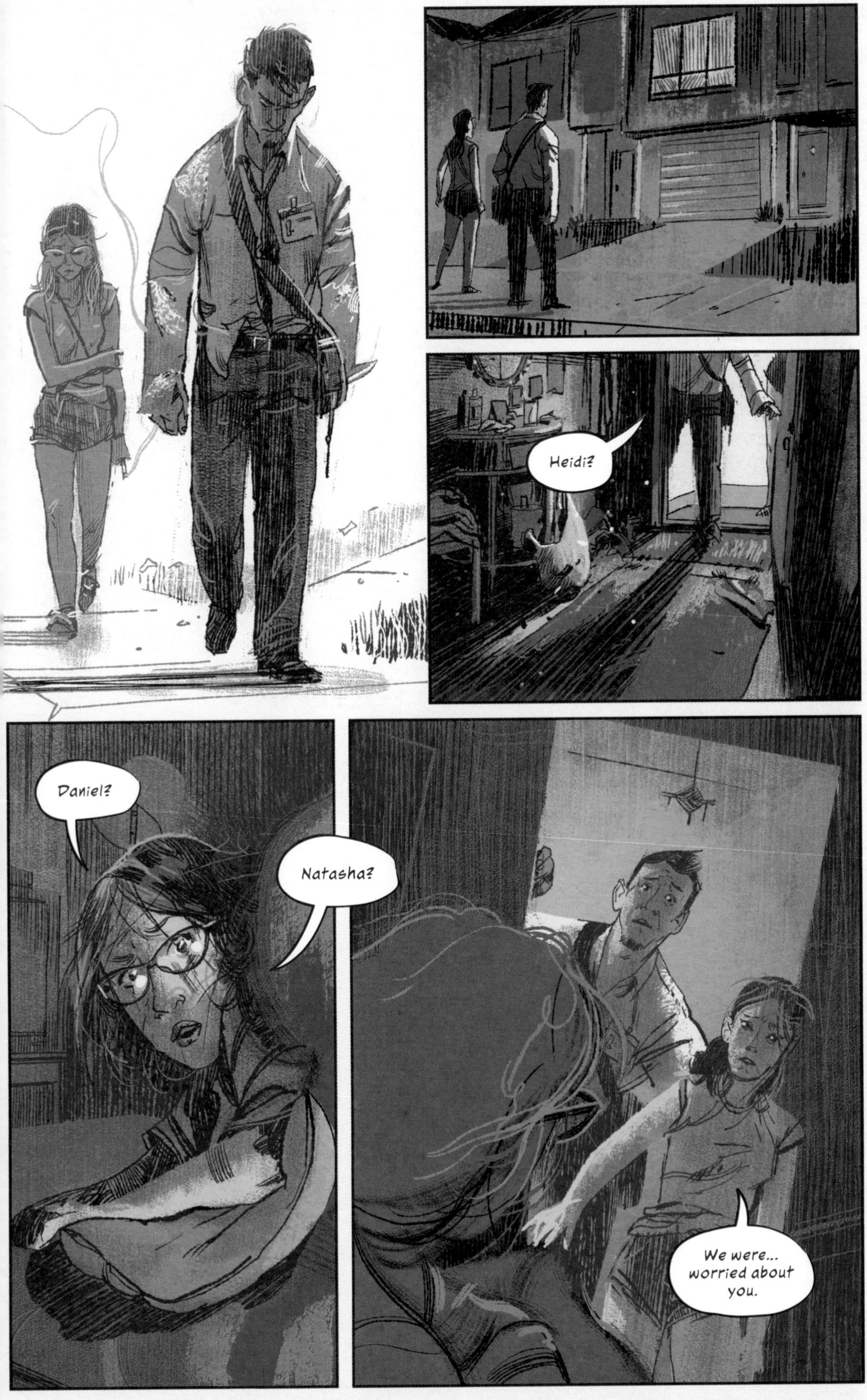
Heidi?
Daniel?
Natasha?
We were...
worried about
you.

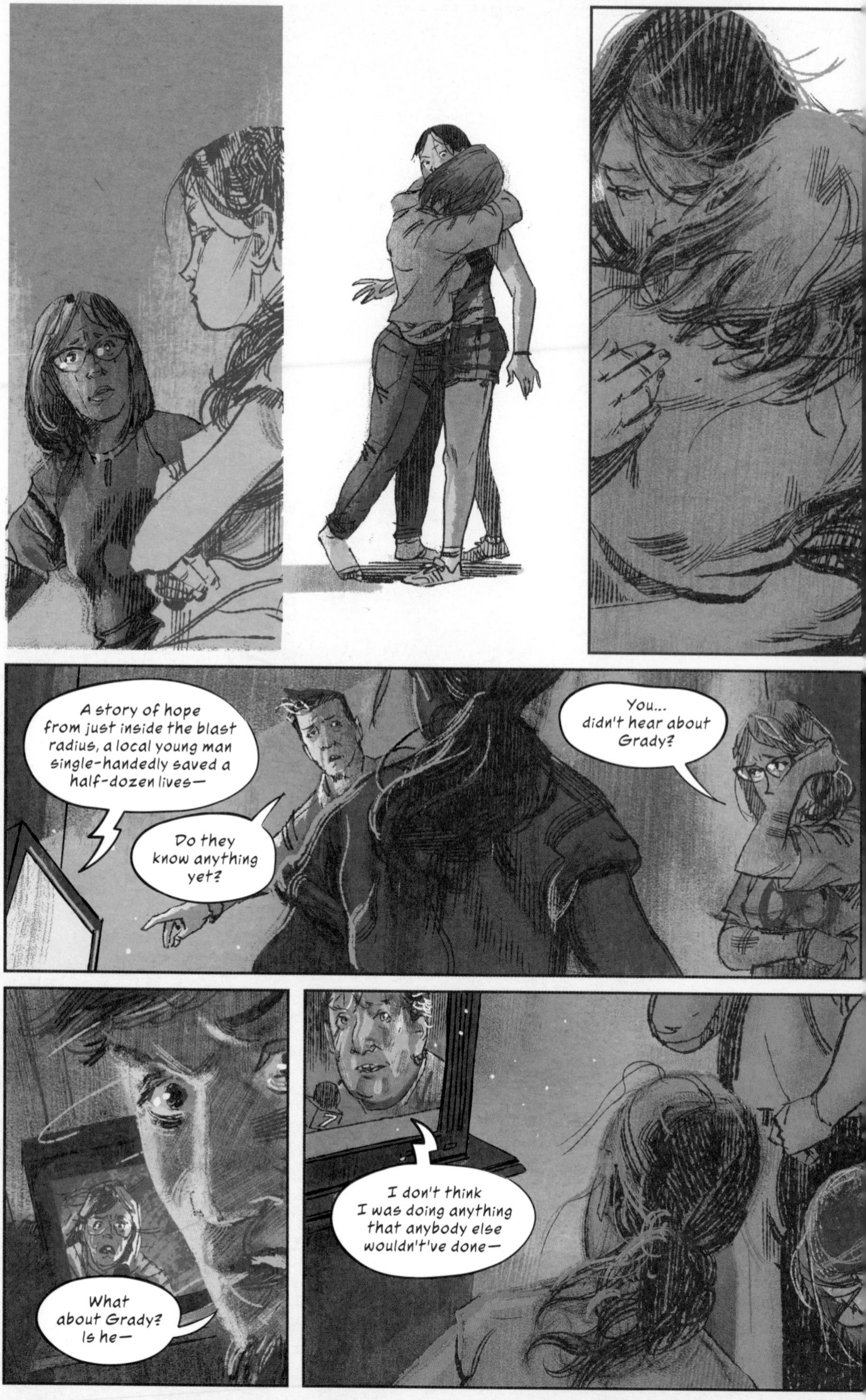
A story of hope from just inside the blast radius, a local young man single-handedly saved a half-dozen lives—
Do they know anything yet?
You... didn't hear about Grady?
What about Grady? Is he—
I don't think I was doing anything that anybody else wouldn't've done—

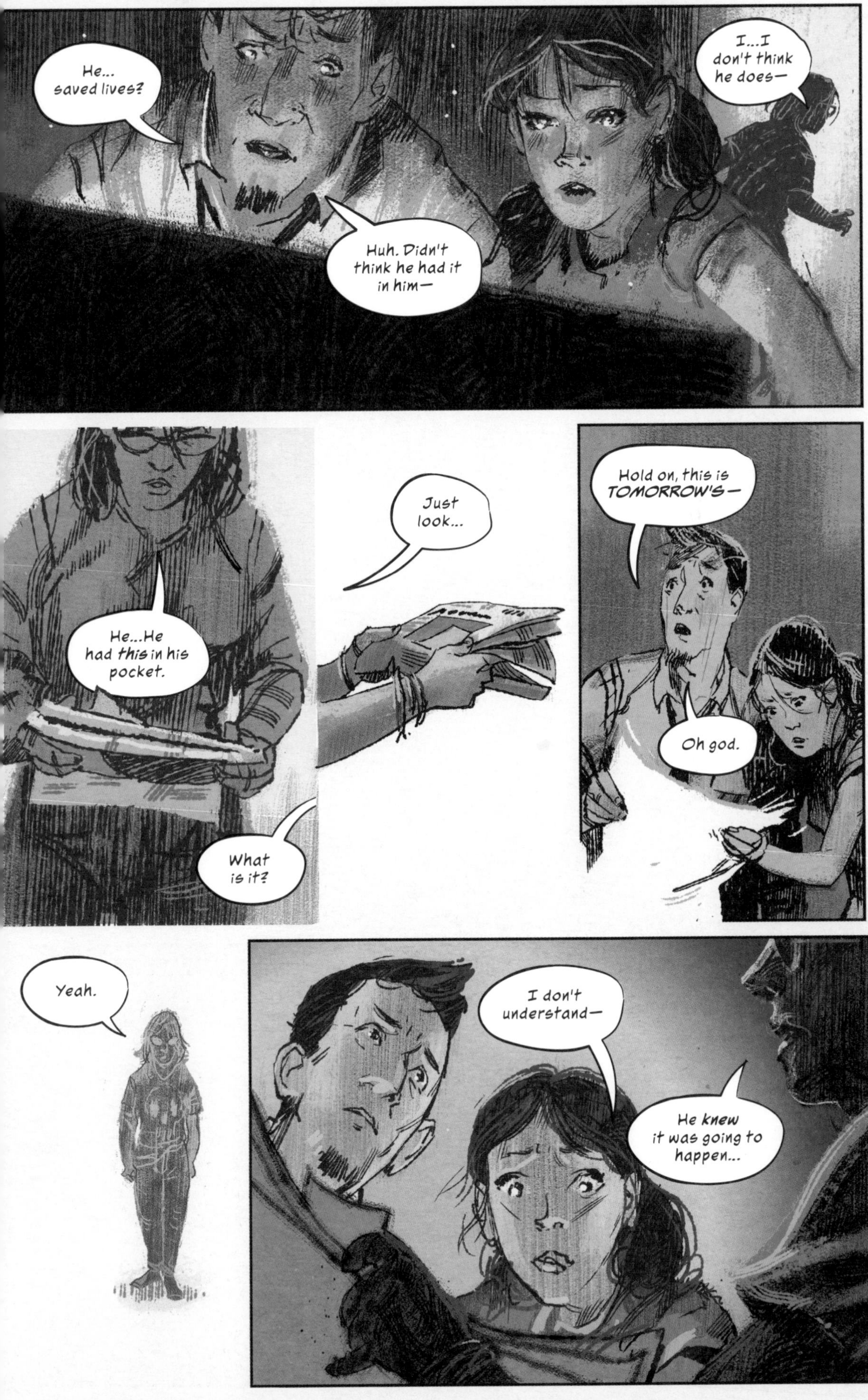
He... saved lives?
Huh. Didn't think he had it in him—
I...I don't think he does—
He...He had *this* in his pocket.
What is it?
Just look...
Hold on, this is *TOMORROW'S*—
Oh god.
Yeah.
I don't understand—
He *knew* it was going to happen...

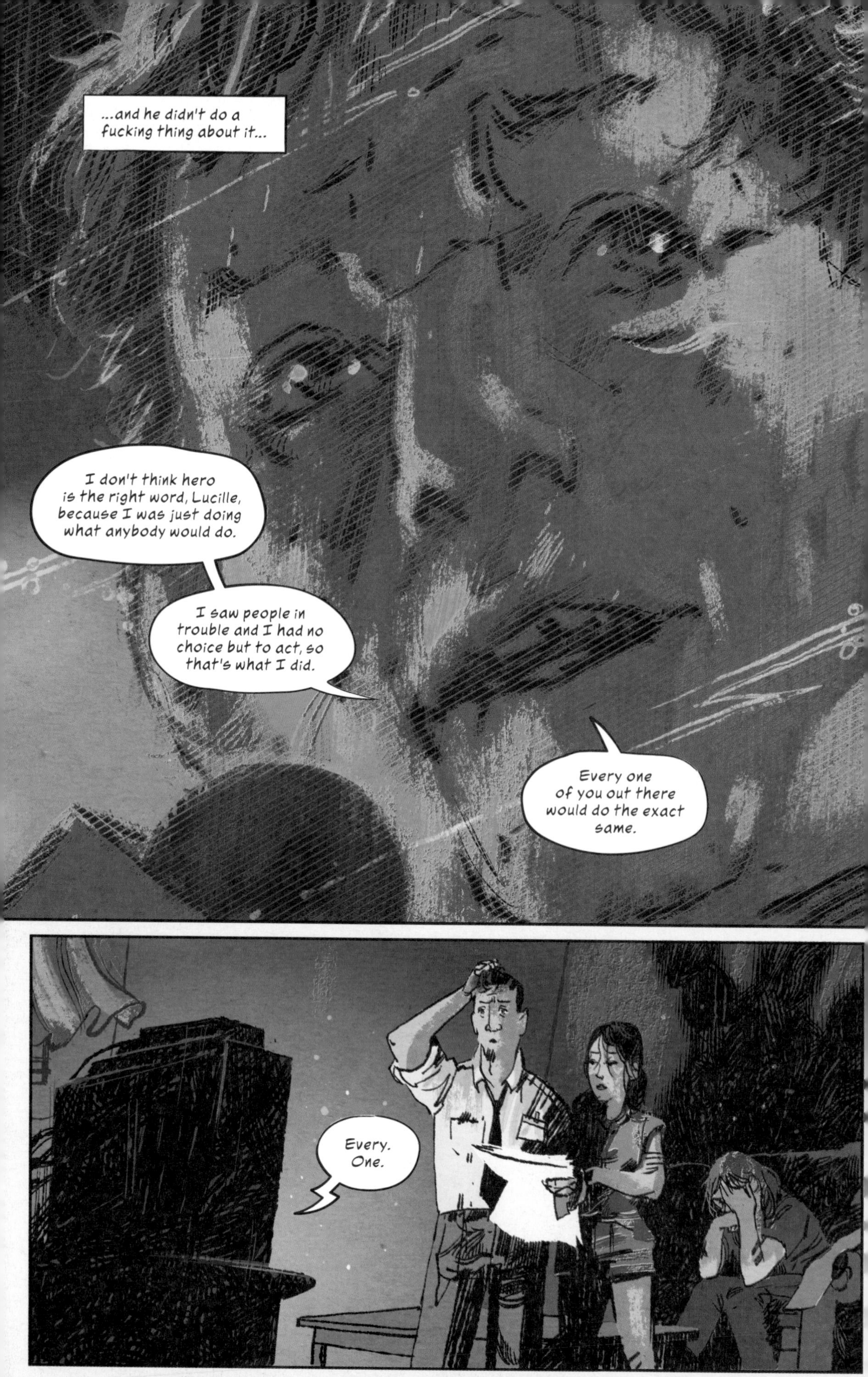
...and he didn't do a fucking thing about it...
I don't think hero is the right word, Lucille, because I was just doing what anybody would do.
I saw people in trouble and I had no choice but to act, so that's what I did.
Every one of you out there would do the exact same.
Every. One.

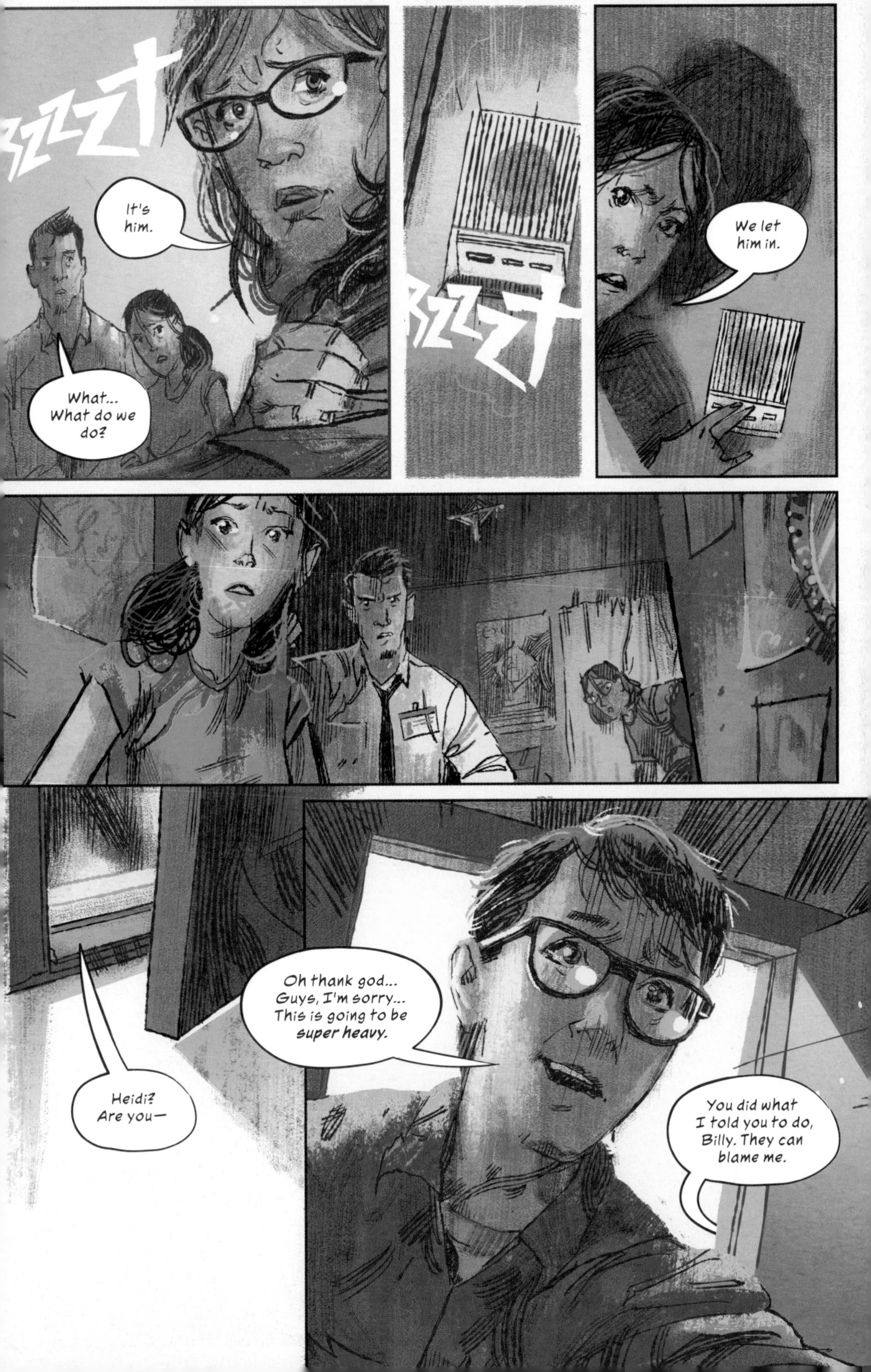
zzzzt
It's him.
What... What do we do?
Rzzzt
We let him in.
Oh thank god... Guys, I'm sorry... This is going to be *super heavy.*
Heidi? Are you—
You did what I told you to do, Billy. They can blame me.

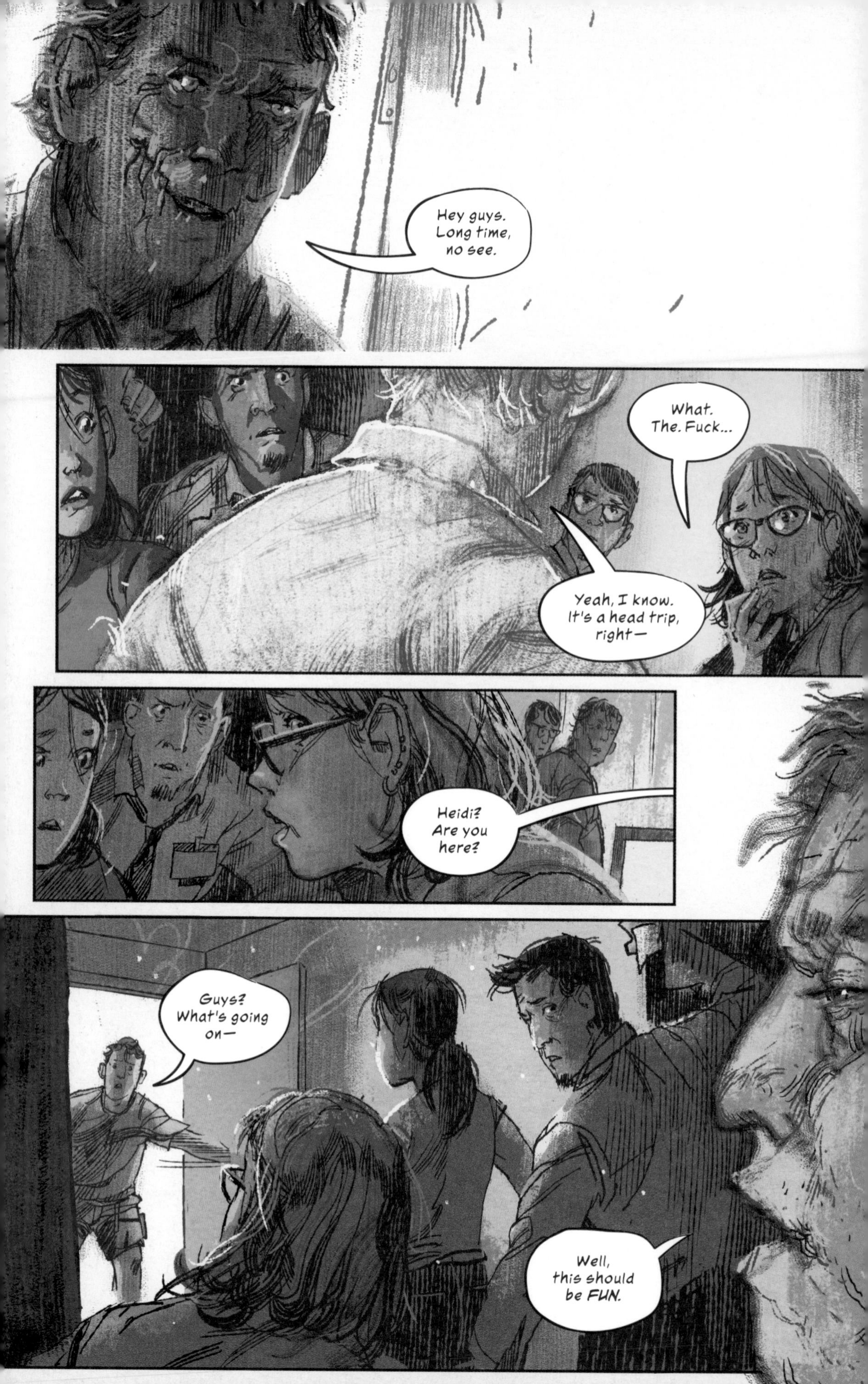
Hey guys. Long time, no see.
What. The. Fuck...
Yeah, I know. It's a head trip, right—
Heidi? Are you here?
Guys? What's going on—
Well, this should be FUN.

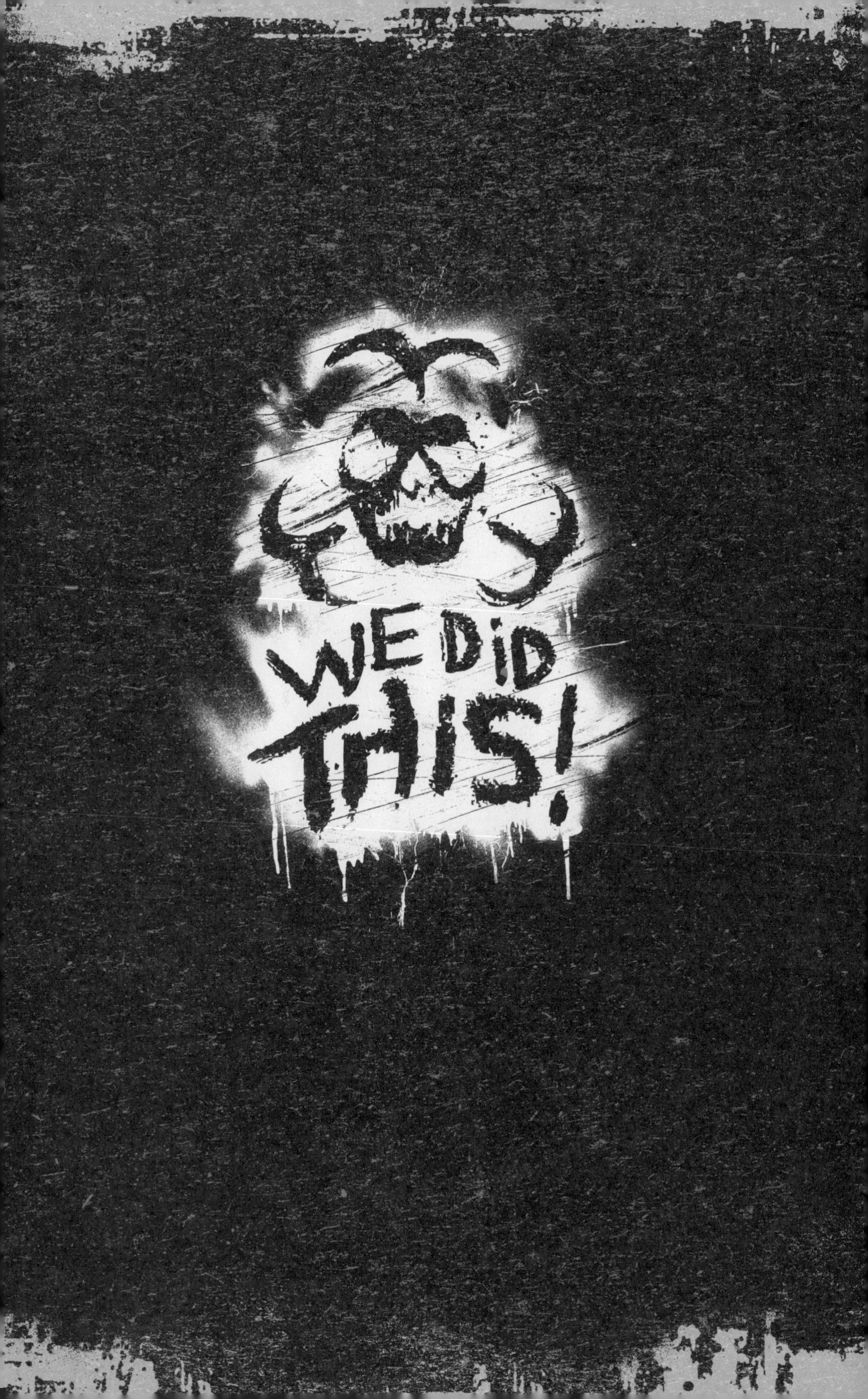
WE DID
THIS!

# COVER GALLERY

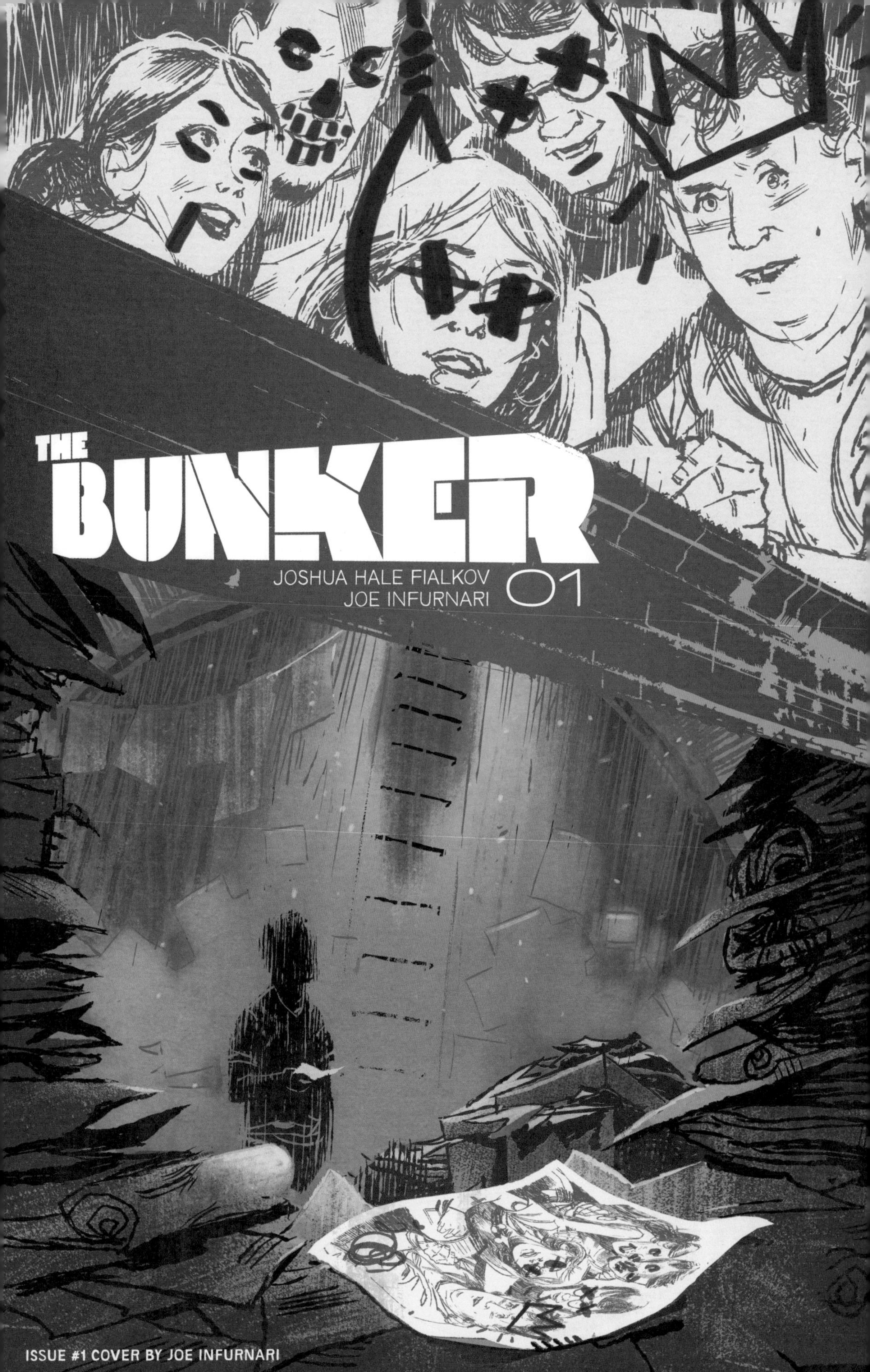


ISSUE #1 COVER BY JOE INFURNARI

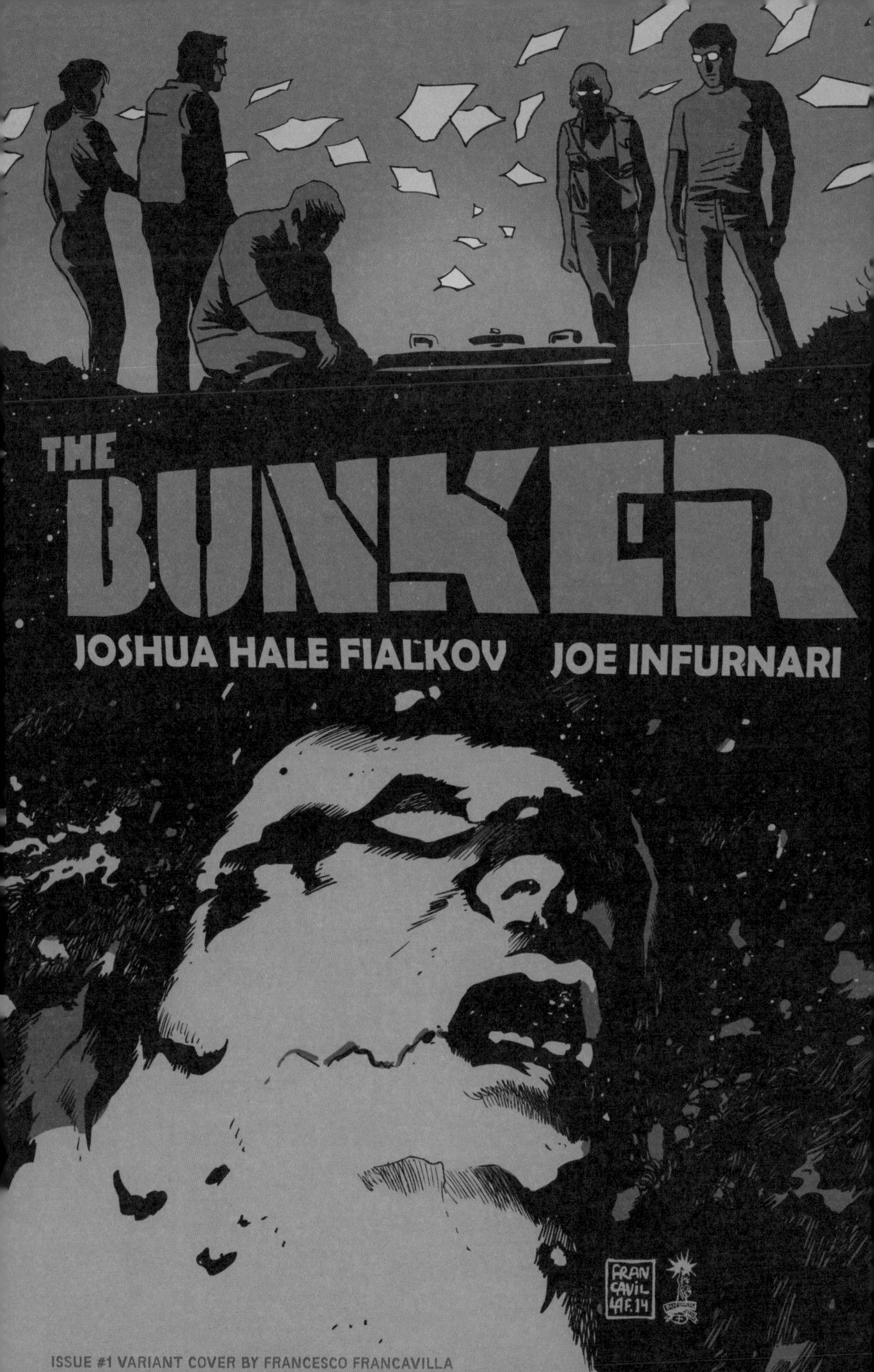
THE BUNKER
JOSHUA HALE FIALKOV
JOE INFURNARI
FRAN CAVIL LA F. 14

ISSUE #1 VARIANT COVER BY FRANCESCO FRANCAVILLA

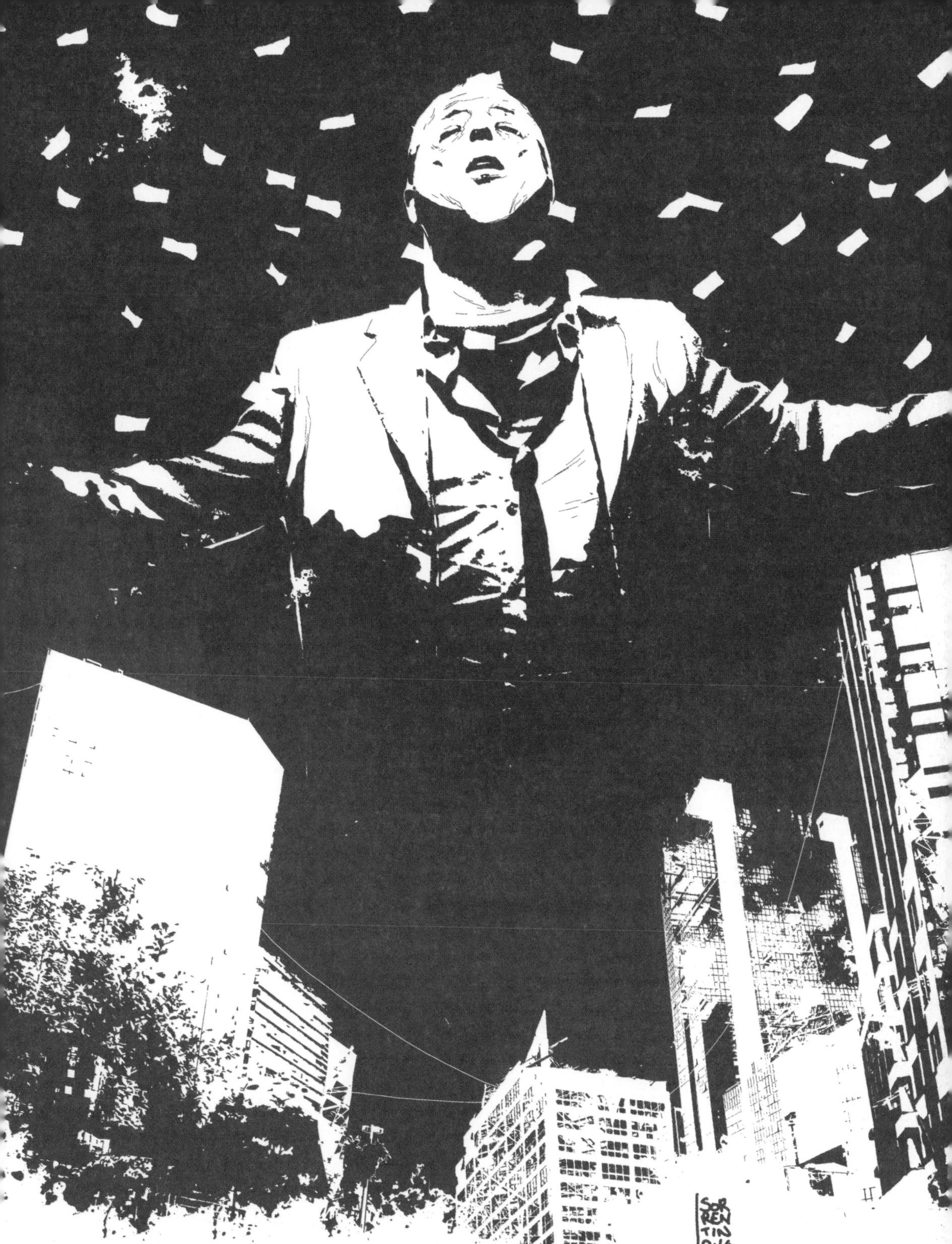
SORRENTINO 0·14

# THE BUNKER

JOSHUA HALE FIALKOV
JOE INFURNARI

ISSUE #1 VARIANT COVER BY ANDREA SORRENTINO

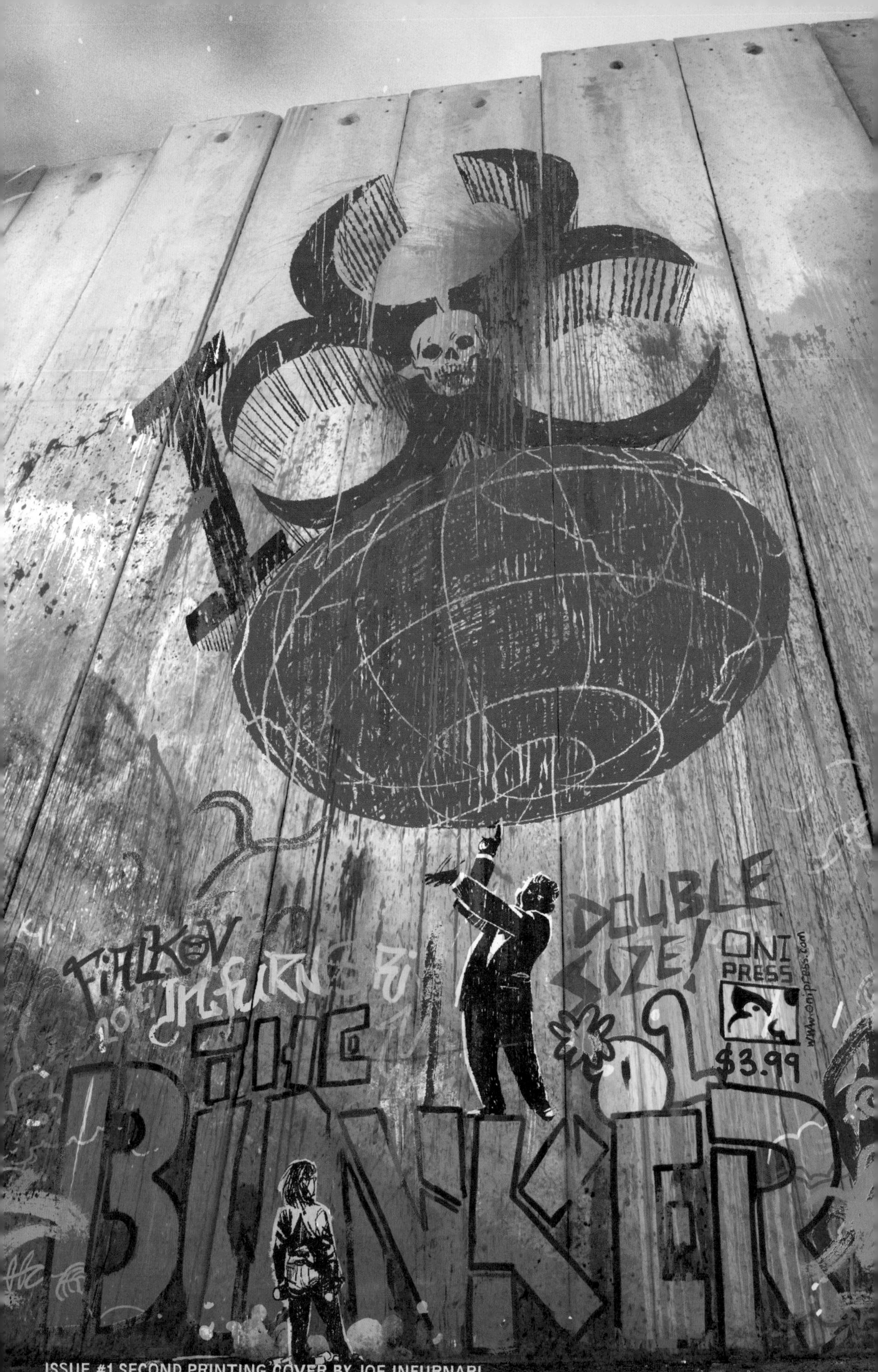
FIALKOV
INFURNARI
THE BUNKER
DOUBLE SIZE!
ONI PRESS
www.onipress.com
$3.99

ISSUE #1 SECOND PRINTING COVER BY JOE INFURNARI

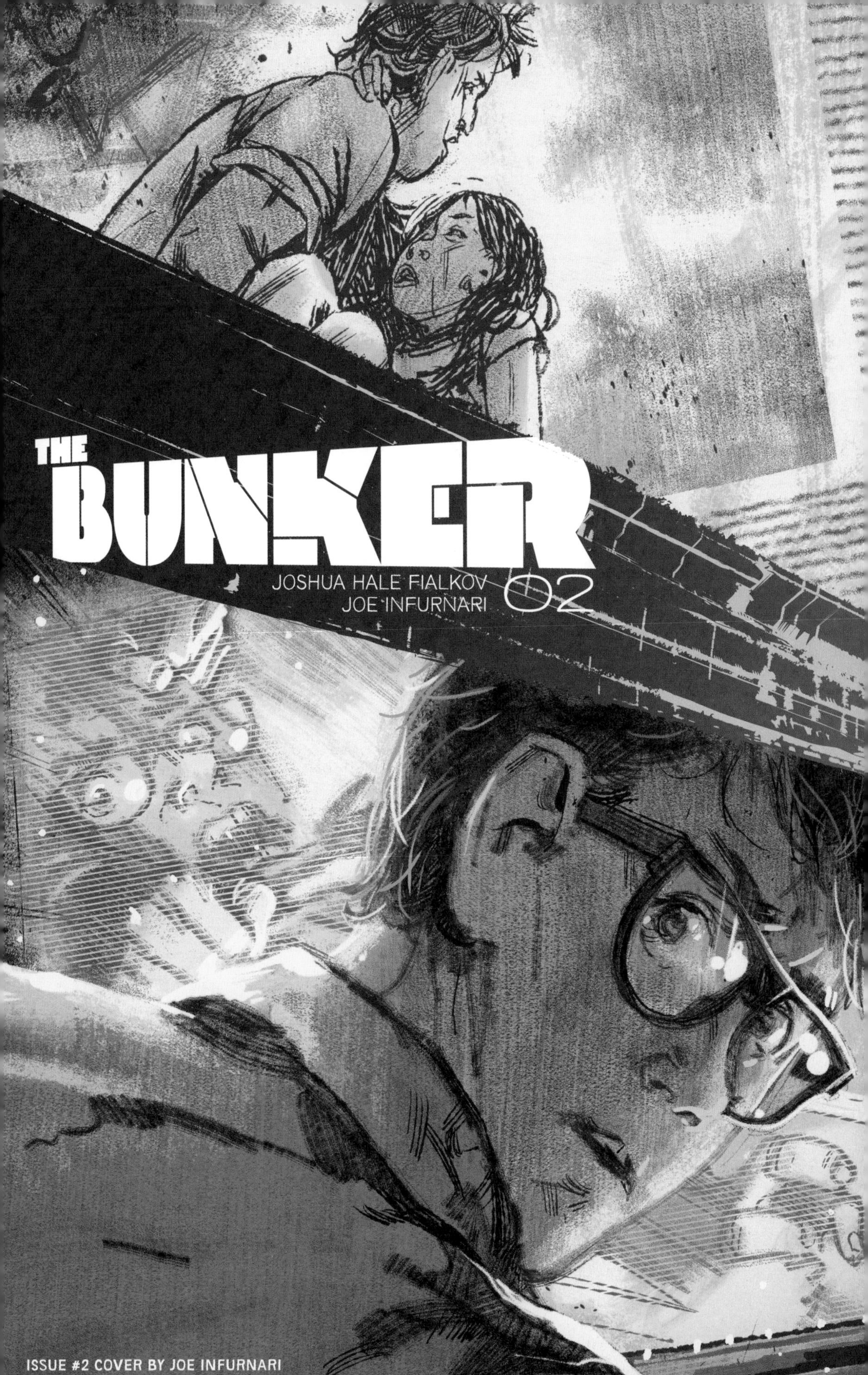
THE
BUNKER
JOSHUA HALE FIALKOV
JOE INFURNARI
02

ISSUE #2 COVER BY JOE INFURNARI

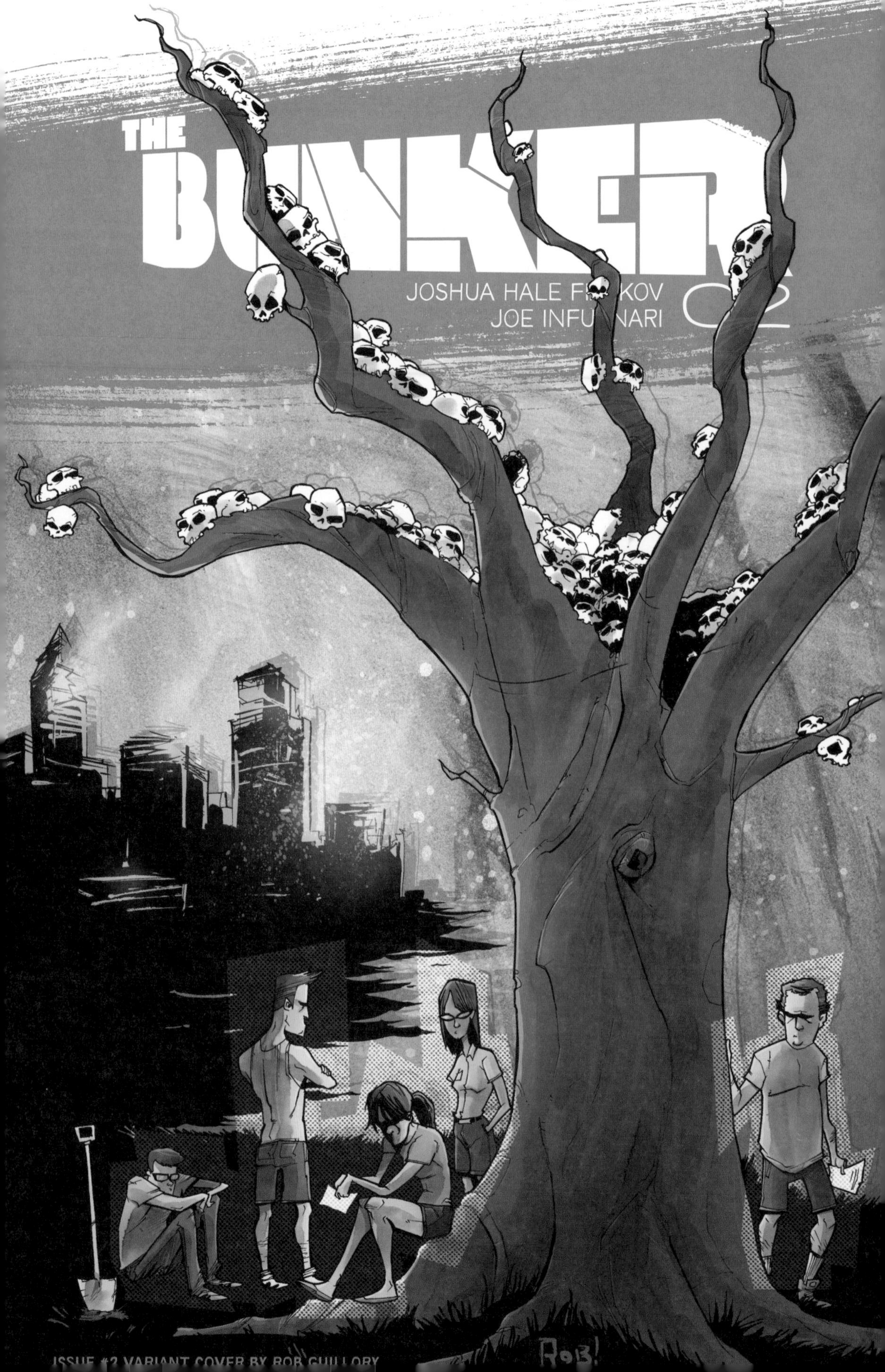


ISSUE #2 VARIANT COVER BY ROB GUILLORY

"PART SCIENCE FICTION, PART HORROR, PART COMING OF AGE STORY, JOSH FIALKOV AND JOE INFURNARI'S *THE BUNKER* SERVES UP ONE OF THE MOST ORIGINAL, THRILLING STORIES OF 2013. ONE OF MY VERY FAVORITE READS. I WISH I'D THOUGHT OF THE IDEA!"

-SCOTT SNYDER (*BATMAN, AMERICAN VAMPIRE, THE WAKE*)

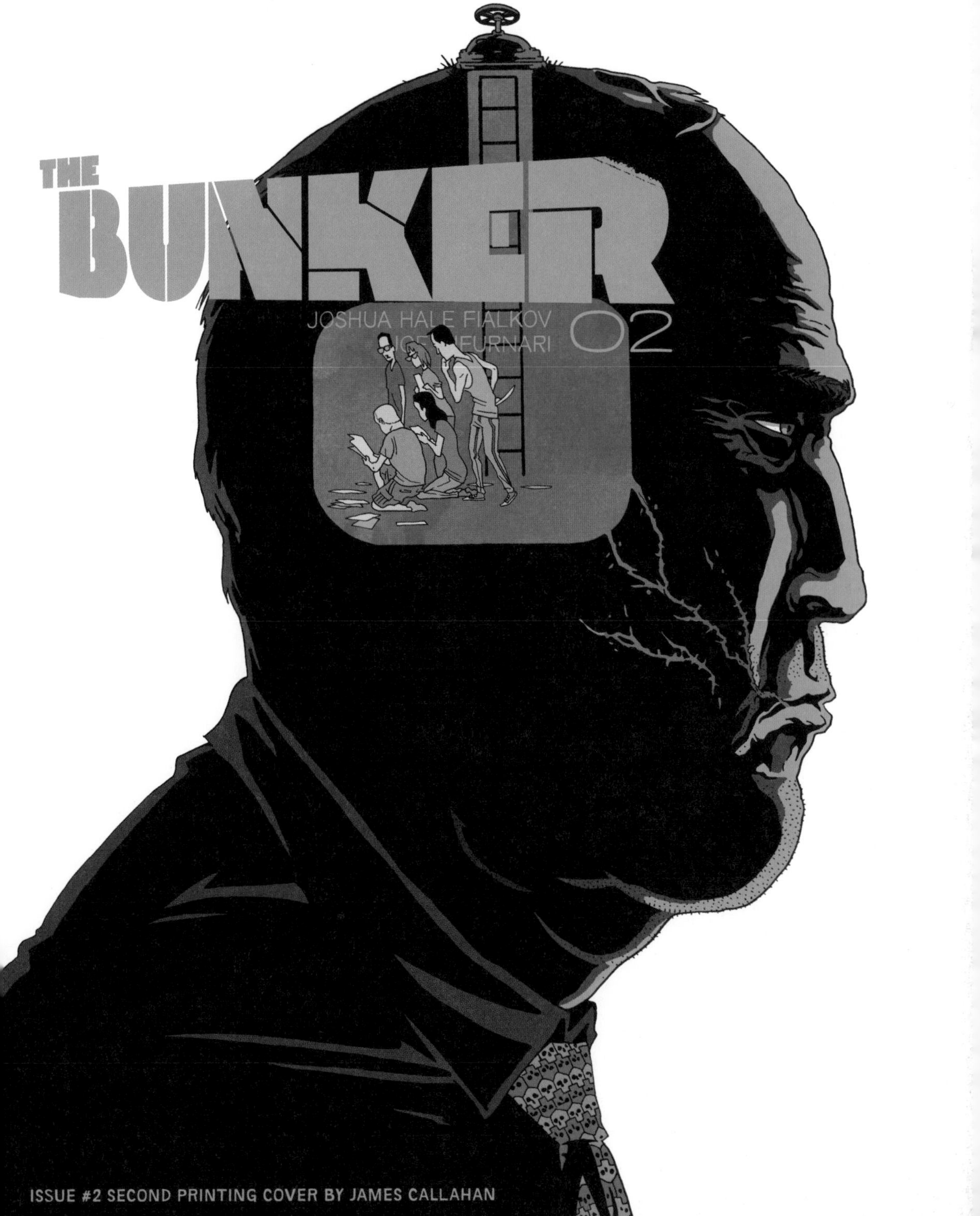
THE BUNKER
JOSHUA HALE FIALKOV
02

ISSUE #2 SECOND PRINTING COVER BY JAMES CALLAHAN

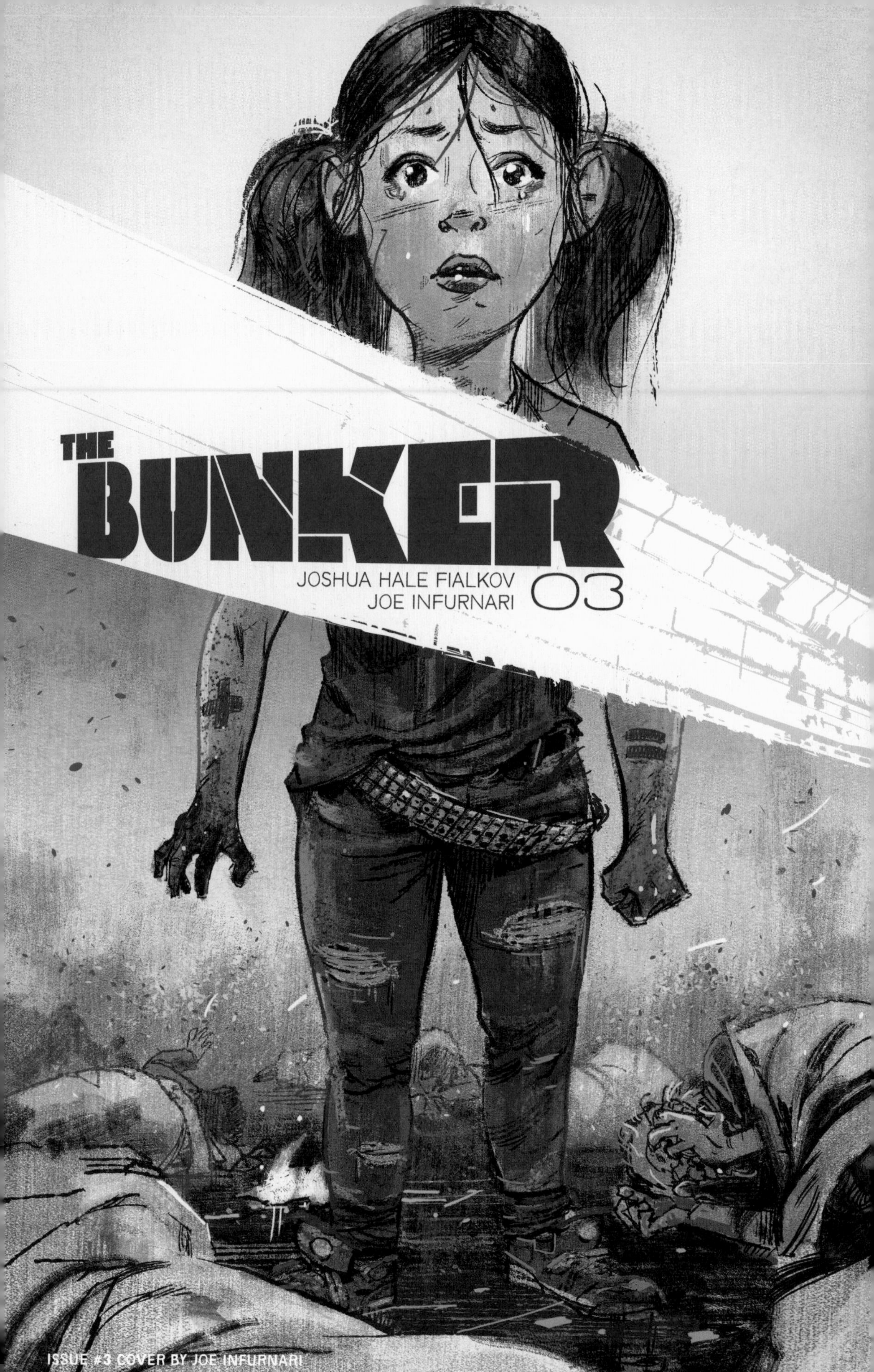
THE
BUNKER
JOSHUA HALE FIALKOV
JOE INFURNARI
03

ISSUE #3 COVER BY JOE INFURNARI

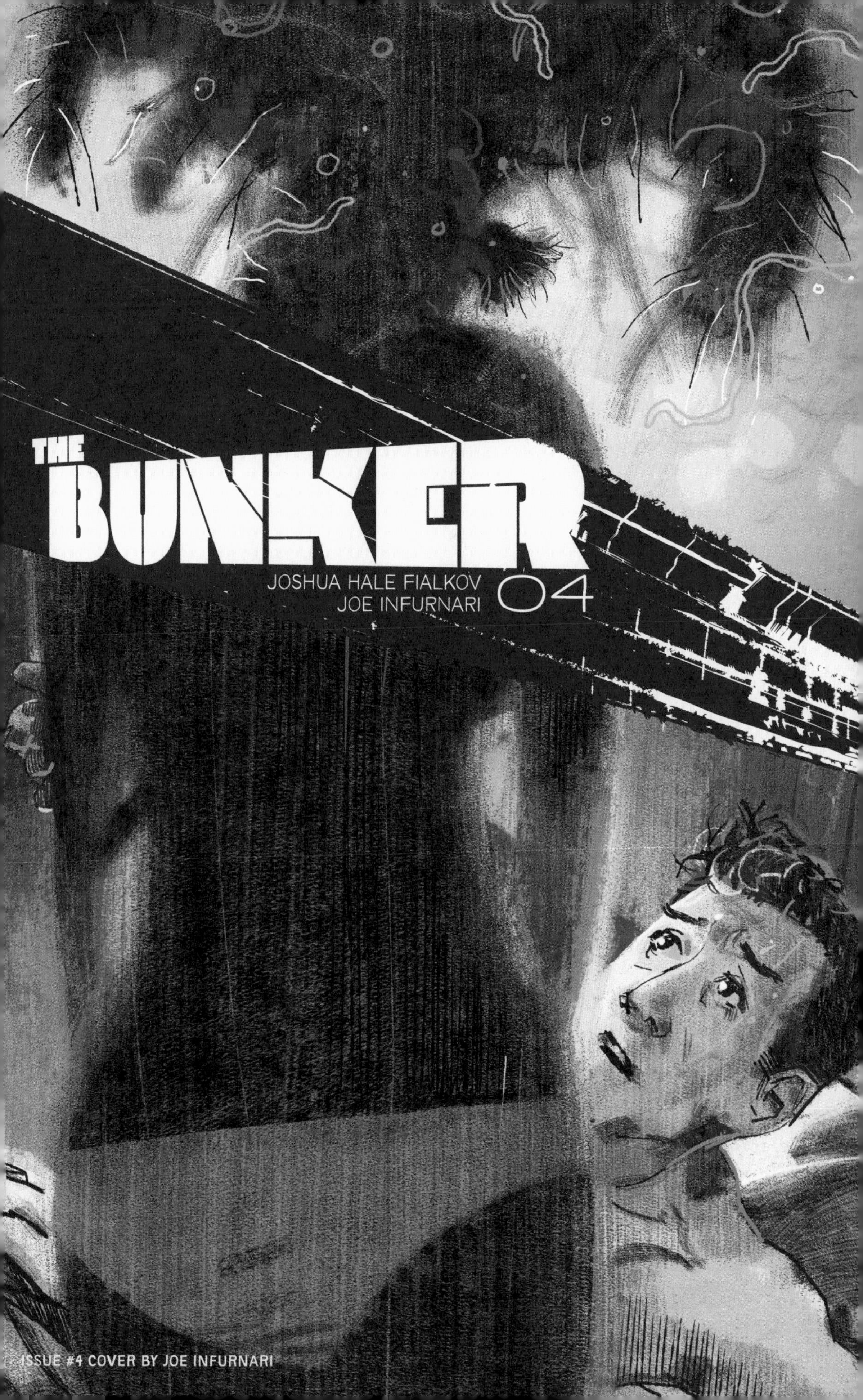
THE
BUNKER
JOSHUA HALE FIALKOV
JOE INFURNARI
04

ISSUE #4 COVER BY JOE INFURNARI

Joshua Hale Fialkov is the Eisner, Harvey, and Emmy award–nominated creator of *Tumor*, *Punks*, *Elk's Run*, and *Echoes*. He was the writer of the critically acclaimed *I, Vampire* for DC's *New 52*, and is an architect of the Ultimate Universe at Marvel Comics. He lives in Los Angeles with his wife, daughter, two dogs, and a disgruntled cat.

Being the singular genius behind the infamous *Time F#©ker*, Joe Infurnari's talents are uniquely suited to the vagaries of illustrating a time travel story. Whether tracing deadbeat dad DNA back to Paleolithic times or propping up a drawing pad in the midst of the apocalypse, Joe's upper lip remains stiff and his focus resolute. It's not all work and no play for Joe 'The Towering' Infurnari! Leisure time is lovingly spent with his new bride and their four crazy cats in a bunker of his own design.

# MORE FROM ONI PRESS...

## A BOY AND A GIRL

By Jamie S. Rich & Natalie Nourigat

176 pages, softcover, 2-color interiors

ISBN 978-1-62010-089-9

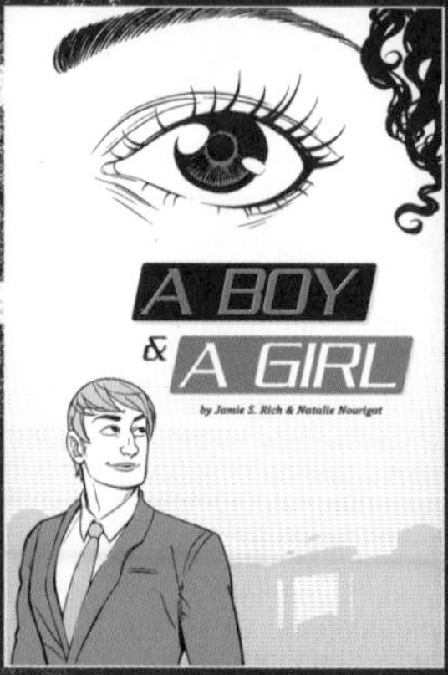
A BOY
& A GIRL
by Jamie S. Rich & Natalie Nourigat

## WASTELAND VOL. 1: CITIES IN DUST

By Antony Johnston & Christopher Mitten

160 pages, softcover, b/w interiors

ISBN 978-1-932664-59-1

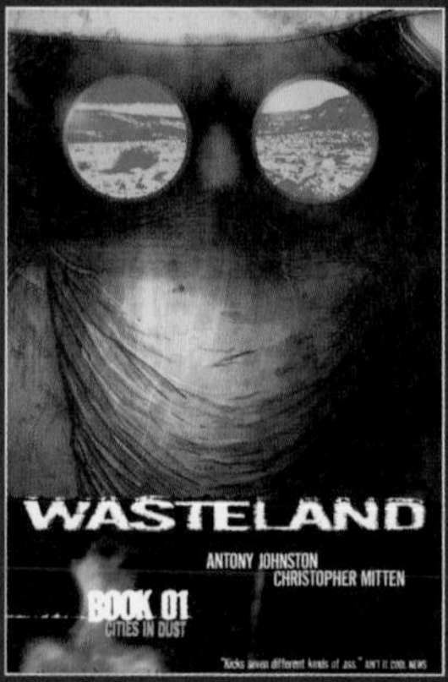
WASTELAND
ANTONY JOHNSTON
CHRISTOPHER MITTEN
BOOK 01
CITIES IN DUST

## THE AUTEUR: VOL. 1

By Rick Spears, James Callahan, & Luigi Anderson

144 pages, softcover, full color interiors

ISBN 978-1-62010-135-3

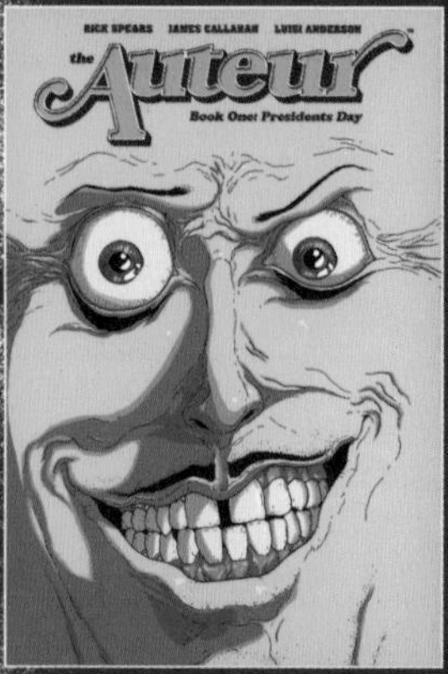
RICK SPEARS JAMES CALLAHAN LUIGI ANDERSON
the Auteur
Book One: Presidents Day

## LETTER 44 VOL. 1: ESCAPE VELOCITY

By Charles Soule, Alberto Jiménez Alburquerque, Guy Major, & Dan Jackson

160 pages, softcover, full color interiors

ISBN 978-1-62010-133-9

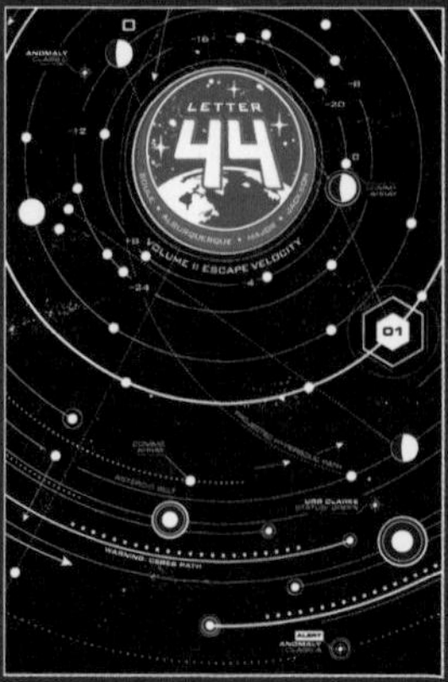
LETTER
44
VOLUME 1: ESCAPE VELOCITY
01

## THE SIXTH GUN VOL. 1: COLD DEAD FINGERS

By Cullen Bunn, Brian Hurtt, & Bill Crabtree

176 pages, softcover, full color interiors

ISBN 978-1-934964-60-6

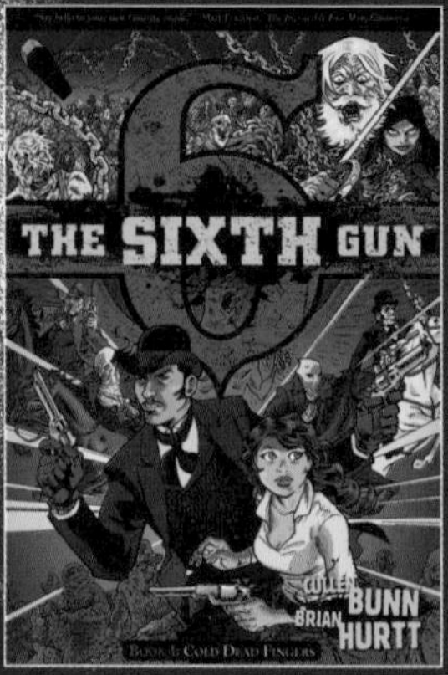
THE SIXTH GUN
CULLEN BUNN
BRIAN HURTT
BOOK 1: COLD DEAD FINGERS

## HELHEIM VOL. 1: THE WITCH WAR

By Cullen Bunn, Joëlle Jones, & Nick Filardi

160 pages, softcover, full color interiors

Includes fold-out poster

ISBN 978-1-62010-014-1

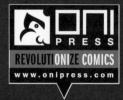

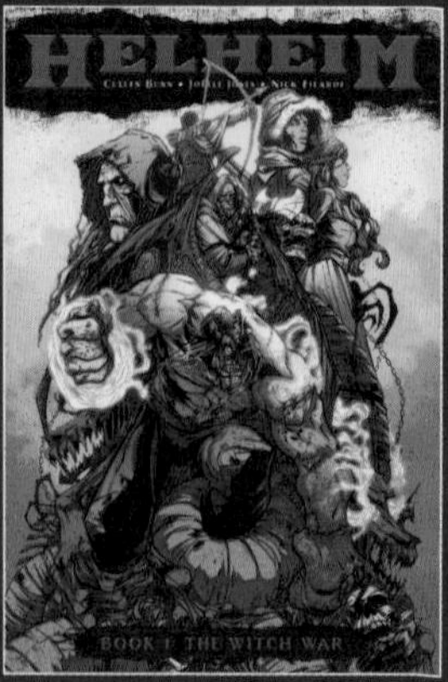
HELHEIM
BOOK 1: THE WITCH WAR

ONI PRESS
REVOLUTIONIZE COMICS
www.onipress.com

For more information on these and other fine Oni Press comic books and graphic novels visit onipress.com.
To find a comic specialty store in your area visit comicsphops.us.